Words and Music

Into the Future

A SONGWRITING TREATISE & MANIFESTO

Words and Music
Into the Future

A SONGWRITING TREATISE & MANIFESTO

Michael Koppy

Good Track Records
West Hollywood, CA USA

Words and Music Into the Future: A Songwriting Treatise and Manifesto.
© Copyright 2019 by Michael Koppy.

Published by Good Track Records, PO Box 461194, West Hollywood, CA 90046 USA

Editorial material prepared, and book printed and bound, in the United States.

Typeset by Jet Set, Studio City.
Designed by Nikki Shein/Shein Design, Los Angeles.
Printed and bound by Formax Printing, St Louis.
www.GoodTrackRecords.com

Library of Congress Cataloging-in-Publication Data

Koppy, Michael
Words and Music Into the Future: A Songwriting Treatise and Manifesto
p. cm.
Includes index.

ISBN-13: 978-0-9966400-2-2   ISBN-10: 0-9966400-2-9

1. Literary Criticism – Popular Songs. 2. Popular Music – History and Criticism. 3. Song Form – Aesthetics. 4. Popular Culture – History and Criticism. 5. Lyric Writing – Literary Form. I. Koppy, Michael II. Title.

LoC: ML3470.K67 2019   LCCN: 2018914504
DDC: 781.6409

To confederates and comrades;
Heretics, Idealists, Misfits, Revolutionaries

Contents

PART TWO: On Performance and Genre

MANIFESTO

PART THREE: Lyrics

Treatise:

A formal exposition on the general state of a subject, treating it in greater depth than an essay and more concerned with investigating or exposing the underlying principles at play.

A look at the way things are.

Manifesto:

An assertive written summons, publicly advocating the determined intentions, motives, and views of its issuer, with prescriptions for producing enlightened progress.

A call to right the current wrongs.

INTRODUCTION

"Not bad, fellas. Let's do one more take, with more emphasis on tone, harmony, melody, rhythm, composition, lyrics, musicianship, tempo, and originality."

Chapter One

No, Don, the Levee Wasn't Dry—and No One Was Drinking Whiskey and Rye

If they cannot be believed even in the very first thing they say and set out to prove, they are not entitled to be believed in anything they say afterwards. — Thomas Paine

D on McLean's "American Pie" has been one of the most celebrated songs of recent decades—do a quick web search and you'll occasionally even encounter it named *the* best song ever written. It's regularly trotted out as a fine example of 'Poetic Lyrics' in popular songwriting, and there've surely been countless precocious high schoolers and callow undergraduates who have written papers of which they're quite proud dissecting the song; detecting references and deducing 'hidden meanings' contained therein.

The chorus—almost always regarded as the most important part of any song lyric, and necessarily repeated several times (seven in "American Pie")—goes as follows:

Bye, bye Miss American Pie.
Drove my Chevy to the levee but the levee was dry.
Them good ole boys were drinking whiskey and rye,
Singin' this'll be the day that I die;
This'll be the day that I die.[1]

What I find so annoying is the utter clumsiness—clumsiness that's not just motored by once and quickly, and so possibly pardonable in rush of more resonant phrases and melody—but repeated, emphasized, hammered home, with all those iterations.

Levees are never 'dry'—or wet—unless we're talking about a recent rain or a dropped soda. A levee is *not* a body of water, but an earthwork that *contains* a body of water. One might note, similarly, that a lake or reservoir might be dry; but not a dam or bridge.

Nor a levee. Period.

And rye? Rye is a kind of whiskey—so "drinking whiskey and rye" is roughly equivalent to "eating eggs and egg yolks" or "watching television and a television show"; a stumbling redundancy.

Again, one *can* perhaps generously excuse a less-well written phrase if it comes in a tightly wrapped package of other ideas and observations, some or most of which stand strongly on their own—or if it comes along just once, possibly, in passing. That's *not* what's happening here, however—we're just getting hit with one inanely half-baked notion after the other, with really nothing worthy of attention along the way, and then we're to endure it all again, and again, and again....

There's little motivation to treat writing of such abysmal execution with much more than ridicule and dismissal—and, more importantly (and perhaps unfortunately), to take seriously anything else delivered in the song. To repeat, the chorus above is the heart of it—the part that needs to be the *most* elegant, precise, evocative, and/or clear. And frankly, if a songwriter can't even clear that fundamental hurdle, his or her extrapolations, illustrations, allusions, and digressions likely do not merit further examination. So, um—ya got anything else, Don?

One can actually find, believe it or not, an apologetics asserting that McLean was referring to a supposed bar called The Levee, in his hometown of New Rochelle, that closed down—so it went 'dry'—forcing drinkers to drive a couple of towns away to imbibe in the town of Rye, and that McLean is actually singing "drinking whiskey IN Rye". I'm not going to waste my time investigating this—for two reasons. (Well, three if you count that life is too short to squander on accommodating obvious stupidities—I also don't spend time pondering if Elvis is still alive, or if he was the Second Shooter firing from the Grassy Knoll.)

First off, he's not singing "whiskey IN Rye"—that's pretty danged clear. (I'll deal with aspects and examples of popular song criticism that are similarly wild-eyed and fatuous—sometimes from otherwise supposedly knowledgeable and respected critics—later on.) Secondly, if he actually were so thoroughly self-referential, it would make the entire song unhinged and self-absorbed to the point of insignificance. (I'll propose some basic public and creative responsibilities in songwriting later on as well.)

Then there's the vacant song title—in that chorus, so also repeated seven times. "Miss American Pie" being a heavy-handed manufacture of hypothetical cultural personification, but with the critical deficiency that it really has no connection to events in the song or to any external touchstone. (Well except *as* a clumsy non sequitur signifier, I guess—a 'signifier without significance'. And so yes, please, "Bye-bye....")

But let's look at that levee a little closer. What's the point of the locale, other than to rhyme his similarly unnecessary 'Chevy'? Unlike, say, the nominal river in Bruce Springsteen's vividly accomplished song, "The River"—which clearly, steadily conveys its seminal meaning—the fumbling 'dry levee' in MacLean's effort adds nothing meritorious. One can *assert* it holds deeper relevance and resonance, of course—one can assert anything—but such an assertion is really quite lacking in support. (One 'explanation' I stumbled on is that it alludes to a 1950s car commercial jingle sung by chanteuse/pitch woman Dinah Shore that also rhymed 'Chevy' and 'levee'. If so, it's a regrettably light-weight precedent off of which to play. Yet that's *not* necessarily objectionable. In passing, once, it can be indulged—maybe even appreciated. But it is certainly *not* worthy of being repeated seven damn times. That's more than 'objectionable', it's tediously insipid. Vapid vamping. No one's impressed.)

The several verses themselves supply a merely innocuous paint-by-numbers inventory of pop culture celebrities and events, sheathed within irritatingly coy obscurations. Again, why? To what purpose? Is anything *served* or advanced by the cutesy conceits (the King, Jester, Jack Flash, etc), other than the songwriter's adolescent hubris?

In the end, there's no reason to seriously favor writing this ineffectual, despite all the volubility and the assertively evangelical delivery. Does one take anything away, really, from the disquisition? Is there even *one* useful insight imparted during the long commentary? For all McLean's obvious aspirations, and the renown the song has attained, it's ultimately really just a laboriously bumbling and unpolished exposition, married to a generally agreeable tune that's dispatched with bumptious assurance, and nothing more. Exanimate loquacity, reflection shorn of insight, recitation sans revelation. At best but a carpentered contrivance.

For someone perhaps kinder, more indulgent, less critical toward the songwriter's lyrical maladroitness in "American Pie", thinking me too exacting or categorical, I'll later also address why such matters are in fact *fundamental* to capable, informed, and effective songwriting.

★

And for those who may think this and selected other negative critiques that follow are simply too scathing, I'm afraid no concessions shall be forthcoming, though rest assured positive examples will be cited as well.

But this is not a sunny Panglossian celebration, a 'fan appreciation'. Seriousness and intellectual rigor are so regularly AWOL in songwriting and surrounding milieux, including in criticism, that it's incumbent for us here to *not* be 'compromising', 'deferential', 'collegial'. We shall be resolutely unswayed by the immaterial and the extraneous—either when castigating incompetence or when saluting rare excellence.

More on such matters follows in these several introductory chapters, and later in some chapters in Part One.

¹"American Pie", copyright 1971 by Don McLean. Quoted here as permitted within the Fair Use provisions of 17 U.S.C.§107.

Chapter Two

There Goes The Robert E. Lee?

Works must be conceived with fire in the soul, but executed with clinical coolness. — Joan Miró

Let's look at another hyperbolically revered song, one that comes to us from the *other* direction, in that it attempts (via fictional first person chronicle) to present a very direct and immediately accessible picture of historical actuality—without "American Pie's" portentous trappings and ostensible poesy:

> Virgil Caine is the name, and I served on the Danville train,
> 'Til Stoneman's cavalry came and tore up the tracks again.
> In the winter of '65; we were hungry, just barely alive.
> By May the tenth, Richmond had fell;
> It's a time I remember oh so well.

chorus:
> The night they drove old Dixie down, and the bells were ringin',
> The night they drove old Dixie down, and the people were singin',
> They went "Na, Na, Na, Na, Na, Na; Na, Na, Na, Na; Na, Na, Na, Na, Na."

> Back with my wife in Tennessee; when one day she called to me,
> "Virgil, quick, come see, there goes Robert E. Lee!"
> Now I don't mind choppin' wood,
> And I don't care if the money's no good.
> Ya take what ya need and ya leave the rest,
> But they should never have taken the very best.

chorus repeat

> Like my father before me, I will work the land,
> Like my brother above me, who took a rebel stand.

He was just eighteen, proud and brave,
But a Yankee laid him in his grave,
I swear by the mud below my feet,
You can't raise a Caine back up when he's in defeat.

<u>chorus repeat</u>[2]

Where to begin? Well, okay, in the beginning….

This song, "The Night They Drove Old Dixie Down" written by The Band's Robbie Robertson, has three verses, all of them serviceable, workmanlike. The (most important) first verse capably sets up the character, the setting, his reactions, torment, and loss. I'm not crazy about this or that line and about some of the words chosen, but it's generally passable work; meriting polite attention—and actually promising, even novel, since I for one can't think of another Civil War remembrance in contemporary or traditional song from either a Union *or* a Confederate vantage.

Good.

Of course, there was no single "night they drove old Dixie down", though the most fitting candidate for such designation would be the day Federal troops finally entered the Confederate capital, Richmond, on—I just now checked—the morning of April 3rd. The night before, April 2nd, saw the panicked mass exodus of terrified residents, against the backdrop of a city engulfed in flames, as illustrated in the Currier & Ives print on the following page.

Digression: So why the mention of May 10th in the song? The only significant event happening on that date was the capture of Confederate President Jefferson Davis, camped with a small group of loyal lieutenants by a stream hundreds of miles away in south Georgia. But his apprehension was essentially an anti-climax at that point, and of far less consequence than Richmond being evacuated, Lee surrendering on April 9th, or Confederate General Joe Johnston surrendering the largest Southern army on April 26th; among other larger and smaller rebel surrenders all across the South, stretching on to June 2nd. Dwelling on the calendrical caprice is unproductive here, except to note that in a song already cataloguing lesser-known historical events—and Union General Stoneman's cavalry raids on the Richmond & Danville Railroad are certainly that—continuing such historical authority is implicitly important; and further, it affords building an even wider foundation. And just tossing out a date without clear reason for it is a wasted opportunity.

These observations and reservations may admittedly be of secondary moment, but they're neither petty nor impertinent. Later, we'll look at similar opportunities that were exploited rather than squandered.

By the way, "Richmond *had fell*"? Here's a construction that does compel comment. It's just plain illiterate. However—and in major contrast to the levee being dry—it comes along just once, quickly, and is immediately obscured by the depth of personal reflection evoked in "It's a time I remember oh so well". It may be charitably indulged, perhaps, if not entirely excused.

Okay, look, I'll be extra nice. Here: I'll stipulate that all the actual history is immaterial. (It *is* material, of course. But we'll pretend it isn't—just so's we can move on. We'll even be happy 'Richmond had fell'. Okay?)

Because it's the chorus as a whole that is such an incredibly consummate disaster.

And after addressing it, we'll even go on to investigate a wholly entertaining and wild-eyed pretext for it. Fasten your seat belts. We didn't chase that hare-brained "drinking whiskey <u>in</u> Rye" earlier, but we'll scamper after this Carrollian white rabbit just for the fun of it here.

THE FALL OF RICHMOND ᴠᴬ ON THE NIGHT OF APRIL 2ᴺᴰ, 1865

This strong hold and capital city of the Davis Confederacy was evacuated by the rebels in consequence of the defeat at "Five Forks" of the Army of Northern Virginia, and capture of the south side rail road by the brave heroes of the north, commanded by Generals Grant, Sheridan, and others. Before abandoning the city the rebels set fire to it, destroying a vast amount of property; and the conflagration continued until it was subdued by the Union troops on the following morning.

The night they drove old Dixie down (whatever date we're agreeing that was, though again the only reasonable one is when Union troops captured the Confederate capital, and it's clear that's the area the singer was in at the time) "and all the bells were ringing". WHAT? Richmond set ablaze by retreating rebels, prison inmates all escaped and on the loose, liquored-up mobs looting the stores, the arsenal blown up in a blast so large it shattered windows and toppled cemetery tombstones over a mile away, the remaining populace braced for even worse from marauding Yankee hordes—and they're ringing bells? Bells don't get rung all over a city in observance of defeat (or by fire departments, none of which are gonna be functional or even staffed in such chaos). They sure weren't in 1945 Berlin, in 1940 Paris, or in 1814 Washington when the British set fire to the White House and US Capitol. (Pretty much the only people in the South celebrating Union victory, and generally doing so with necessary circumspection, were black—clearly not at all the populace the singer of this song is representing.)

And "the people were singing"? Really? The South in ruins, its capitol city engulfed in flames, drunken rioters on the streets—and if you didn't know that, you'd surely have assumed as much, no? (You didn't think the women were all tossing flowers out windows to the hated Northerners; the remaining old men and boys on the street offering whiskey to the detested invaders, did you? Or that everyone calmly *left* their threatened homes and possessions—to walk to church, and they all joined in song there?) Except for the strictly mechanical aspect—they rhyme—the lines are utterly ignorant.

But again, look, let's *not care* when or where all them danged people—whoever the hell they are—were a-singin', okay? Maybe it *was* on May 10th, for whatever reason. Maybe it's a year later and they're gathered in song up in Detroit. We'll go with whatever—ANYTHING! I Don't Care <u>Who</u> is singing—and I Don't Really Care <u>Where</u> they are singing, okay? Agreed? Let's just get to the revelation the song promises. I mean yes, it's pretty much a clueless mess, but we've come this far, and ya hope the reward at the end will make it all worthwhile.

And yet, believe it or not, we're *still* not at the most insipid part of it all—this song that did begin with potential.

Because *what*, exactly, was it that "the people were singing"? This is the climax of the chorus, after all—the place where the song should reasonably be expected to have its greatest insight, it's most profound and lasting resonance and revelation. So maybe it'll all come together here—to somehow justify those preceding couple of lines and wrap everything up in an epiphanic resolution.

Oh, no it won't.

Incredibly—*pointlessly, frivolously, idiotically*—the people were all singing "Na, Na, Na, Na, Na, Na; Na, Na, Na, Na; Na, Na, Na, Na, Na."! (Even while typing this—and having heard the song countless times over the years—I can't help but shake my head in disbelieving derision.)

This is songwriting so ineffectual, so nonessential—so ultimately *impotent*—that it should be laughed at in contempt.

Full stop.

Yet—and get this—here's what a few major, widely-respected(!) critics have written about it:

> Ralph J. Gleason: *"Nothing I have read…has brought home the overwhelming human sense of history that this song does…'The Night They Drove Old Dixie Down' is a remarkable song…It has that ring of truth, and the whole aura of authenticity."*[3]

> Greil Marcus: *"What it says was clear from the moment it was released…its power, though, is too great to take for granted… You can't get out from under the singer's truth…to this day none of us has escaped its impact, what we share is an ability to respond to a story like this one."*[4]

> Gilbert Cruz: *"One of* Time Magazine's *Top One Hundred Songs of All Time."*[5]

My heart goes out to these fellows. They're all surely bright, generally perceptive guys, no? And they all certainly and sincerely *wanted* to hear and engage a substantive, intelligent piece of lyric writing on this unusual topic, from this unheard quarter—as would I, myself a white Southerner. So they ignored the actuality…and wrote about what they'd *liked* to have experienced. (There'll be more unfortunate critical sloppiness—even incompetence—examined later.)

Okay, fine.

So, ya ready to dart down the rabbit hole? Hold on, here we go!

You can encounter an 'interpretation' of the song from fervent fans who realize it's a mess and so desperately want to reconcile it with facts. It goes like this: our narrator, plainly so concerned with immediate events ('the night they drove old Dixie down'), the fall of the Confederacy, his family and dead brother, has, for some reason, suddenly whipsawed his focus to describe things up in far off New York and Massachusetts and Ohio—*they* were ringing bells and singing. Or maybe it was those invading troops in Richmond? Those are clearly *not* 'the people' to him, and there's not a single word to support this—no "meanwhile, up north", "on the other side" or similar, but the reasoning is that *because* it's so incredibly stupid the way it is, and as surely the songwriter *couldn't* be so blundering, then this *must* be what's going on. (Are you enjoying things so far? Well here comes the real fun part.)

So those "Na-Na-Na-Na-Na's" presumably aren't really *that* at all. I think here's apparently what you're supposed to picture: start with a bunch of third graders out in a schoolyard taunting a playmate, sashaying side to side, all with thumbs in their ears and fingers wiggling, sticking out their tongues and chorusing in a sing-songy, "Nyah-Nyah-Nyah-Nyah-Nyah-Nyah!" Okay? Now substitute lines of grizzled, bearded, uniformed soldiers for those kids. (Laughing yet?) "Nyah-Nyah-Nyah-Nyah-Nyah-Nyah!" I honestly love this. It's right out of Monty Python. "The Lumberjack Song"! Priceless.

With any of this 'interpretation'—and quite obviously, the word should remain in quotes—the song suddenly does acquire a kinda weird schizophrenia, of course. But yes sir, the Yankees *are* now ready to taunt and mock the Southerners—with butts swingin', fingers wavin', and tongues waggin'. Nyah-Nyah-Nyah-Nyah! Neener-Neener-Neener!

But let's get serious again. If Robertson wanted to move us into another direction entirely, he could've done so in countless ways, but perhaps the easiest would've been to just replace "people" with "Yankees"— no heavy lifting, no big rewrite. "And all the Yankees were singing". Two syllables squarely replacing two syllables. Simple. Done. But he didn't do that—or anything like it. He was happy with what he had.

(Another 'defense' advanced for the 'ringing/singing' foolishness is that April 2nd, 1865, was a Sunday, so folks were gathered in churches that morning. But that's the morning *before* 'the night they drove old Dixie down' — a day before the Yankees marched in — so another distraction.)

Enough.

And what we've engaged in over the past few paragraphs, really, was being suckers — we allowed ourselves to indulge apologists for the writer's ineptitude and laziness. The internet is rampant with this kind of thing, of course — obsessed and gullible fans can easily spend many contented, self-indulgent hours 'interpreting' and 'deconstructing' and debating among themselves, much like moon landing conspiracy buffs, determined to make sense out of nonsense. It's middlebrow credulity mixed with idol worship, resulting in pseudo-scholarly masturbation — and another sign of the inculcated intellectual poverty so pandemic in contemporary popular songwriting and criticism.

★

Though it usually in fact is, a song's chorus actually doesn't necessarily *have* to be the lyrically strongest part of a song. In an effort like "The Night They Drove Old Dixie Down", for instance, with so much description and information set in the verses, the chorus could indeed be something simple — and so the divergent but inane "Na-Na-Na"s replaced with something equally as divergent and simple, but genuinely evocative; like the sentiments found in a religious hymn perhaps, or maybe general reflections on the senselessness of war or the panic and uncertainty born of defeat. Imagine first jettisoning the "bells were ringing / people were singing" jabber and replacing it with another angle of personal or general reflection from the narrator (in similarly patterned rhyming couplet), then following with a direct lift of a few lines from a Baptist hymnal over the extant tune — or even a large part of an actual hymn or pastoral folk song, *including* that melody or a recognizable variation on it. I'm not asserting any of this thinking is necessarily the strongest way to go, but just about *anything* is stronger — more integrated, consistent — than the maundering silliness there now. Later on, we'll also take a look at the general folly of using "la-la-la" and similar in a song which attempts to be a serious piece of work.

(Speculation here, but I wonder if Robertson didn't just simply get bored with his efforts. He'd done some library research — to learn about General Stoneman, certainly, and to get some overall knowledge about the collapse of the Confederacy, perhaps—and maybe had enough. Time to just finish this up and move on. The heavily degraded application evinced between the work in the verses and the work in the choruses is so marked that it does sorta smack of "Damn, can I go home now? Time for a drink. Hell, we'll just pad this out with something-something / ringing-singing' and a whole big ol' shitload of 'na-na-na-na-na'. Good enough!" Again, just a gut suspicion—and who really cares—but when you look at the lopsided whole, something like that seems plausible.)[6]

★

As for the heading of this chapter—"There Goes The Robert E. Lee?"—this quotes one of Joan Baez's at best ignorant bastardizations of the song in her hit version of it; a song that's already, as established above, largely a piece of confused babble. "The Robert E. Lee" was a paddle-wheel steamboat plying the Mississippi River in the latter 1800s. While one can obviously accept seeing it might elicit bystander interest, so what? This has NO CONNECTION AT ALL to ANYTHING in the song. I'll not take time here dwelling on the incoherencies she cavalierly inflicts on the piece, and how simple laziness (just not caring enough) brought them about—it's admittedly a bit of a divagation—but do some web searches if you're curious. (Didn't *anyone* working on her album know how to use a danged telephone—to call The Band, their management, roadies, attorneys, record company, *anybody*—to get the proper lyrics? Of course they did—ah, but who gave a damn, eh?)

The song may not deserve great respect, but her departures and interpolations only compound its problems—and it all underscores, *again*, the overwhelming superciliousness and superficiality so rife in popular song and popular song criticism.

[2]"The Night They Drove Old Dixie Down", copyright 1969 by Robbie Robertson. Quoted here as permitted within the Fair Use provisions of 17 U.S.C.§107.
[3]*Rolling Stone*, October 1969.
[4]*Mystery Train: Images of America in Rock and Roll* (New York: Penguin, 1975), 55.
[5]*Time Magazine*, 10/21/2011.
[6]Oh, the grunt work I go through for y'all. I had the library send a copy of Robertson's autobiography, *Testimony*, to my branch, and just went over to spend an hour searching through the ponderous danged thing—512 pages (no index, table of contents, or chapter titles; none of these good signs). Robertson states the chorus actually came *first*, and he was thrilled with it. So now I just throw up my hands and look to heaven in beseeching exasperation, resting my case. Wow.

Chapter Three

To What End?

I'm patient with stupidity, but not with those who are proud of it.
— Edith Sitwell

Perhaps the point has been sufficiently made in the previous two chapters—but let's quickly dispense with a few more typical examples from the two equally inarticulate schools of practice in contemporary songwriting that we've exposed, before moving forward.

So, ladies and gentlemen, may I present to you some absolute crap—er, I mean 'brilliantly imaginative writing'? I give you John Lennon's "Come Together":

> Here come old flat top,
> He come groovin' up slowly.
> He got joo joo eyeballs;
> He one holy roller;
> He got hair down to his knees—
> Got to be a joker
> He just do what he please.
>
> He wear no shoeshine;
> He got toe jam football;
> He got monkey finger;
> He shoot Coca Cola;
> He say "I know you, you know me—
> One thing I can tell you is
> You got to be free!"

chorus:
> Come together, right now,
> Over me.

He bad production;
He got walrus gumboot;
He got Ono sideboard;
He one spinal cracker;
He got feet down below his knees[7].......—

Okay, enough, enough....

We certainly don't need to continue. Lennon himself says, "The song was created in the studio. It's gobbledygook".[8] (Yes it sure is, John—but admitting that doesn't absolve you of responsibility for it....)

This travesty would make a fine 'Exhibit A' in illustrating how bad things can get when an act Knows It Can Get Away With Anything—and Simply Does Not Care. The lyric writing, er, um—technique?—used here is one I call Refrigerator Magnet Songwriting.

"Come Together" does have an unusual overall sound to it, about that there should be little disagreement. And it's a well-produced recording. A well-produced recording of—well, yes, "gobbledygook". Like a really great-looking classic automobile—without an engine or a steering wheel, sitting on four flat tires. (We'll look at the differences between songwriting and production—picture and frame—later.)

And let's not just exempt it as some 'nonsense verse'—declaring it simply an example from that genre of poetry, and that such assertion exonerates it. It isn't, and it doesn't. (Someone who's perhaps attached to the notion, however, is counseled to read some actual and first-rate nonsense verse, by Edward Lear or Lewis Carroll, among others.)

We'll deal directly with the loathsome 'But It's Poetry!' 'defense' of inept songwriting later, by the way. And we'll examine the basic difference between a poem and a song later on as well. More pertinently, we'll also address the fact that there's such a thing as *bad* poetry—and that calling something 'poetry' does not bestow automatic gravitas.

One can think of so many of Lennon's songs that were similarly concurrently both endowed and crippled. A fascinating one, for example—musically, I mean—is "Lucy in the Sky With Diamonds", a great sounding composition, with an arrangement that's stunningly unique and expertly, inventively produced. And plagued with lyrics that are preposterously self-indulgent and in-your-face stupid. (We'll carefully separate lyrics from music—and both from production—in later chapters as well. This may strike one as obvious and unnecessary, but it's the *failure* to properly do so that licenses, enables—even allows unquestioning consecration of—so many dumbfoundingly trivial efforts.)

And there are *multitudes* of other extremely successful—read: well-known, covered by other acts and commercially lucrative, but ultimately banal—songs like "Come Together". This, folks, is where lauding stream-of-consciousness idiocy and nominal 'Poetic Lyrics' has gotten us—as abetted by the lethal combination of intractable hero worship and celebrity self-entitlement, both of which we'll also address later. And let's keep in mind that John Lennon could be—could be, when he restrained and applied himself—a capable and occasionally even affecting songwriter. But "Come together, over me"? "Come together, over me"? Does a refrain of that repeated adage—or whatever exactly it is: A maxim? A motto? A rallying cry?—make *any* sense?

★

On the other side of the coin, here's one of a zillion available examples accentuating how depressed the bar is in the 'Trying to Say Something Meaningful When Low on Talent' department—this by the persistent but under-equipped John Mellencamp—and another song that I'm sure you've endured far too many times:

Well I was born in a small town.
And I live in a small town.
Probably die in a small town.
Oh, those small communities.

All my friends are so small town.
My parents live in the same small town.
My job is so small town.
Provides little opportunity.

Educated in a small town.
Taught the fear of Jesus in a small town.
Used to daydream in that small town
Another romantic, that's me.

> But I've seen it all in a small town.
> Had myself a ball in a small town.
> Married an L.A. doll and brought her to this small town;
> Now she's small town just like me[9]......—

Again, fine, okay, just—STOP. Please let's not go on.

Utterly *abysmal* writing—competent, at most, on the level of a diligent grade schooler trying his or her best. But OH-so-self-important. This vehicle isn't even a working automobile—it's an empty parking spot. A waste of time. (And elaborating on that last observation, is the song really an extollation of the virtues of small towns and rural life—or of Mellencamp himself? He gives no reasons at all why small towns are great places, does he? But there's a lot of him strutting about and bragging about how supposedly down home and authentic he is—though he <u>also</u> makes damn sure we know he snagged himself a cliché big city Trophy Wife.)

★

How about one more piece of saccharine tripe before we move on—some rubbish from Bob Dylan. One could really never credibly put the words 'Bob Dylan' and 'articulate' in the same sentence—elegance, eloquence, and economy lie outside his compass. But as we'll look at some of his more spasmodically incoherent 'Poetic Lyrics' later on, for now let's briefly address a klutzy waddler from when he attempts to be plain spoken: the Hallmark Card called "Forever Young". (Admittedly, that's not a fair characterization: most Hallmark Cards are better written.)

> May God bless and keep you always.
> May your wishes all come true.
> May you always do for others
> And let others do for you.
>
> May you build a ladder to the stars
> And climb on every rung.
> May you stay forever young.
>
> <u>chorus</u>:
> Forever young; forever young;
> May you stay forever young!

May you grow up to be righteous.
May you grow up to be true.
May you always know the truth
And see the lights surrounding you.

May you always be courageous;
Stand upright and be strong.
May you stay forever young.

chorus repeat

May your hands always be busy.
May your feet always be swift.
May you have a strong foundation
When the winds of changes shift.

May your heart always be joyful.
May your song always be sung.
May you stay forever young.

chorus repeat[10]

There's a foul smelling odor of middlebrow sanctimony exuding from this song. It's maudlin mush. The dopey benediction here—or whatever you want to call it—does nothing but wallow in bankrupt bathos. And it goes absolutely nowhere.

Yet, to be clear, cheap sentiment is actually *not*, in itself, a definitive indictment—if there's *also* something on offer; something new and larger to be gained elsewhere within the package.

You can delight in every present moment, Bob. You may try to guide and properly teach. You can recount your own tests and trials so a child might prepare and prevail when similarly challenged. You may imagine the future man or woman in the face of the child. You may simply long for times past—if you, please, don't just glory in your self-pity; and give us reason why this nostalgia is in fact expansive or ennobling. (And along the way, sure, you might hope the enthusiasm and innocence of youth can be maintained deep into majority. Just one, or a couple, of lines of dead-end sentiment are surely not asking too much of us—as opposed to the *grinding* fucking ordeal of them you've piled up here.) And if you'd taken *any* of those routes—or maybe the lead of wistful, bemused but confident resignation summoned in Malvina Reynolds' touching song, "Turn Around"—you might might have come up with something worthy.

But, as noted, even what you're doing here is *still* potentially okay, *if* you can bring some poetry, some well-written evocations, to surround and expand upon the ultimately pointless title line with which you otherwise unremittingly batter us into insensate apathy.

Here, however, we get the pedestrian tedium of mawkish platitudes—a relentless parade of somnambulant empty clichés—wedged between that banal title line that's pounded over and over again. Puffed up schmaltz. There's no reflection on, or celebration of, current circumstance—the present situation Bob would like to see last forever. (It's also rather sing-songy—not an attribute in a song that would like to be taken as a statement of earnestness and depth.)

By the way, if writing a song in which it's necessary to rhyme 'young', one of the few words available is 'rung'—which naturally makes citing a ladder an easy and fitting choice of image, and climbing it an obvious metaphor for life. Great luck, this. And most any songwriter would surely, happily head in the same general direction with it as did Dylan.

But is "and climb on every rung" the best you can do with that, Bob? I mean what else is someone going to *do* with a friggin' ladder but climb the danged thing? That's pretty much a given, dontcha think? How 'bout we replace your demonstrably feeble "and climb on every rung" with, say, "and gain purchase on each rung", eh? (Or perhaps "<u>find</u> purchase....".) The suggested replacement uses a far more interesting word, adding the connotative element of wishing a demonstrably certain and secure ascent, in place of your anemic tautological mundanity. "And climb on every rung" says nothing. "Find purchase on each rung" is a different matter. I've not given it a lot of thought—there may be yet stronger ideas for that line and couplet. (The additional syllable in my suggestion isn't a problem, as consistent meter isn't obtained elsewhere in the song either.) I cringe at that truly hokey "ladder to the stars" pablum itself, but there's not time here—nor inclination—to rewrite the whole tepid concoction. Yet just about anything is better than this brain-dead "and climb on every rung".

And it all just drones on. "May your wishes all come true." "May you always be courageous / Stand upright and be strong." "May your heart always be joyful / may your song always be sung." It's one gooey, cheese-ball clunker after another.

Is anything said that offers fresh insight? Is anything expressed with such eloquence that we're surprised and delighted, even though the essential observation itself may understandably remain a commonplace? Do we learn one interesting notion, or enjoy just one thought expressed poetically—or even with entertaining novelty? In short, is there *any* reason to indulge this syrupy and laboriously thudding mediocrity?

Yes, surely Bob *deeply* feels the thoughts he's clumsily trying to express here. No doubt. But listen up, please: Sincerity is Not Depth. We'll look more closely at that critical distinction later on. But for now let's just agree that he may be *utterly* sincere with "Forever Young". So what?

It may be proposed, as it was to me by a correspondent, that we might judge or receive "Forever Young" as one does a so-called 'Irish Toast' or 'Irish Blessing': as something gracefully avuncular and light-hearted, (and so somewhat inconsistent with the ponderousness of Dylan's own performances of the song).

But that doesn't help at all.

The best known of those constructions, surely, is the one that goes "May the road rise up to meet you. May the wind always be at your back. May the sun shine warm upon your face, and rains fall soft upon your fields. And until we meet again, may God hold you in the palm of his hand."[11] There's no question that even if this has a legitimate pedigree (and that's doubtful) it is certainly a cliché—it's been over-quoted, over-produced, over-exposed. It borders on kitsch. But that *doesn't* mean that it's actually poorly written. Shakespeare's *Sonnet 18* ("Shall I compare thee to a summer's day?...") is also over-exposed—as is the *Bible's* 23rd Psalm ("The lord is my shepherd, I shall not want...")—but few would deny they're well written. This "Irish Blessing" may or may not be in that league, but it is unquestionably more resonant and poignant—much better written—than Dylan's unctuous song. "Forever Young" is *pure* kitsch; drivel.

★

Maybe you're thinking, "Well, it's way too easy to criticize songs like those looked at so far; anyone can do it. They're lesser efforts." If so, you're partly correct; yes, it's like blasting away at a barrel of minnows.

But 'lesser efforts' implies they're secondary aberrations—and that they most certainly are not. Indeed, these are revered, inflated exemplars of what's held to be the *best* in popular songwriting, written by ostensibly consistently luminous 'artists'. Just think about that for a moment. Because *were* they generally recognized as either secondary efforts by competent writers or as the best work possible from marginally talented hacks—so in either case endured simply as filler material—the situation here would be significantly different.

Or perhaps you're thinking, "Christ Almighty! All the criticisms so far have been *much* too picky. I think these songs are great!". If so, you may not wish to continue reading, as we're attempting to engage in a serious examination of the generally disheartening state of popular song, *divorced* from personal affinities. If you disagree with the characterization of the state of the medium as generally dismal—if you're usually satisfied with, regularly even excited by, what you hear via the internet, radio, film, and television—perhaps even a salute, a nonplussed nod in your direction, may be in order as we part company: you're exactly the 'audience' (i.e. the market) the cynically vacant entertainment industry and its eagerly adhering applicants cherish. And so, um…congratulations?

★

Do we just continue to endure the tsunami of bilge water deluging us daily—and must we complacently resign ourselves to doing so because that's simply what constitutes the overwhelming majority of efforts with which we're presented?

I say we shouldn't. I say no.

[7]"Come Together", copyright 1969 by John Lennon and Paul McCartney. Quoted here as permitted within the Fair Use provisions of 17 U.S.C.§107.
[8]*All We Are Saying: The Last Major Interview with John Lennon and Yoko Ono* by David Sheff. (New York: St Martin's Press, 2000), 201
[9]"Small Town", copyright 1985 John Mellencamp. Quoted here as permitted within the Fair Use provisions of 17 U.S.C.§107.
[10]"Forever Young", copyright 1973 by Bob Dylan. Quoted here as permitted within the Fair Use provisions of 17 U.S.C.§107.
[11]It seems, by the way, that whether of older vintage or recent creation, the first line is actually a mistranslation of the Gaelic. A proper translation apparently renders the more prosaic but operative "May your journey be successful".

Chapter Four

A Personal Remembrance

When I was a child, I spake as a child,
I understood as a child, I thought as a child.
But when I became a man, I put away childish things.
— Saint Paul, *King James Version Bible*

When I was in my mid-teens, I performed—regularly, determinedly, earnestly performed—various songs by the Byrds, Beatles, Rolling Stones; "Blowin' in the Wind" and "The Times They Are A-Changin'", "Don't Think Twice, It's Alright" and others by Bob Dylan; "The Sounds of Silence" by Simon & Garfunkel; and whatever other purportedly serious and thoughtful songs I and others like me were told at the time were 'important' and 'meaningful'.

But frequently—almost always, actually—nagging at me was the feeling that something was missing, something was off or even hollow in most of what I was singing and playing. I outwardly deferred to the judgments from on high that these were great anthems of progressive, even revolutionary, political, social, and musical importance. I mean, clearly and a priori, the acts and their songs seemed to all be on 'the right side' of the severe and multiple great societal divides of the time—and the Important National Media, the Record Industry, and Other Big Successful Acts all said Dylan's songs, especially, were 'brilliant', 'revolutionary', 'towering'; and he himself 'The Voice of A Generation', writing 'true poetry' and so on, and so on.[12]

Yet why didn't I fully subscribe to that? Why did so much of it all just seem to me to be jejune, self-satisfied navel-gazings on one end, and inarticulate and directionless rambles on the other?

The songs pervaded the entire culture. I could hear 'em on the radio a few times in a day, and friends do their own renditions a couple of times that evening. In the face of such overwhelming and inescapable confirmations, my reservations and gut caveats were, surely, simply products of adolescent ignorance, no? Maybe I just wasn't sophisticated enough, or smart enough, or cool enough to get it.

But still, I wondered, could my doubts be warranted?

★

Reaching young adulthood in the oppressively provincial North Florida panhandle, I was a particularly zealous fan of the Buffalo Springfield—a band which included Stephen Stills, Neil Young, and others who almost all subsequently continued on through successful music industry careers. And I was, believe me, Neil Young's Number One Biggest Fan— to me he was a Great Artist, and could simply Do No Wrong.

And now? Now I can barely stand to hear the guy—and roll my eyes at his generally erratic songs, be they more recent or those very same efforts about which I rhapsodized so extravagantly Way Back When.

What happened to my enthusiasm for Neil and his work?

Well, I got older, wiser—more exposed to and knowledgeable about the world. I became more discerning, discriminating, and demanding.

He didn't.

Period.

This book is specifically directed to those who've experienced comparable growth and accrued sapience; who are similarly willing to cast aside convention and cant.

And, as it turns out, we'll even examine Mr Young's work more directly later on. I hadn't expected that going in.

[12]Bob Dylan's deleterious influence on contemporary songwriting is so extensive— and so unchallenged, despite the work itself inconveniently being remarkably shallow and clumsy—that he and it will be frequently referenced and revisited. We'll naturally focus directly on the songs—and on songs by others who've been influenced by him—at length. But unfortunate diversions along the way are that he's *also* properly spotlighted in the chapter on plagiarism, and we'll elsewhere shovel past the mountains of blind celebrity worship from his most obtusely rabid fans and eager disciples. While neither his personal and professional ethics nor the prostrate adulation of his adherents is of direct substance when discussing the work itself, those peripheral considerations are necessarily germane in any discussion of the conventionally imputed merit and impact *of* that work.

Chapter Five

A Later Kick in the Pants

The continual dumbing down of America is most evident in the slow decay of substantive content...it's a growing celebration of ignorance.
— Carl Sagan

Many years following, an acquaintance asked why he never heard me play songs by current songwriters. As I was then slowly preparing to record my next album, I replied that I wasn't averse to learning recent songs, or even including a rendition of one on my coming album, but I hadn't really been listening to much popular music at the time and so was pretty ignorant about what might be a good fit.

No, I didn't intentionally avoid what was popular. Hell, over the years, I'd enjoyed hearing the occasional specific song by mainstream acts like the Beach Boys, Ramones, Lefty Frizzell, the Four Tops, Eminem, Chet Baker, the Who, Snoop Dogg, Celine Dion, Lovin' Spoonful, Norah Jones, the Yardbirds, Gene Pitney, Garth Brooks, the Go-Gos, and others—an almost schizophrenically eclectic assortment I here realize—even the occasional Broadway show tune and French chanson. As we'll note in a later chapter, that a song may be light-minded is not necessarily an indictment, nor an indictment of those who enjoy it. There should always be room for divertissements and escape. The common critical error with all such material, though, is thinking them more than merely enjoyable trifles. And the fatal mistake is glorifying them as Great Art.

But it might be fun to work up something similarly light, mainstream, and current, to record. Hey why not? (This was a little after Johnny Cash garnered renewed attention by recording Trent Reznor's song for Nine Inch Nails, "Hurt". I wasn't an admirer of the recording or of the song—and the match struck me, really, as a kinda cheap gimmick. But the basic idea of doing something outside the expected, *if it can be made to work*, is one that'll always intrigue me.)

The following morning my friend walked in with a gift: two CDs he'd burned for me the night before. One was a compendium of about 20 songs by different current acts he thought were doing the best songwriting at the time. The other was devoted entirely to songs written and performed by Beck. So the next evening, driving a rental car from LA to San Francisco, I studiously listened to them both several times, hoping to hear something that might arouse my enthusiasm.

As with so much in popular music, and even when I turned the treble up and the bass down, it was hard to understand the lyrics to a lot of what was sung.

Strictly as melodies, however, one song out of the 35 or 40 got my interest—a song by Beck, though here again it was hard to get much of the lyrics despite repeated plays. But I became enthused about the possibility of working it up and possibly recording it, as I quickly thought I could do a solid job with the music on guitar. If the lyrics worked, or could be made to work with a little tweaking, then maybe this'd be a good song to include on the album. Hey, great!

So I got home, checked the mail, returned a couple of calls, showered and changed, poured a glass of wine, sat down, and slipped the CD into the computer while finding the lyrics on the internet to follow along.

And?

Well, I guess it might have been expected, really. I've been around.

Unfortunately, the 'writing' was just incredibly stupid. Pretentious, insufferable, meaningless garbage. A complete waste of any intelligent person's time and patience.

(Wonder if maybe I 'just didn't get it'? See footnote 167 on page 278.)

It was honestly just sad that some smirking clown could manufacture this stuff, proudly put his name on it, expect people to buy it, hear it, and cheer it…and they would. I mean, really?

> *It's hard to argue with success.* — Alexandre Dumas
>
> *It's even harder to argue with contented ignorance.* — MK

Chapter Six

Don't Shoot, Dammit!
I'm Just the Messenger!

*In a time of universal self-deception, telling the truth is
a revolutionary act.* — George Orwell

In 1798, a book of poems titled *Lyrical Ballads*, by William Wordsworth
and Samuel Taylor Coleridge, was first published. For the second edition, three years later, Wordsworth
inserted a long and sweeping Preface—in which he attempted to point
out and emphasize the importance of
the foundational thinking that had
premised the book. (The basic thrust of
the Preface, as was intended to be ex-
emplified in the poems themselves,
was to move poetry towards a more
vernacular language, a revolutionary
leap away from the elegant and ornate
writing styles dominant at the time.)

He even fully recognized the imposing Preface might be seen as crass
sales craft—as an attempt to garner favorable reactions to the poems independent of their intrinsic quality. Yet the urgency of what he had to
say about poetry was so important, he felt, that a full presentation of was
incumbent upon him, and necessary to advance the entire art....

In 1954, in the pages of the French film magazine *Cahiers du Cinema*,
then critic (and, of course, within a few years internationally renowned
director) François Truffaut wrote what became recognized as the seminal

call to arms for the nascent Nouvelle Vague (New Wave) in French cinema. In his critical essay entitled "Une certaine tendance du cinéma français" ("A Certain Tendency in French Cinema") he documented and ex-

coriated the ossified so-called 'Tradition of Quality' then prevailing in French filmmaking. His central thesis was germinal in the development of the auteur theory, in which the director—the director who had both talent and the force to maintain a consistent worldview throughout his or her works—was asserted to be the most important creative participant in filmmaking. The director, not the screenwriter, producer, or actors, was the true 'auteur'—author—of a film. Film and film criticism in France—and soon around the world—were never the same again....

Two centuries after Wordsworth and sixty-plus years following Truffaut, I take inspiration from both efforts, and similar revolutionary manifestos, to examine the recent and current state of American popular songwriting (and attendant non-American Anglophonic songwriting generally—so we'll also be including a lot of work from the UK, Canada, and maybe elsewhere). And we'll address the two complementary but equally wrong-headed directions found in general practice: simplistic and impotent lyric writing on the one hand (e.g., "The Night They Drove Old Dixie Down", "Small Town"), and those so-called 'Poetic Lyrics'—poorly-crafted and inarticulate babble, as epitomized in songs by Dylan and so many others, certainly, which've been held in highest critical and often popular esteem in recent decades—on the other (e.g. "American Pie", "Come Together"). I'll offer some thought on why they may actually be two sides of the same coin—why they may derive from the same cultural impulse. And I'll propose some principles and practices that might lead English-language songwriting to more resonance and significance.

This book is a defiant proclamation, a statement of creative and ethical principles, an artistic manifesto.

Most men and women, by birth or nature, lack the means to advance in wealth or power. But all have the ability to advance in knowledge. — Pythagoras

Among the emails that arrived as I was writing, there sometimes came the charge, "You're so negative!", or "You seem so angry!" — really just variations of blaming the messenger for the message. Sure, it's understandably somewhat disorienting, disconcerting, to be confronted with a fact we avoid, but actually already *do* know: that so much of what we've been conditioned to expect in songs is insultingly expendable. Yet it *is* ultimately liberating — and necessary both for our own self-respect, frankly, and for songwriting itself to become more substantive, illuminating, intelligent. So no, I'm not cheaply 'negative'. I am serious.

And it'll slowly become apparent — once we navigate past as much of the industrial pollution and cultural garbage as we can — that there are actually sporadic positive signs here and there as well. You'll see.

The large part of what we'll engage in is literary criticism — treating songs as serious writing — albeit most definitely lit crit sans the usually attendant academic bells, whistles, and occasional misguided frivolities. And when inferior or questionable writing is encountered, we'll go so far as to regularly present alternative conceptual ideas, and even offer very specific writing suggestions for how the song lyrics might be made more effective. We'll also attend to musical aspects, and to some performance matters, as well as to many of the baser peripheral cultural trappings, including popular song criticism. And we're even gonna focus in on some critically important ethical matters along the way.

I hope you'll enter this as one might begin an informal inquisitive dinner dialogue with perceptive friends, or a thoughtful afternoon conversation with trusted pals over coffee or a couple of beers at a neighborhood hang-out — meaning we're gonna jump around, explore tangents, speculate, offer examples positive and negative, digress, and backtrack whenever it may be warranted or productive — en route to some generally hard and fast conclusions. We'll even throw in an occasional funny story.

In other words, this is gonna be rambling, idiosyncratic, and opinionated — intelligently opinionated. And as noted earlier, it won't be just another buoyant celebration of commercially profitable crap.

I expect both the general reader and other practicing songwriters and musicians may find many observations and insights helpful, and occasionally even instructive. I hope so, in any event.

By the way—a stylistic note: Throughout this book, when song lyrics are directly quoted, they'll appear in a way that surely isn't unique, but is admittedly unusual: thoroughly punctuated—periods, question marks, exclamation points, commas, semicolons, colons, dashes, parentheses, brackets, and quotation marks inserted as they may best help define and convey the ideas in those lyrics. Versions of the songs will be, as best as I can determine, as they are performed by the original writer(s), with respect to exact lyrics and the schedule of verses, chorus, bridge, etc. (If a big hit recording is how it's best known—and that differs from the presumed original—the revised presentation may be the way the song is subsequently performed by the original writer(s) as well; meaning they've adjusted it to mirror the hit rendition. Yet I've tried to track down the earliest finished constructions when possible, with some note of significant later versions when of interest.)

And in the effort to find common familiarity in the material considered—most of the songs examined—like those addressed above—will be ones that've been around for a long while: songs the vast majority of which will be well-known by most readers, with only the occasional more recent or obscure title. It's helpful to find as many *shared* exposures in examinations like this as possible. So we'll not look at anything by Jason Mraz, Taylor Swift, Max Martin, Kendrick Lamar, Ed Sheeran, Meghan Trainor—or Whoever-Etcetera-And-So-Forth-Else—but with the adjuvant observation, however, that things are definitely not improving.

In most cases, I'll attempt to keep music and lyrics distinct by using 'composition' and 'composer' when discussing music, and using 'writing' and 'writer' when discussing lyrics.

Also, please be advised:

A recorded song is a marriage of lyrics, music, recorded performance(s), and production. And the best way to gain optimal exposure to that is in an authorized, official release—simply because that's where the creators were most likely to retain some measure of control. They 'signed off' on it, in any event. In fairness to the songwriters and acts whose songs are quoted, in Appendix I appears as good a list as I could compile of the original albums that include the songs examined, and so delivering preferred results. Most operations like YouTube are essentially rip-offs, delivering low-quality sound reproduction while concurrently exploiting—effectively cheating—songwriters of proper, fair royalties.

As a writer and guitar player myself, I may cite an occasional minor example from my own work in passing, as a positive or even as a negative example. (If you wanna hear someone Really Beat the Livin' Hell Outa Himself, though, just get me to critique my *own* songs—I can go on ad-damn-infinitum on things that I think ill-conceived, unmusical, untenable, inarticulate, confused, poorly concocted or executed, or just plain old flat-out fuckin' dumb! I'm a much, *much* tougher critic of my own stuff than you or anyone else could ever be, believe me. And I sure as dang hell ain't no Big Name With A Big Résumé. Yet I hope I'm also perceptive enough to recognize when something of mine may have bearing.)

Finally, I wish to thank the many people who've helped me through the years to ponder through and arrive at the formulations herein—I'm one who tends to think best when bouncing ideas and notions back and forth with someone else, someone for whom I have respect and whose intelligence and insight I find particularly acute. So I'm in lasting debt to Michael Robertson, Morrie Bobrow, and Ken Bullock (San Francisco), Garrett Soden, Michael Varhol, Uri Hertz, and Tré Giles (Los Angeles), Rebecca Chalker and Richard Leslie (New York City), Steve Arwood (Nashville), Frank Lindamood and Karen Graffius-Ashcraft (Tallahassee), Lynne Magin (Chicago), Dan Simberloff (Knoxville), Karl Lundeberg (Washington), and Tom McFarland (Merritt Island). Most of these poor people endured some long (and surely often disruptive) phone discussions and/or email exchanges over the years on ideas that are gathered in this book; though I emphasize that *none* of them agree with everything here. And some may disagree with just about *all* of it. So don't hold anyone but me accountable for factual errors as you may find them, or culpable for intellectual lapses as you may judge them to exist. And I sincerely thank each of the folks above for their forbearance, taste, and intelligence.

I'm also indebted to the many people, some of who are named in Appendix IV, who emailed with their insights, arguments, corrections, and suggestions as this work evolved, posted on my web site, with such input eagerly solicited. So much of what came in was pivotally helpful.

And one last minor stylistic matter just before going to press: as readers have perhaps already noted, I simply prefer British punctuation practice, finding it more clearly logical, as concerns a) no periods after Mr or Ms, etc, b) commas and periods placed outside quotation marks rather than inside, and c) no apostrophes used when writing decades: so 1990s instead of American-Canadian style 1990's. So there.

★

But before we even get into critical specifics of songwriting, I think we need to dispose of much of the accumulated sludge and encrustations that surround and suffocate the topic. Of all fields of entertainment and the performing arts, popular song is perhaps the *most* larded with extraneous nonsense—from imbecilic posturing and ludicrous marketing of acts themselves to pandemic insufferable fan worship. It's inanity ascendant. One of course finds crass preening, cynical calculation, and vapid idolatry everywhere in the performing and fine arts—hell, one finds it to greater or lesser extent in every human endeavor—but probably nowhere is the cancer so metastasized as in popular song.

So first—and, admittedly, a long 'first' it's gonna be—let's look at several quagmires will try to avoid on our journey. Popular music, so ubiquitous and available, is rarely examined coldly—and the common desire for heroes, villains, authority, and vicarious nobility is so determined that it's a field overflowing with breathlessly delivered superficial appreciations. I'm going to take a patient tour d'horizon of many inconsequential pretentions that regularly preclude or undermine what might otherwise become serious discussions of popular song. While many of the things I'll address—perhaps most—are surely obvious to most, I think it's important to expose them deliberately, decisively, one by one.

If you don't wish to take time to revisit what should be the indisputable foundations for a discussion of this sort—and find an attempt at such to be tedious or even condescending—please accept my apologies and go on to Part Two, beginning on page 75, or even skip the Treatise entirely and go on to the Manifesto half of all this (page 121).

But, with sincere respect to my readers, even a quick scan of the immediate chapters following may still be helpful. We're in somewhat uncharted critical waters, after all, and so getting initial bearings.

Thank you.

TREATISE

PART ONE: Distractions, Diversions, Deceptions
— CLEARING AWAY MOUNTAINS OF CRAP —

Chapter Seven

Politics? Religion?...
How About SONGS?!?

Never discuss politics or religion in polite company!
It always starts an argument!
— Your Mother

What your mom and mine both neglected in our educations was teaching us that judging a song almost always gets the same result. You can disagree about a film, painting, or novel, for instance, and easily maintain civility. But start dissing a song someone 'likes', or the act that performs it(!), and All Hell Breaks Loose. It underlines the two primary properties of most songs that can cause such momentous disagreements.

So let's address them before we start out in earnest.

The first is that songs are usually slight—there's regularly not really much going on. The ideas imparted, generally, are so simple, and so simply put, that there's little need for them to even be stated—except perhaps as cheap reinforcement for what we already know or feel. That's if what they're ostensibly about is even clear at all. So much of what's passed off as a song lyric makes such tenuous actual sense that *any* affinity is gonna be similarly subjective, even though it may be inflexibly believed by its holder. It's so often little more than just a title and a melody, stuffed with lots of blurred filler. Challenging the trivial conceit explodes the entire house of cards and leaves little standing—not always something easily accepted.

The second is that, because of the tremendous power of music, even the most pedestrian song can quickly become profoundly memorable, lodging itself into protected places in our lives, with earworm snippets repeating over and over again. The familiarity breeds investment—even if it wasn't originally welcomed.

And so songs become Important. Widely current. Canonized. They can take on a magnitude of authority and reach a level of societal esteem far out of proportion to what may be intrinsically warranted—and so often without any really reasonably productive foundation whatsoever.

Throughout this book, the attempt will be made to divorce *as much as possible* from all influence of current popular opinion. Nothing is sacrosanct; everything on the table. And I'll return to remind on this regularly.

★

Think of how stupid the average person is…and realize half of them are stupider than that. — George Carlin

There's one more line of 'thinking' we should dispose of in this chapter—but one *so* moronic that I'm forced to stress it isn't a straw man argument, but something that was actually encountered more than once while writing.

As noted, the constantly evolving work was posted on my web site, along with an invitation for comments. In significant ways, this book was crowd-sourced—or 'crowd debated', in any event. Due to the many thoughtful, perceptive emails that were kindly sent in, some errors were uncovered, many supporting facts were added, and a few lines of inquiry modified or even discarded as immaterial. All very positive.

Yet it was also surprising how, every once in a great while, a negative commentary on a song was met with a vehement castigation—but, and here's the point, *based entirely* on a variation of "You're wrong about that song…because I like it!", as if such an empty statement had merit.

It doesn't. 'Like' whatever you want. I'll 'like' what I want. And everyone else can do the same. (We'll address this more fully in a later chapter.)

At least those who subscribe to patent pretexts for their personal partialities—'drinking whiskey IN Rye', 'it's the Yankees who were singing', and so forth—are *trying*, though club-footedly, to couch their attachment to this or that poorly written song. Those too intellectually lazy or incapable to attempt even that deserve, I don't know what—resigned pity?

And so yes, the investment by a few correspondents in Being a True and Loyal Die-Hard Fan—defending their (so unfairly disrespected!) pop idol and his, her, or their masterpieces No Matter What—was an occasional annoyance. And we'll deal with the blind banality of fandom and its stubborn delusions in chapters throughout Part One.

But for now, let's digress for a moment:

It so happens that I very much like eating saltine crackers with a big glass of milk—all on its own, as a complete meal. I don't do it often, but it's been an entire lunch or dinner quite a few times in life. I really, really *like* a big pile of saltine crackers with a tall glass of milk.

But I *don't* presume for even one danged minute that this somehow constitutes a compelling argument that it's therefore 'good food', 'nutritionally complete'—or *anything at all* other than my own oddball taste (or admittedly embarrassing complete lack thereof).

No one with half a brain should care what you or I personally 'like', if that's all we can contribute. We're here to discuss substance.

I sure hope as we go along we'll successfully perforate many spurious but conformist arguments concerning songs and songwriting—and a few incredibly, obstinately, dimwitted 'arguments' like this one as well.

★

Unhappy the land in need of heroes. — Bertolt Brecht

Finally, concerning Loyal Die-Hard Fandom itself, we should also stay aware that there's an uncomfortable but undeniable 'fascist element' to it—or another way to put that is that both fascism and devoted fandom would seem to spring from the same mob psychological impulses. Yes, the connection may be easily overstated (and I can almost actually *see* some readers recoiling while reading the previous sentence!) Most certainly, being a committed fan is ordinarily a *benign* dereliction of critical independence—but it is at heart a dereliction nonetheless, a subordination of intellectual independence to fetishism and groupthink. The common, understandable human insecurity that brings forth ready adherence to easy answers which incorporate flatly ridiculous truisms— embodied by savior heroes, and supported by reassurance the strength in numbers of a community similarly committed brings to that capitulation—is what leads to (usually) innocuous exuberant enthusiasms exhibited in mass attendance pop music events and gargantuan sports spectacles. But it also leads, in extremis, to virulent affirmations at Nuremberg Rallies, enlistment in Scientology, Mormonism, and similar ridiculously obvious rackets, North Korean Juche fanaticism—and other patently authoritarian declarations feeding (to admittedly much greater or much lesser extent) on such eagerly blind and assertive allegiances.

Yes, we're ranging *very* widely here—and there's a vast large expanse between being a bubbly, smiling enthusiast of this or that transient pop act and goose-stepping down the boulevard in brown-shirt uniform.

But the point remains that in <u>all</u> matters, it's far better to question— even cynically question—than to suspend critical judgment and be just another self-contented enthusiast; a placid, predisposed, gullible consumer.

And this does directly pertain to serious examinations of popular entertainment and songs.

Chapter Eight

Ground Rule Number One

When not applied strictly to painters, 'artist' has a pretentious sound to it.[13] — Steven Moore

I agree with Mr Moore, above. The term 'artist' is elitist and exclusionary, and should be avoided, even in casual discussion. I'll here consciously try to use the terms 'songwriter', 'lyricist', 'composer', 'performer'—even the rather clinically distancing 'practitioner'—and similar.

The characterization of someone as an artist is an easy handle, of course, but it also abets legitimization of a lot of impertinent and pernicious nonsense. In everyday conversation, we so often use the word as a superlative descriptor: "The guy's not just your regular plumber, he's a real artist!" or "She's not a simple gardener, she's an artist!" The two people are lifted above their peers into an ennobled realm, 'above the riff-raff', when all that's actually intended is to compliment the person in question for doing generally capable or even excellent work in his or her field—he does excellent plumbing, she grows some great vegetables. Good for them both, and good for us who benefit from their efforts.

But artist is indeed a very loaded term, conferring an almost blanket license and excuse for grandiosity and outré self-indulgence—as if someone who's admirably mastered singing in public, for instance, is deserving of specially preferential and coddled treatment; as though we should almost expect, and certainly applaud and reward, diva behavior. It allows—sanctifies—excess, because (again) they're NOT just like you and me, they're lovably crazy, unpredictable ARTISTS. Calling someone working in entertainment (and the so-called performing arts—which is, with similar pretense, really just high-brow entertainment, albeit stationed elsewhere on the cultural continuum, no?[14]) an 'artist' is an insidious elevation. It contributes mightily to the tawdry celebrity culture so prevalent in contemporary society—and hallows a lot of second-rate work.

★

There is no essential difference between the artist and the artisan. An artist is really just an exalted artisan. — Walter Gropius

Songwriting can be an art—it can result in a work of art—and when that happens, it's providential. But sorry, any wide-eyed romantics along for the ride here: good songwriting and good songs are more properly, accurately, carefully considered and crafted work. Inspiration really *is* ninety-nine percent perspiration. And creating a song is, in the end, organized and thoughtful problem solving to reach a desired result, though the solving of the schematic and thematic obstacles—owing to the *technical* exigencies of the task at hand—can often severely alter what had been initially presumed to be that ultimate objective, that ultimate message. Yet whether intended from scratch, or arrived at serendipitously, if an overarching and insightful vision is achieved, then the work may even be properly lauded as a work of art. The effort to get there, however, isn't glamorous. It's a complicated and demanding job.

Similar to rejecting the inadvertent or deliberate aggrandizement perpetrated by so casually throwing around the word artist and the expanded importance it bestows, I recall writer Garrison Keillor intoning in his commanding baritone to comparable end some years back—I'm paraphrasing from memory here—"Writing is a great and noble calling!" (long pause) "Writing is a great and noble calling!...But so is dentistry. And so is nursing. And road repairing."

Yes.

We do ourselves and songwriting a disservice when we call those engaged in it (or working in related fields—including singers, instrumentalists, and producers) artists. We cheat listeners and actually demean the hard work of songwriters when we mystify the complicated process of writing and composing a successful song.

[13] *The Novel: An Alternative History* by Steven Moore. (New York: Continuum, 2010), 7
[14] We'll briefly look at the regularly posited differentiation between 'popular art' and 'high art' in a later chapter.

Chapter Nine

I'm Your Biggest Fan!
You're My Hero!

Only fools have the habit of believing everything written by a famous author is admirable. — François-Marie Arouet (Voltaire)

The Number One Single Biggest Malignancy that enables the vapidity, superficiality, and incoherent posturing so pervasive in contemporary songwriting, criticism, and performance is, as alluded to earlier, Fan Idolatry. Over-the-top adulation. Celebrity ass-kissing. Hero worship.

And as we'll address later, that kind of insipid awe-struck reverence — eager, willful ignorance, really — is found just as often in academics and critics who one should reasonably expect to be past such unseemly displays. This isn't the place to psychoanalyze the popular desperation that finds satisfaction investing stars with veritable supernatural authority, but it is appropriate to expose it as the thoroughly detrimental, even outright destructive, addiction that it is.

It's a common thing to hear "I'm a Beatles fan" — or a Katy Perry, Faith Hill, Bing Crosby, Joni Mitchell, Bruce Springsteen, Queen, Supremes, or Whoever-the-Hell-ELSE fan. But if that enthusiasm, as it easily can, prevents or significantly colors otherwise intelligent appreciation — particularly precluding ready dismissal of inferior (or even downright incompetent) works by that practitioner when warranted — there's no clear benefit in hearing someone's judgments on the act's efforts. One has little legitimacy as a critic if he or she is predisposed to liking blindly (or, far more perniciously, manufacturing or advancing doubtful justifications for) everything this or that act puts forth. Such opinions are obviously bereft of discernment. This person is a fan — an unblinking, unthinking consumer.

Over the years, I've very much enjoyed a lot of what I've heard by Buck Owens and the Buckaroos—friends might understandably call me a 'Buck Owens fan'.[15] Yet I'm well aware he also wrote some really—and yes, I mean *really*—embarrassingly bad stuff, along with the good and the truly great. I submit to you the A-side of a 1967 single, a song of his called "Where Does the Good Times Go?":

Where does the good times go?
Where does the river flow?
Where does the north wind blow?
Where does the good times go?[16]

This is Plain Bad, on just about every level. (Anyone disagree?)

And the really sad news here—as it was with the "American Pie" lyrics quoted earlier—is that this is the chorus. So it's heard three times in the just over two minutes of the recording. YIKES!

I've also immensely enjoyed recordings and live concerts by the Clash back in the day—I still think their first-ever US concert, at Temple Beautiful in San Francisco and to which I went, ranks as the most electrifying rock performance I've attended. And I continue to find their work engaging these many years later. But it's quite unlikely you'll ever hear me lecturing on how uniformly great their writing or composing ostensibly is, or find me performing one of their songs.

Look, we all have our individual enthusiasms and personal preferences; as we all have our guilty pleasures and transient fancies. And with a little study we can ferret out legitimate factual evidence to serve an illegitimate prefabricated notion—that they're just so gosh-darn innovative and creatively dazzling. And even if we can't find it—and whether some actually exists or not—we can make it up. Such is the mental agility and application that is fundamental to everything from brilliant doctoral dissertations to hare-brained conspiracy theories. (We'll delve into this a little more in Chapter Twelve.)

And we've also all been buffaloed in the supermarket checkout line— our curiosity morbidly ensnared, and our eventual bewildered continued attention garnered—by this or that bit of tabloid weirdness perpetrated by this or that act; for whatever reason extraneous, or even integral, to the actual material created by the act.

Divorce yourself as much as possible from all that, please. We're here to evenly examine the work itself.

So while I'll occasionally use the facile agency of a practitioner's name as an easy way into a general discussion of his or her work—standing in for all the collective actual work done *by* that practitioner—it's something else that should be only carefully invoked in serious discussion. While not all of Ernest Hemingway's stories were masterworks, and not even close to all songs by the Beatles were outstanding; yet we calmly speak of loving Hemingway, or the Beatles—or Rembrandt van Rijn, Eero Saarinen, the Rolling Stones, Louise Nevelson, George Balanchine, Elizabeth Barrett Browning, or Whomever. Not a single one of them created only masterpieces. So careful with the praise; too much of it and we've become that unthinking fan, that intellectual cripple. There's a big connotative difference between the words 'customer' and 'consumer'—you never hear of a 'tough consumer'—and I'm urging us all here to be the former. Fans are largely the latter.

And on the other side of the coin, there will occasionally arrive a piece of work from a second-rate act and second-rate songwriters that rises far *above* their usual uninspired efforts. And it's imperative, here as well, to divorce oneself from prejudices about the source and to consider the material itself. Later, as much as I admit it pains me to do so, I'll favorably note the significant accomplishment in an extremely well-known song by the Eagles, an act I utterly detest on just about every level as the apotheosis—rather, nadir—of swaggering commercial mediocrity.[17] But the song in question merits appreciation, and such it shall be properly accorded.

Elsewhere, when discussing the *musical* side of songwriting, I'll similarly and I hope fairly recognize the melodic gifts of composers whose public personas, in apparent but absolutely immaterial contradistinction, may even radiate plain doltishness; in acts I think thoroughly celebrate mindless vapidity.

One does well to remember the lesson so ably imparted by Peter Shaffer in his play, *Amadeus,* and in his subsequent screenplay for the film version, directed by Milos Foreman. But it's one we all instinctively already know, even if the specifics of Shaffer's play (and the very short play by Aleksándr Púshkin upon which it was itself based) are entirely fabricated and fictional. The world isn't patently guaranteed, everything black and l white, all the actors easily pigeonholed; intelligence, morality, and various talents distributed to any individual or throughout society in equitable or predictable measures.

In this examination—other than to expose how such concerns derail the quest for literary-lyrical and musical significance—we're not interested in the messenger, but in the message.

And so we'll close this chapter by reiterating the decisive point made at the beginning: The Number One Single Biggest Malignancy that enables the vapidity, superficiality, and incoherent posturing so pervasive in contemporary songwriting, criticism, and performance is Fan Idolatry.

[15] I produced Buck's first two concerts after Dwight Yoakam coaxed him out of retirement many years back. "Michael Koppy presents Buck Owens and the Buckaroos", in Sacramento and San Francisco: both SRO, hundreds turned away. Buck, his manager, and I got along famously, and it was one of the more rewarding projects I've taken on. (The shows also got me on heavyweight promoter Bill Graham's radar, by the way—but that's a story for another essay one day.)
I mention the association not to name-drop but to underscore that my critique of "Where Does the Good Times Go" is *not* a result of personal animosities or pique—we really *are* here to discuss the work itself, divorced of subjective prejudices or preferences.

[16] "Where Does the Good Times Go", copyright 1967 by Buck Owens. Quoted here as permitted within the Fair Use provisions of 17 U.S.C.§107.

[17] News report from South Carolina: "Police: Eagles Tunes Lead to Bread Knife Brawl", *Charleston Post and Courier*, 9/16/2013, by Christina Elmore:
Police in North Charleston arrested a woman Monday night after she allegedly stabbed her roommate multiple times for refusing to stop playing music by the Eagles. According to the official report, Vernett Bader, 54, became irritated with her 64-year-old roommate (and one-time boyfriend) after he kept rejecting her pleas to turn off the Eagles, telling her to "shut up". Bader finally went to the kitchen and grabbed a knife, which she subsequently used to come back and stab him several times in the arm, hand, and elbow. He managed to wrestle the knife away from her, but she quickly retrieved another from the kitchen and returned to continue her efforts. Bader was held at the Charleston County jail Tuesday pending a bond hearing. The report did not detail which Eagles songs were being played.
What?!? Why was <u>she</u> put in jail?!? Who's *really* the victim here?

Chapter Ten

Herds of Wildebeests Stampeding Across the Veldt!

Fifty Million Elvis Fans Can't Be Wrong!
— Title of a 1958 record album

If fifty million people say a foolish thing, it is still a foolish thing.
— Anatole France, 1880

Similar to blanket idolatry is the argumentum ad populum 'proof' that this or that song—or this or that act—is unquestionably wonderful because it's just so dang popular and commercially successful. Everyone goes to the concerts; the act is pulling in zillions of bucks each week; the songs are all high on the charts!

As I've written elsewhere before, there's also no doubt that McDonald's hawks the most hamburgers and that Procter & Gamble sells the most toilet paper.

So what?

That Buck Owens song, "Where Does the Good Times Go?", mentioned in the previous chapter? Well, it was the Number One Song on the *Billboard Magazine* sales charts for four straight weeks, and sold millions of copies. And? Does that mean it *is* well-written, insightful, and essential after all? Of course not. Or that it's unambitiously pleasant and infectiously painless? Well, maybe—I guess, to some extent, for whatever that's worth. But it was primarily just product—product quickly marketed to pull in as much money as possible while the act was the biggest draw in country music, at the very zenith of its popularity. Bad product—distressingly bad product.

Countless writers, composers, and performers who (and songs that) were wildly popular in past eras and decades have been completely forgotten by history—mention of their names today draws only uncomprehending stares. The same will come to pass for the great mass of the exceptionally popular practitioners and their efforts of today. Hell, the vast majority will be forgotten by next week, as the tightly packed herds of au courant tastemakers and conformist fans dash madly en masse, first this way and then that, in desperate, panicked search for the next serving of packaged, processed acclaim.

For so many reasons, popularity is an extremely feeble metric to invoke in any assessment of artistic merit.

Chapter Eleven

Science Explains Why Peeing Your Pants Beats the Hell Out of Nostalgia

Any of us who are worth anything spend our adulthood in unlearning the follies and expiating the mistakes of our youth.
— Percy Bysshe Shelley

In everyone's life—and especially during stages of adolescence and early adulthood—there's a soundtrack of popular songs associated with specific events and people: a love affair, a memorable afternoon or evening, a political awakening, an unusual incident, etc. The songs become emotionally invested with far more personal involvement than any musical or lyrical appreciation of intrinsic merit might legitimately warrant. We are partial and attached to all with which we associate the song; it has become inextricable from and wholly woven into the memory, whatever that memory may be. Critical detachment is obviated and a warm feeling of self-absorbed engagement and reflective satisfaction is provided.

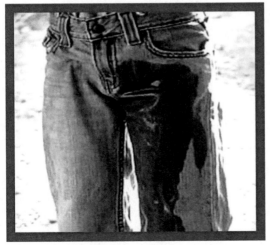

No news here.

Peeing in one's pants also provides a warm feeling all over. But it additionally rids the body of material that no longer has any nourishment. Nostalgia simply revels in the unleashed warmth.

We absolutely gloried in this or that song when newly investigating the world, in love, and 18 years old. It underscored all we were thinking and experiencing. It was the soundtrack of our emerging maturity.

That's just wonderful—but doesn't mean it's good work. I mean hell, it might be. But it most likely isn't.

Okay?

Chapter Twelve

Madonna, Kanye, Coldplay, Bieber, Maroon 5, Lady Antebellum, U2, One Direction—Effluvia, Ephemera, Etcetera, Etcetera

There are few cases in which mere popularity should be considered a proper test of merit; but the case of songwriting is, I think, one of those few. — Edgar Allan Poe

It's easy to kid yourself about how clever a lot of second-rate stuff is...Bullshit is the true American soundtrack.
— George Carlin

The often-great Poe is exactly dead wrong, and the often-great Carlin is precisely right on. (In innocent Edgar's defense, the very lucky guy was never bombarded by decades of "In-A-Gadda-Da-Vida", "Funkytown", "SexyBack", and "Boom Boom Pow". And we'll consult his undeniable wisdom on more important matters later on.)

★

As observed earlier, we all indulge in guilty pleasures—work that provides not even an emotional connection to particular life events, and that we candidly know to be patently inferior, but that we still find amusing, soothing, welcomely unchallenging or similar. (Quite often it's simply stuff with which we've been assaulted so many times that it has become familiar—and therefore unthreatening, safe.) One might just plain

Have A Soft Spot for an "American Pie" or "Small Town" or whatever, *fully* aware they ain't no great art. Fair enough. My own list of guilty pleasures in popular music might be said to include songs and recordings by Gene Autry, the Yardbirds, Ricky Nelson, the Doors, Ernest Tubb, the Cars, the Buzzcocks, and others more recent. The songwriting is almost invariably simple journeyman concoctions—nothing more was considered or even likely—as are most of the performances. So while I personally find it occasionally comfortable—and may even sometimes perform one or more of the songs I first heard by these acts—I wouldn't for a moment presume to champion many of them as more than pleasant trifles, light filler. I hope you'll recognize your own such diversions, and affectionately dispatch them as well.

★

Garbage is always. We will die, civilization will crumble, life as we know it will cease to exist, but trash will recur and endure.
— Robin Nagle

And then there's the Daily Dreck—from a plodding army of disposable acts incapable of more than the most one-dimensional postures and hackneyed trivialities; unequipped at displaying even a remote indication they might be other than subcontractors in the cynical marketing department of a major industrial polluter. This is the innocuous and insidiously invasive rubble that clogs radio, shopping malls, web channels, movies and television. The less time spent here, the better.

One can *try* to intimate artistry, and depth—and convince oneself it's truly there—but crap is crap. Having a weakness for this or that expression of it is all too human—and while properly disconcerting, is grudgingly harmless so long as one doesn't wallow in it to the exclusion of works of actual value, or insecurely defend that vulnerability to it by going on to waste time imputing meaning that doesn't exist and asserting stature that doesn't obtain.

Chapter Thirteen

See You at the Grammys!—A Note on Industrial Smarm Festivals

These things are fiascos. It's all just dimwits taking themselves much too seriously. — John Lydon

This chapter is directed as much, probably even more, to fellow practitioners as it is to general readers, because it's people who work *in* entertainment who are really the biggest advocates and suckers for the repulsively low-rent buffoonery of awards and awards spectacles.

While I've never read anything divulging Woody Allen's reasons for not participating in the Oscars, I suspect his thinking on such events may parallel mine. I know when I've done good work; I know when I've done lesser or even really bad work. And come on, admit it, you do (or should) as well. It's always nice to get praise for one's efforts— maybe even a bit necessary to some social extent. But I sure's

hell don't need—nor even want—confirmation of any of it in the form of a tawdry award, or lack thereof, from purported peers, or via public vote. Yes, such things can be viewed as 'all part of the game'—ways to help sell more merchandise—but is the game, really, simply to move product? If it is, then deck yourself out in a 'meat dress', wear modified motorcycle helmets and claim you're robots from outer space, have someone else (someone more technically capable) write and sing and play the instruments for you, put on diva airs and the most revealing attire you can find; and have at it.

Though all of such affectations and conceits are obviously peripheral to the actual acts of writing, composing, and performing—and so have no direct effect on the quality of the work (and can perhaps therefore be defended as 'harmless fun')—involvement in such industrial smarminess in fact rubs off; one becomes what one has beheld. One perforce buys into prevailing enthusiasms and celebrity, competes with it—and slowly becomes champion of, and commodity in, the basest of swap meets.

Some years ago, I wrote to a major pop music critic, chastising him for a particularly myopic article. His indignant response closed with what he undoubtedly thought was the perfect put-down, the *ultimate* kiss-off: "See you at the Grammys!" he scoffed. When I read the line, alone in my office, I burst into an audible laugh. But I honestly felt a little sad for the poor guy as well. The Grammys clearly meant something conclusive to him; having one presumably the ultimate sine qua non of creative substantiation and legitimacy, and not being part of, or beholden to, that scene at all a defining damnation. Without the Grammys, however would we know what's good, what's 'successful', what's worthwhile?!?

Personally, I've never even watched more than a short stretch of a Grammys telecast—or a Tonys, Oscars, Emmys, Golden Globes, People's Whatevers, MTV Whichevers, Kennedy or AFI Whoevers—and would never participate in person in such an embarrassingly shallow and ostentatiously oleaginous industrial circle-jerk.[18]

Look, the entertainment industry has pretty much the same percentage of folks in it who are plain hacks as does any other line of work—meaning the vast majority generally do what's reasonably expected, with not many readily capable of much beyond that. And while I'm an admittedly very demanding critic, very few of my so-called peers ever actually do something for which I really have honest unqualified admiration. It does occur, most certainly, and when I encounter it I'm loudly effusive with my recognition and praise, believe me! But it's rare. And so for me to even accept the vast majority of hacks *as* peers is to effectively denigrate my own efforts. There are opinions I very respectfully consider— but placing value on what the mass of the industry thinks is simply an abrogation of responsibility, a cry of desperate high-schoolish insecurity.

But let's go a little further. For an award to be welcomed as authoritative confirmation that this year one has done masterful work *equally* requires implicitly accepting that not being handed an award next time around means one's work wasn't so good that year—when in fact the actual creative accomplishment may be far more significant. Again, you should *know* when you've done the best you can, when you may have found, through diligence and application (and occasionally actual inspiration), an innovative idea or presentation; and when you've successfully or unsuccessfully completed the work within all the availabilities and limitations present. Doesn't a patronizing pat on the head and a pot metal paperweight actually somewhat cheapen things?

I strongly expect that in a hundred years or so, our current societal fascination with asinine awards and awards show spectacles will be seen as a laughable proof of our present vapidity and hubris. Awards and awards participation are not worth nothing; they're worth *less* than nothing. This goes for those considered more high-brow as well: Pulitzers, MacArthurs, OBEs, Nobels—does anyone honestly think a war criminal like Henry Kissinger or the unctuous and deplorable Mother Teresa deserved *Peace* Prizes, Nobel or other? Or that Barak Obama properly merited the same award—just a few months after becoming president, having at that point actually achieved virtually nothing of international consequence? Laughably, in fact, the Nobel nominations closed only eleven days after he took office. (In Obama's case, obviously, his greatest accomplishment at the time, to the Nobel folks, was in merely *not* being his mentally-challenged predecessor, George W. Bush. While that's an entirely laudable quality—and he is recognizably brilliant and apparently an admirable human being—you and I ain't Bush either, and we didn't even make the short list. We might also note that, aside from any personal qualities he may or may not possess, by the time he was handed the award, Obama had already launched more drone strikes than Bush had during his entire eight years as president, and by the end of his two terms had been at war in seven countries compared to Bush's four.)[19]

Do not take the fulsome flummery of awards and industry accolades as anything other than low rent celebrity schmooze, devoid of merit. I repeat, awards are not worth nothing; they're worth less than nothing. No one should care how many Grammys or other statues some act has stockpiled—while not definitively exclusionary to having created good work, it's on balance possibly more indictment than accomplishment; and in any event it's certainly a meaningless distraction from evaluating any supposed intrinsic merit in the work itself.

In general, all the calculation, posturing, and preening done jockeying for whatever award is coming—not to mention TONS of money burned to promote jealously covetous egos in the bigger extravaganzas—exposes the entire repulsive mania. In my own experience, I've learned from dealing with various Award Winners on multiple occasions that doing so may require *more* care and studious circumspection—not only to challenge 'rest on one's laurels' complacency or high-handedness (inadvertent or deliberate), but to try to ascertain if there is, or ever was, much real talent, or responsible professionalism, there in the first place.

Enough said; moving on....

[18] I should probably explain that this chapter isn't prompted by a cheap case of sour grapes. Many years ago, relatively naïve and still new to the Entertainment Industry in The Big City, I was even handed an award myself, for "Best Show"—or maybe "Best Overall Production", I can't recall—but it was spoken of as 'the biggie' at some critics' affair in San Francisco. (This despite that I was the only producer and director in Northern California who as a matter of policy never gave out even one free press pass—every single critic attending one of my shows came in holding a full price, paid-for ticket, though of course each was treated professionally. The principled reasons for why and how I successfully engineered that policy is another story for another essay one day.) Someone phoned to report my show had been selected, so I went to the event—held in a 1,400 seat theater—said a few words, and left shortly after. Really, it was pretty much a waste of time—and the award itself was tossed into a dumpster on the walk back home. I mean Christ, who needs that stuffy pretense? (While inserting this footnote, I suddenly flash with a laugh that the story recounted here is a bit reminiscent of the 'Yardbirds scene' in Michelangelo Antonioni's film, *Blow-Up*. No?) But again, seriously, it all really is just tasteless nonsense—who needs it?

[19] For a long list of Nobel disputations, underlining the regularly brutal nitwittedness of that popularly most-revered of recognitions, here's a Wikipedia entry on the topic: https://en.wikipedia.org/wiki/Nobel_Prize_controversies. (web search terms: Nobel controversies Wiki)

Chapter Fourteen

Ethics? In POPULAR MUSIC...?

*The music business is a cruel and shallow money trench, a long
plastic hallway where thieves and pimps run free,
and good men die like dogs.* — Hunter S. Thompson

A primary point I'm trying to make throughout these opening chapters is that one place to *not* seek to find heroes and demigods is in the entertainment industry — popular music in particular, and songwriting as a specific handicraft and livelihood within it. The essential insignificance of *so* much of the work, the capricious permutations of luck, and the potentially vast amounts of money to be gained all conspire to generally boot higher aspiration and principle from the field. (There's an old saying: "The three places you can make a *lot* of money quickly are the stock market, crime, and entertainment". You can also quickly lose a lot in all three.) It's actually common knowledge to even the general public — and despite the robust romanticization bestowed on practitioners by that general public ('artists', see above) — that entertainment, and again, especially popular music, is a demimonde of hucksters, incompetents, parasites, cheats, sleaze-balls, and corporate accountants. Those many who're not fully compromised by the incessant debasements and ethical assaults — and even those wholly impervious to them — must all still navigate around them regularly.

So while Elvis Presley's manager, Tom Parker, famously told associates — only a couple of hours after Presley's death — "This changes nothing!", performers (and songwriters) can themselves be just as cynical, calculating, and avaricious. The tremendous odds against 'making it big', the stifling competition to be the one who hits the jackpot (and then keeps on hitting it), and the jealousy of those others who have actually scored big time financially and critically, altogether severely dampen much if not most of any initial innocence and altruism a novitiate may have once had.

Sure, songwriting can pay big financial and other dividends if fortune responds—but that response is bestowed with only little reference to talent or application.

All too often, a songwriting credit (and remuneration) is taken by someone—a manager, star performer, producer—who had absolutely nothing at all to do with the writing or composing of a song. Sometimes, more artfully, the credit is properly proclaimed—but the financial stipulations contractually required of the writer(s) and composer(s) in order to have the song recorded do the same damage. And sometimes, as we'll note later, a song is plain outright stolen. It's all just part of the power politics of the music business.

And though elegantly reinforced revelation—designed or stumbled upon—is most often the dominant factor in what makes a *great* song great, the day-to-day challenge is more down-in-the-dirt engineering (and, businesswise, simple self-protection!) than receiving divine architectural intervention and concomitant proper recompense. And on the other end, a *lousy* song, well-promoted, can make a career.

For a look at the greedy financial chicaneries and machinations surrounding and infecting just one hallowed act of recent decades, the case of Nirvana is typical.[20]

I hope that with just the couple more chapters we may have properly punctured and deflated all or at least most of the romantic illusions, obsessive exaltations, and impertinent prejudices found when addressing popular music, so that we may begin to tighten focus in on the actual work of songwriting itself. Bear with me....

---

[20]There've been several exposés written—and danged if I'll read 'em all—but one that seems to cover the story well is "A Piece of Kurt Cobain", by Jim DeRogatis, *Chicago Sun-Times*, 3/10/2002. (Web search terms: Piece Cobain DeRogatis)

Chapter Fifteen

Dunno Much 'Bout Art, But I Know What I Like

When small men attempt great enterprises, they always end by reducing them to the level of their mediocrity. — Napoleon Bonaparte

In most of these introductory chapters, I've attempted to place some limits on unsupported enthusiasms. Here I wish to open up the other side a bit, to expand appreciations—and knock off *negative* predispositions.

Don't like rap? Absolutely *hate* Broadway musicals? Simply *can not stand* grunge? Delta blues? Bel canto? Funk?

Really? Reminds me of a proclamation I hear all the time from people about a certain kind of television program—and perhaps you've said it yourself: "I hate sitcoms!"

My response? "It's not the *form* in which the piece arrives, it's the *execution*. You've allowed your understandable habitual disappointment with what you've been offered to make you incorrectly dismiss what is simply a theatrical structure."

Don't believe me? Okay, let's play a little game. I'll list a bunch of live three- and four-camera sitcoms from the past many years—no animation (*Family Guy*, *The Simpsons*, etc), no single-camera show (*M*A*S*H*, *The Office*, *The Games*, etc). There's no doubt whatsoever that we'll disagree on which ones we think 'good' and which ones 'bad', but I have absolute confidence you'll agree some of these shows were well-done, first-rate work. You actually enjoyed—*admired*—this one and that one.

Ready?

Some from the UK, some from the US, in alphabetical order: *All in the Family*, *The Andy Griffith Show*, *Blackadder*, *Cheers*, *The Cosby Show*, *The Dick Van Dyke Show*, *Fawlty Towers*, *Frasier*, *Friends*, *Gilligan's Island*, *The*

Honeymooners, I Love Lucy, The Mary Tyler Moore Show, Mork and Mindy, Parks and Recreation, Roseanne, Seinfeld, Will and Grace, Yes Minister.

No, I didn't say they were all great. (To me personally some of these are simply unendurable.) But as with me, I guarantee that you also didn't hate every one of them; because the ones you liked were, well—and I'm quoting YOU here—"the exceptions".

Yes, they were. And so it turns out you don't actually dislike sitcoms. But what you really dislike is incompetent work and stupidity—not situation comedy as a genre. And you're right that 'incompetent work' and 'stupidity' are terms that most certainly and accurately describe the overwhelming vast majority *of* sitcoms. But it's really the execution that was insufferable, not the format.

The same self-aware openness should hold for genres of song. Yes, most of the stuff in (country, cabaret, bluegrass, heavy metal, R&B, fill-in-genre-here) is garbage. But it's not the form—the style—it's the execution. And that even goes for styles in *which* the presentation—death metal, anyone? opera?—seems to be, or even actually is, determined to be as off-putting as possible to all but an intended narrow fan base.

I suspect that much of the resolute blindness found in genre preferences basically derives from a kinda 'haughty laziness'—just an Iron Determination to peremptorily dismiss anything and everything recent, and/or anything not falling easily within a strictly pre-determined bias. Why do that? Because it's just easier, quicker. And in the lazy listener's defense—as we'll note here again and again—most of what we're presented with in *every* genre is, indeed, cynical fly-by-night ridiculousness.

But good work—incisive, entertaining, relevant, well-crafted work—can be done in just about *any* format by a talented songwriter who applies himself or herself. It's not the style that matters, it's the work that is achieved *in* the style. After all and for example, the well-known singing cowboy song, "Don't Fence Me In"—the kind of thing one might reasonably expect to have been churned out of early Nashville or to even be a traditional folk song—was written by that ultimate urbane sophisticate, Cole Porter. And I bet if he'd tried he might have written and composed a great song in *any* genre.[21]

[21] A few of the lyrics were adapted, quite loosely, from "Open Range", a 1936 poem by 'cowboy poet' Robert Fletcher.

Chapter Sixteen

Ever Notice the Worst Writing in an Insightful Pop Music Review—Even a Rave—Usually Shows Up When the Critic Quotes the Band's Lyrics?

Writing about music is like dancing about architecture. — Martin Mull

A quick digression to begin this chapter: There's little actual music discussed in a review or article on popular music or musicians that is directed to a general readership. And that's logical, of course, insofar as even the rare musically knowledgeable critic faces the brick wall of an overwhelmingly musically illiterate readership. Less than 2% of the population can read music at even a rudimentary level, and the percentage that understands even a loose general lexicon of musical terms is still quite small. So our hypothetical musically conversant critic is precluded from entering into a full critique of the actual music. What's left for him or her to comment upon and fill out the article is the act's lyrics, the record production, and—most easily mined for presumably factual material by the critic but of least significance—the biography, posturing, and industrial marketing of the act. This can perhaps then extend on to the critic's posited cultural antecedents or impact of the act being examined. It's a challenge to not waver off track into press agentry on one side, and speculative cultural fantasy on the other. Neither is popular song criticism.

While the preceding may not strike as particularly contributory to the general discussion here, the tendency of those involved throughout popular song to talk about 'popular *music*'—practitioners characterizing themselves foremostly as musicians, and often the general dwelling on instrumental virtuosity and public performance—has in fact a detrimental effect on songwriting itself. We'll address that insidious diversion in a later chapter.

(And one might properly have sympathy for critics, constantly flooded—*overwhelmed*—by the promotional hype zeroing in from every direction. Ya hafta wonder if the job wouldn't be easier—and better for all concerned?—if pop music critics were able to practice an anonymity similar to that regularly engaged in by major restaurant reviewers. How in hell a conscientious professional can stay 'in charge' and not become overly-jaded, flummoxed, irritated, on occasion even unconsciously compromised—or *all* the foregoing simultaneously—must be an ongoing challenge.)

★

These critics with all the illusions they create about artists—it's really just idol worship. — John Lennon

Limitations imposed on a musically educated and serious pop music critic by his or her musically illiterate readership are unfortunate but understandable. Of far greater note—another dimension entirely—is authority invested in ostensibly sober-minded academics and professional critics who turn out to be plain incompetent, or desperately panting lovesick groupies.

But the frenzied infatuation of over-anxious fandom can be encountered anywhere—from the patriciate to the hoi polloi.

And so I give you just one example, from probably THE most prominent deliriously swooning academic of them all: former Cambridge and Oxford University (now Boston University) professor, past president of the Association of Literary Scholars, knighted by Queen Elizabeth, author of over thirty books on poets and poetry—and insufferably cretinous Bob Dylan fanboy—Sir Christopher Ricks:

> *I think it's an immense privilege simply to be <u>alive</u> at the same time as Bob Dylan! We should all be so grateful!...Not a day goes by when I don't listen to him or at least think about him!*[22]

Yes, academics and intellectuals can be just as embarrassingly besotted with celebrity and corrupted by hero worship as anyone else. There are literally thousands—thousands—of books about the Beatles, for instance, over 900 Dylan hagiographies, and many hundreds of books on Elvis and the Rolling Stones. Few of any of these rise above being simple endorsements of celebrity. (Why Dylan and his songs are such an ideal hobby for the regnant crop of baby boomer academics, however, is particularly noteworthy and will be looked at in a later chapter.)

But let me also be clear that finding meanings hidden in artistic works, diving beneath the surface to unearth resonant, internally consistent alternate readings and applications of what the writer has provided—whether such was intentionally created by the writer or wholly imputed and supported by careful critical analysis—is a valuable and, if successful, a vastly rewarding scholarly venture. (The key phrase in the preceding sentence is "supported by careful critical analysis"—meaning half-assed ravings stemming from unbridled idol worship don't make the grade.) Secondary meanings and allusive harmonies in a creative work can be a sobering substantiation of artistic accomplishment—though, importantly, a work may be admirably insightful and eloquent without them. Does Michelangelo's *Pietà* require subliminal messaging to be properly considered breathtaking? Any questions? We're not philistines here.

★

Those who can do, those who can't become teachers.
— George Bernard Shaw

Within popular music academia we find a lot of frustrated de facto conspiracy theorists—scholars and would-be scholars who can (and will) find and pound together the most absurd connections, concordances and extrapolations from the most tenuous evidence, all to support his or her pre-existing fetish. Religious zealots do this kinda thing all the time—and so can the ambitious, assertively dense academic drone.

Let's look for a moment at the aforementioned Mr Ricks and his galumphing, utterly dreadful 528-page homage to Bob's lyrics, *Dylan's Visions of Sin*[23]. It's one of the best-known examples of what might be termed a Dylan Devotional—and a book so poorly written and smugly self-satisfied with its juvenile half-clevernesses that one quickly wants to simply throw the damned thing across the room in utter disgust. Aside from the just plain vaingloriously sophomoric writing, it's packed with disheveled sophistry and servile genuflections—comparable, perhaps, to a lengthy North Korean news chronicle of the Dear Leader's latest divine intervention. Ricks, as with so many enraptured fans, is the ecstatic parasite finding immortal magnificence everywhere he looks. And I do mean *everywhere*. Forget about 'careful critical analysis' as mentioned above; this guy suffers from childish over-excitement, proudly trumpeting whatever half-baked disconnected notions enter his wide-open head at any given moment. One presumes the fellow may be an infectiously enthusiastic teacher to bright-eyed college freshman out in the Big Wide World for the first time. And that's wonderful. But he's an utterly *lousy* student—a walking personification of 'literary confirmation bias': his preconception dictates his judgment. Dylan wrote it? It is, ipso facto, dazzling. But this Ultimate Eager Fan—his pious, penitent attendance is de rigueur at every performance his idol plays within driving range[24] (and, of course, each one of these performances is life-changing)—is more than just your average tormented groupie. He goes so far—and yes, I know this is hard to believe, yet it's true—as to write the most mawkish, insipidly juvenile fan letters to his hero. No, not at all of the "let me ask about the literary antecedents or poetic intentions of this line in (insert song title here)"-type, but complaining, with deep personal anguish, about Bob's moustache—like some lovelorn pre-pubescent girl moping beneath a bedroom wall of cherished boyband posters, or a young boy (in this case, rather, an octogenarian academic) tormented by homoerotic obsession.[25]

(In case you wonder: yes, I became curious about Ricks after suffering his jaw-droppingly inane book and recalling I'd just seen a similarly muddled piece by him on another matter in *The New York Review*. So I clicked around to get some background, and the weirdness just piled up higher and higher. And as I argued earlier in the section on awards and awards shows, my advice to readers is to not be cowed by credentials and résumé. Intellectual bantamweights like Ricks—like other occasional high-voltage/low-wattage characters prominent here and there around the world—can sometimes build impressive careers. Good for them. But let's withhold respect until we encounter genuine ability. On paper, Sarah Palin and Donald Trump have also had impressive careers. So what?)

I'll go on a bit here, because the puppy love of this 'academic authority' is so ridiculously revealing, and it's *emblematic* of the fact that with bozos like this we're *not* dealing with thoughtful analysts at all but simply with ordinary armchair fans and smitten hobbyists. Ricks not only owns nearly 2,000 bootleg Dylan albums, tapes, and studio outtakes, but he keeps in his office—and again, I am *not* making this up—the actual bathtub that came from Dylan's childhood home in Minnesota, purchased on eBay, "It's where the baby Bob made his first splash!" gushes Ricks. Wowie.

Yes, *this* is what we're up against, folks.

I'll stop making fun of hapless Sir Christopher after this final sample of, um, 'sober analysis' from him:

> *Bob Dylan is unquestionably the greatest living user of the English language!*[26]

Holy friggin' crap. Yep, he's talking about the fellow who gave us the klutzy "Forever Young", among other graceless embarrassments. What can you say? This is *not* a competent critic, nor even a capable intellect; this is an undisciplined, scatterbrained fan. But enough; comedy's over.

And no, while out-and-out creepy infatuation with his hero obviously doesn't rule out sad sack Ricks as a possibly knowledgeable commentator on Dylan's writing, his critiques unfortunately (but predictably) are fully consistent with what one expects: rapturous, unhinged, acrobatic panegyrics supported by the thinnest of conceits and the most pretzeled of arguments, interspersed with the occasionally curious but effectively immaterial factual notice. In the end, an over-caffeinated confusion of giddiness and plain idiocy. An in-depth appraisal of *Dylan's Visions of Sin* is outside the scope of this effort, but to get an idea of the grandstanding speciousness displayed, a few reviews are cited in footnote 27 below.[27]

Okay, sure, the poor Ricks is perhaps singularly cringe-worthy. But there are many, *many* more hopelessly swooning superfans like him spread throughout academia. Do not think the guy unique. He ain't.

And as noted earlier in the chapter entitled "I'm Your Biggest Fan!", idolatry is not criticism—even when wrapped in scholastic sanctifications. And you know something more? It's not really even appreciation.

★

...and those who can't teach become critics. — H. L. Mencken

Finally, we come to the Eighth Circle of Hell,[28] the exclusive back-stage VIP lounge of fungible 'rock journalist intellectuals'—almost an oxymoron, this—like (again), veteran Greil Marcus, to pick just one:

> *I'm not interested in what the songwriter thinks he or she is do-ing, what their desires are, what their intent is. What I'm inter-ested in is what happens to the song when it's out there in the world...Performance is more important than composition to me.*[29]

With the absolutely stunning remarks above, Marcus fairly disquali-fies himself as a critic of popular song. Yes, a song should arguably stand on its own—generally, that is, though most certainly not always—and we'll get to that later. But that's not what Marcus is arguing, as he's pa-tently not really interested in the real world, but in his own tail-wagging-dog solipsistic pseudo-anthropology. (See his take on "The Night They Drove Old Dixie Down" on page 11.) And, of course, performance is ob-viously quite *secondary* to composition when analyzing a song—indeed composition, the writing, is the inextricable *foundation* of any discussion of performance.[30] His many books, including *Mystery Train*, the re-release of which was the focus of the above interview quote, while superficially interesting here and there, are essentially the purple prose of the impetu-ous infatuate who's just not really listening—and he's obviously in water way beyond his depth when opining on popular songs themselves.

Not convinced? Here's another bit of ruthlessly tough, rigorous criti-cism from Mr Marcus:

> *If by classic blues you mean <u>any</u> recording from the '20s and '30s, I'm not sure I've ever heard a bad classic blues!*[31]

Hopeless. But *not* unusual.

★

The problem with rock criticism is the lack of criticism of the criticism — Jon Landau

I don't know and have never dealt with either of the two fellows whose ridiculousness I expose here, and surely Marcus and Ricks are well-intentioned and not deliberately obtuse. And, again, I could have easily chosen from among *many* others to find comparable exemplars of so much that's bankrupt in the world of popular music criticism—no, they're *not* at all outliers, and their staggering, swaggering goofiness is *far* from unusual.

They're simply run-of-the-mill starry-eyed fans, after all—run-of-the-mill starry-eyed fans with credentials. So perhaps a proper fit for their talents would be writing regular columns in *Seventeen* or *Tiger Beat*; their breathless ejaculations wedged between similarly gripping articles on "Beating Acne For Good!" and "Planning the Perfect Slumber Party!"

For popular music to rise above the inconsequential, the clueless, the puerile, it'd be helpful if writers *on* popular music also rose, en masse, above the inconsequential, the clueless, the puerile.

★

But back to the immediate matter at hand: the rhetorical question posed in the heading to this chapter, because journeymen examples like Marcus and Ricks do know the language, and of the two at least Marcus can on occasion also capably use it. The writing in popular music criticism itself is regularly to a higher standard than the writing in the songs being examined.

The Parable of the Blind Leading the Blind
Peter Breughel the Elder

And so, how many times have you delved into a music review in a reputably literate publication and/or by a presumably knowledgeable critic only to find, down deep in the piece when the act's lyrics are finally looked at, that those lines are totally or near-totally lacking in intrinsically worthy observation or insight? They just lie there, leaden.

The worst writing in the article, yes, ends up having been those quoted lyrics—providing yet another anecdotal illustration of the pandemic unfocused poverty currently ascendant in American songwriting.

[22]*New York Times*, 9/9/2004, "Dylan, Master Poet? Don't Think Twice, It's Alright", by Charles McGrath.

[23]In deference to William Morris' famous instruction, "Have nothing in your house that you do not know to be useful, or believe to be beautiful", stuff this brazenly bad should certainly be neither purchased nor despoil someone's bookshelves. (If you've simply got to see what could warrant such disgust, your local library may have a copy; see it there. Email me with your own reactions.)

[24]Similarly, see former New Jersey Governor Chris Christie's obsession with Bruce Springsteen (reportedly 141 concerts and counting), or any ardent Deadhead's devotional pilgrimages.

[25]*New York Times*, 9/9/2004, McGrath, "Dylan, Master Poet? Don't Think Twice, It's Alright": **After the release of Dylan's *Time Out of Mind* album in 1997, Mr Ricks was upset by the thin little mustache that Dylan had begun sporting. "I just don't think it looks good," he said. "Do you?" He added that he thought about getting up a petition reading: "Mr Dylan, please remove the stipple from your upper lip." "I didn't send it," he said, "because my students said it might hurt his feelings."**

[26]*Writers and Company*, CBC Radio, 10/16/2016, interviewed by Eleanor Wachtel.

[27]Some perceptive and intelligent reviews include ones by Eric Ormsby in *The New Criterion*: https://www.newcriterion.com/articles.cfm/blowinwind-1483 (web search terms: Blowin' Wind – New Criterion)
Christopher Hitchens in *The Weekly Standard*:
https://www.weeklystandard.com/christopher-hitchens/americas-poet (web search terms: America's Poet – Weekly Standard); and a somewhat lighter but also generally on-target review by Andy Fogle in PopMatters:
http://www.popmatters.com/review/dylans-vision-of-sin/ (web search terms: Visions Sin – Pop Matters)

[28]Fraud. (And, okay, to detractors this book may seem to have originated in the Sixth Circle of Hell: Heresy. Great.)

[29]ASCAP.com, 7/28/2015, "Rock Critic Greil Marcus on the Power of Songwriters", interviewed by Steven Rosenfeld.

[30]Similarly, in another field, here's comic actor Jason Alexander on the success of the television show, *Seinfeld*: **"Well, 90% of the journey was in the great writing. The four of us (actors) just took it the last 10% of the way."**

[31]RockCriticsArchives.com, 3/12/2002, "Online Exchange with Greil Marcus".

Chapter Seventeen

Those Pesky, Over-Idealized Nineteen-Sixties

During the 1960s, I think, people forgot what emotions were supposed to be. And I don't think they've ever remembered. — Andy Warhol

The rise of the Beatles, Stones, Hendrix, Dylan, CSN&Y and other popularly successful acts in the 1960s—combined with the political and cultural uncertainties and re-evaluations that pervaded the period—have given it a glamorized importance in popular songwriting beyond what's actually merited.

The revolution in song lyrics ascribed to the 1960s was in reality a principally cosmetic and superficial development. Discard all the over-romanticization, and probably the primary *lasting* positive accomplishment of the turmoil of activity was in encouraging longer songs, this due largely to the incorporation of folk music into the popular mainstream.

The important complementary introduction of greater musical sophistication—this unrelated to the influence of folk music—is also significant, though the musical stagnation of immediately preceding years pretty much *mandated* such inexorable progress. Thank god for the arrival of and subsequent growing capabilities revealed on occasion by the Beatles, Brian Wilson, and other new musical minds and influences as well, because popular music—melody and harmonies—had effectively reached something of a dead end. (More on this in Chapter Forty-Two.)

But while efforts had regularly been made to liberate popular songs from the iron-fisted demands of radio programmers for short compositions, that enabled wedging more commercials onto the air, and jukebox

owners, because shorter plays meant more coins in slots over time, legitimate folk songs—so many of which derived as reportage of real events,
and so necessarily governed by the desire to provide a full recounting of
the facts and effects of those events—came without such industrial prohibitions. This is not to say that folk songs, when occasionally packaged for
popular commercial exploitation, hadn't been severely edited to conform
to mercantile expectations of length (and content—cf. the nominal 'house'
in "The House of the Rising Sun", another aspect of which song is discussed in a later chapter, transformed from a whorehouse into a more
publicly palatable gambling venue), but they initially arrived fully-
formed, without the prior restraint of compression for length universally
expected as a matter of course from Tin Pan Alley efforts. The onslaught
of songs from this quarter, and of original efforts partaking of those
somewhat unfettered configurations folk songs had introduced—coupled
with the changing landscape of radio itself—was truly expanding.

Unfortunately, other than in that one simply superficial mechanical
aspect—length—neither the literal song constructions nor the depth or
proficiency of the writing in original lyrics was really affected. Song structures, with few notable exceptions (and even those all-too-often simply
rudderless self-indulgences and 'jams') were still regularly predictable
and formulaic—with those most adhering to folk music archetypes arguably the most retrograde. (By 'song structures' and 'constructions', here, I
address the simple scheduled use and placement of verses, chorus, introductory verse [in older song structures], bridge, refrain, pre-chorus and
etc—not melody and harmony, which is another matter, and which, as
noted, did attain greater sophistication. We'll address song structure later,
in Chapter Fifty-Six.) Lyrically, in place of where there had earlier been
banal simplicities, were lodged undisciplined meanderings that were similarly banal—and the widespread ratification of pretentiously inchoate,
inarticulate nonsense and near-nonsense, i.e. those 'Poetic Lyrics'.

It's of course understandable that the suggested freedoms from the
extremely limited palette of lyrical ideas found in doo-wop and similar
coincident 1950s popular songs birthed by exposure to folk songs should
be deliriously welcomed by both songwriters and audiences. And good
for that. But what was accomplished with the newly revealed options is
a whole other story—probably as much due to the iron grip of cynical

corporate machinations as to the entropic cultural dumbing down regularly wrought by celebrity affectations. Both influences inevitably incline toward mediocrity. As we'll see when looking at high-profile examples from the singer-songwriter school licensed by the new freedoms inaugurated, very little of it merits the respect it was so readily, eagerly accorded. In fact, it can be posited that what derived was really more smoke and mirrors, cloaked in portentous hype, than any actual revolutionary progression. Rampant pretense—simply subsuming the previously ascendant rampant lack of ambition—in a broadly ersatz 'revolution'.

Chapter Eighteen

So Where Are We?

When I hear a song that gets my attention I kind of right away want to see the lyrics, because it's sometimes hard to understand them all and I don't want to become attached to something that's just stupid.
— Marika Lundeberg

We're now going to look at a well-known song, and we're going to adhere to the proscriptions and admonishments in the immediately preceding chapters in Part One. We're *not* going to be influenced by:

1. Our personal nostalgia
2. The songwriter's fame and public success
3. Various awards and critical plaudits the song or songwriter may have garnered
4. How many times it's been recorded or performed
5. The amount of money it's surely earned

We are also not going to be concerned—yet, anyway—with:

1. The melody
2. The vocal performance of the song we know best or personally prefer
3. The instrumental performances
4. The original recording

It's a test.
Are ya ready? Here we go:

I give her all my love;
That's all I do.
And if you saw my love

You'd love her too—
I love her.

She gives me everything;
And tenderly
The kiss my lover brings;
She brings to me;
And I love her.

A love like ours
Could never die,
As long as I
Have you near me.

Bright are the stars that shine;
Dark is the sky.
I know this love of mine
Will never die;
And I love her.

Bright are the stars that shine;
Dark is the sky.
I know this love of mine
Will never die;
And I love her.[32]

I'll presume that every reader here almost immediately, within the first line or two, recognizes this song is "And I Love Her", by Paul McCartney, and so the tune, evoked personal connections and re-awakened memories, admiration for the Beatles generally, and other impertinent peripherals clog the mind while one reads the lyrics.[33]

But now that we've gone through that beclouded experience, however, perhaps read them again—*divorced* from all that. Go ahead.

★

McCartney has said "It's the first ballad that I impressed myself with."[34] Sad to note, he's apparently not chagrined when he says that, and he continues to regularly, confidently perform "And I Love Her" precisely as originally written.

This is writing so pedestrian, so thudding, that we surely don't really need to take it apart; yet a quick dissection may still be in order, if only to unequivocally substantiate the obvious crudeness.

If "I give her all my love" needs to be followed just a couple of lines later with "I love her", someone obviously hasn't been listening to what's already been said, Paul—or you don't realize you're being redundant. You give her all your love…AND you also love her? Did we miss something? (The first time there's no "and" before the "I love her", which might allow someone to aver the line is simply an acceptable reiteration, a summation, of the preceding, and not a pat redundancy. I think that 'someone' would be foolish. This is decidedly *not* well-wrought writing.)

And the "If you saw my love, you'd love her too" line rather demotes the level of ardor, Paul, as you're just saying she looks good—a superficial and fleeting basis for the sublime love you wish to proclaim. "If you *knew* my love" would be much better, certainly—and on a practical level also a) sings better, and b) provides an additional, interior rhyme for the lines ending "do" and "too". Good. After the second verse—filled with some more clunkers—we learn your love "could never die"…ONLY as long as you have her near you? So when she goes to visit her dying Aunt Agnes, that love will basically evaporate, eh? That's what you're implying. A true love would presumably be one that would easily weather a little distance and time apart, so *that* is what you should be celebrating.

And we end with the gooey, but twice-sung(!) "Bright are the stars that shine; dark is the sky" verse—which reminds, frankly, of a "Roses are red, violets are blue" bit of trite boilerplate. It's filler. Just plain yuck.

But 'yuck' that's been performed and recorded by others *thousands* of times. It's one of the *most* venerated songs of the past half-century.

What more needs to be said about the stunted state of popular song?

★

Oh, I do hear you, McCartney Fans and Beatles Fans: HOW can I presume to separate the lyrics from the rest of this song?!? What about Paul's melody? And his singing of the song? And George Harrison's memorable guitar riffs? It's plain wrong to separate the music and lyrics like this—the song is a complete piece! That's what a song *is*!

And you're sorta right. Well, superficially, anyway. The finished song—and the original recording—are certainly 'of a piece'.

But no, we most definitely *can* separate music and lyrics. And we *should* separate music and lyrics. And—guess what—we already *do* separate music and lyrics. I'll prove that to you in a later chapter.

A friend suggested we might kindly—but *steeply*—lower our standards and excuse "And I Love Her" as a song targeted at 13-year olds. But as we'll also note later on (Chapter Thirty-Seven: The Kids Are Alright!), that's really just a pseudo-justification for inferior work. I myself remember wincing, or the childhood equivalent of wincing, certainly, when I first heard "And I Love Her"—and I doubt I was alone in that reaction.

Later on, we'll look again at this very song, to examine other aspects of it—everything else substantive that's part of it. But I said "everything else *substantive*", so no, we still won't care *who* wrote it, composed it, sang it and played on it; how big a hit it was/is; and so on and so on.

It has also been proposed by a correspondent, that, because it's an 'early period' Beatles song, it might be received more charitably than later efforts that aspired to greater gravitas. But again, it's one of their two or three (depending on your source) *most* covered songs, and it's regularly praised as great work. So no.

★

Despite the heterodox positions advanced throughout this Treatise and Manifesto, it's at heart simply an appeal to intellectual integrity. So be entirely honest and candid: is there any plausible world in which the above song lyrics themselves can be properly characterized as anything other than second-rate dreck—or your choice of words saying the equivalent?

Someone can certainly still 'like' the song anyway—I think we've sufficiently hammered that unsubtle point home in earlier chapters. But if a reader remains unable to look objectively at the lyrics to "And I Love Her", severed from extraneous considerations, to engage the writing on its own merit—or rather, its embarrassing *lack* of merit—he or she is beyond the reach of what we're involved in here.

---

[32]"And I Love Her", copyright 1964 by John Lennon and Paul McCartney. Quoted here as permitted within the Fair Use provisions of 17 U.S.C.§107.

[33]John Lennon contributed a little work on the chorus section of "And I Love Her", but the extent of that secondary contribution was contested by him and McCartney.

[34]*Paul McCartney: Many Years From Now*, by Barry Miles. (London: Secker & Warburg, 1997), 122

PART TWO: On Performance and Genre

Here we inspect the popular song landscape: where bodies are buried, who's digging the graves—and how thick the concrete is that covers it all. We'll also light on occasional 'cracks in the pavement'—actual positive inclinations and practices hidden within the various otherwise generally barren environs—that will solidly inform the overall direction of our effort.

Chapter Nineteen

"Yeah I Know It's Crap, But You Really Hafta See 'Em Live!"

You can fool some of the people all of the time, and all of the people some of the time, but you can't fool all of the people all of the time.
— Abraham Lincoln

We'll now start to look at how popular songs are presented to us, as well as whence they derive.

And to start off this short chapter, let me quote myself—a dictum I attempt to present, whenever appropriate, in as close an approximation as I can to Charlton Heston playing Moses thunderously parting the Red Sea: A Recording Is Not A Performance. I'll repeat that—forwards and backwards, with doubled exclamation points at the end: A Recording Is Not A Performance! A Performance Is Not A Recording!!

Excitement elicited by a live performance is entirely unrelated to excitement elicited by a recording. In basest example, there's no doubt one can be lifted to congenial enthusiasm drinking beer with friends, listening to or dancing to some practiced bar band covering hits of the day and yesterday. A fun evening is had.

A recording, however, has nothing whatsoever to do with that or any other live performance—and if the act, and the material of the act, actually merits recorded (meaning strictly aural) presentation, a whole other set of considerations derives.[35]

What works on stage doesn't necessarily work on record—and vice-versa. A wrong or slurred note on stage will be imperceptible to 99.9% of the people there—on record it will likely stand out like a glaring, flashing red light to everyone who hears it. Such 'imperfections', so-loved by starry-eyed purists and academics, can drive the actual performers nuts, of course—because if he, she, or they had it to do again, the mistake wouldn't be there. "Hell, every other time we played it right, dammit!"

Similarly—and of particular note to the objectives of this book—a lyric that is pretty damn trite or just plain idiotic when heard on a recording can be mitigated, obfuscated (indeed effectively buried) by purposeful slurring, rushing through, an instrument playing a particularly loud or intrusive note or riff at that moment, an eccentric physical mannerism or stunt, or other diversion when performed live. But it remains *there* in the actual song, an artifact and proof of inferior songwriting.[36]

A live presentation is called a live 'performance' with good reason.

[35]Within the recording industry, business-wise, the live album has been traditionally considered a kind of holding action in an act's stream of product—a way to stay in the public eye, and ostensibly 'stay current', without having to actually write and prepare new material. It also served, naturally, as a promotional device to help the act sell more tickets out on the road. (Quick note here: I one time asked a performer who'd put out one of the most successful live albums ever released how it all transpired. He chuckled and revealed that they'd only actually used one song recorded at the live gigs, and everyone then went into the studio a week later to record all the songs again in that controlled environment. The audio engineer added an audience track to each cut—cutting in crowd hoots, hollers, laughter, applause—and it was all edited together and released as a massively successful 'live album'. The wowed critics wrote about how exciting, magical—and necessary—the record was; because, of course, "Man, you gotta hear 'em live!" Not even one, naturally, saw through the artifice, the de facto hoax.)

[36]Many tricks, though obviously not all, that are used to distract from inferior writing in a live performance can also be implemented when recording, of course. This will be dealt with in a later chapter.

Chapter Twenty

Over the Top? Ya Think?

Beauty of style—and harmony, grace, and good rhythm—depend on simplicity. I mean the true simplicity of a rightly and nobly ordered mind and character. — Plato

I'm gonna continue on performance considerations here, because obviously it's the vocal that brings the actual writing to our ears.

And a great vocal instrument—a voice that hits the notes squarely and rhythmically—is but the first step. The subsequent and far greater measure of a singer is his or her ability to deliver the intention of the lyrics without drawing attention to that delivery itself. Two educative cases come immediately to my mind: Eric Burdon's well-known vocal on "The House of the Rising Sun" (sung to a memorably effective orchestration by the Animals, especially on guitar by Hilton Valentine and keyboards by Alan Price; of Dave Van Ronk's from-the-ground-up re-arrangement of the traditional folk song) and the similarly well-known "I Will Always Love You" written and first performed by Dolly Parton. Again, these are songs with which every reader is certainly familiar, so good.

The traditional "Rising Sun" is a folk song in simple 4/4 time generally arranged across three chords (Woody Guthrie, Lead Belly, others) that we presently know, primarily via the Animals, as a song in 6/8 time arranged across five basic chords—and which is, incidentally, the first real example of folk-rock, easily antedating efforts by the Byrds and others.

And while Burdon certainly has a powerful voice and solid intonation, it's his phrasing of the lyrics that fail to fully express the sentiments of the song. He allows the 6/8 meter to chop his delivery into an almost galumphing staccato: "There is......a house......in New Orleans......they call......The Rising Sun......and it's been......the ruin......", and so on. Given all the positive attributes of the rendition, and his natural gifts, it's unfortunate that he turns the effort into more a rote recitation than a powerful admonition. Don't get me wrong, it certainly works as presented, but I'm not being picayune in pointing out the definite vocal deficiency here. And it is unfortunate. But it's an aspect of singing just about any song that can be effectively anticipated and countered with enough attention and care. Stretching this or that word or syllable, anticipating the beat here and there (meaning singing the last word in a lyric line ahead of the beat upon which it naturally falls) and/or retarding the lyric elsewhere, as may be found helpful there—all these things help to overcome any natural 'sing-songy' tendency of a specific song lyric. While discussing phrasing may seem to be a minor and peripheral matter, it's what has kept Frank Sinatra and Billie Holiday (for just two examples of great singers) in highest regard for so many years. Sinatra's actual intonation—his nailing of the notes—wasn't perfect or even consistent; and Holiday's vocal range was really quite limited. I think the argument could be seriously advanced that Burdon was gifted with a more capable innate vocal instrument than either. And yet Sinatra or Holiday—singing to the Animals' great arrangement—likely would have diminished his exertion to insignificance.

★

Dolly Parton's "I Will Always Love You" offers textbook illustrations of so much of what has gone wrong in English-language popular singing. The song itself is precariously—but in Parton's very capable writerly hands,[37] quite effectively—balanced between fey and heartbreaking. And it's that innate slippery purchase that has made hearing so many other renditions of it such an endurance test. Yes, I'm looking at all of you Whitney Houston wannabes and various contestants on *The Voice*, *American Idol*, *Britain's Got Talent* and other repellently déclassé TV spectacles. And also at all you Amy Winehouse manqués.

The musical term 'melisma' means holding a word or syllable for more than one note—perhaps its most common manifestation to those of us in the U.S. is in the two notes allocated to the very first syllable of "The Star Spangled Banner". There's nothing at all inappropriate, cheap or deficient in employing it—either through intentional writing or, if carefully invoked, in singing. What *is* insufferably dissolute—and almost always *profoundly* detrimental to a well-written song (as "I Will Always Love You" most certainly is)—is the addiction in recent years to over-the-top melismatic grandstanding as if such irksome showboating somehow actually adds depth to a song. It does the exact opposite. Compare Houston's tacky, over-wrought singing of the song to, in particular, Parton's own earliest 1970s performances of it. Yes, Parton uses melisma—again, it's *not* the vocal application that's objectionable, it's the garishly assertive *intrusion* of that vocal application on a song itself that's so pernicious. Parton's melismatic delivery is simple, effective; in contrast, Houston's peremptorily tosses all sincerity and resolution into a dumpster so she can show off like an impossibly spoiled adolescent. Ridiculous and altogether painful—and again, detrimental to the intrinsic actual emotional effectiveness of the song.[38, 39]

★

Let's go on to some other ruinous performance affectations.

[37]By the way, a quick note back on "The House of the Rising Sun": Parton recorded her own version of that song—unfortunately in a musical production that's just plain awful—but in which her rewrite of the lyrics does a thoughtful job of both making the song more easily sung and more lyrically coherent. Dolly Parton—to those who may not know—is a *very* capable songwriter; one of the current true masters.

[38]What does work, and to electrifying effect, in that 1992 Houston effort, however, is the uncued a capella key change 2/3 of the way through. It's such a powerful device, however, that melding it with a properly self-aware and deferential performance of the rest of the song would require a lot of prudence—and it may admittedly still be ultimately quite hard to square the two objectives. But had she and her producers been able to restrain themselves, just this single device, correctly integrated, would have given them *both* a potentially great performance of a memorably romantic ballad—Houston certainly had the vocal instrument—*and* the hooky 'star vehicle' treatment they coveted. (En passant excursus: as to the occasional charge that a modulation—a key change—is a cheap trick, its use just a cheesy obviation of the otherwise possible necessity of writing an additional verse, I've several thoughts. But without taking too much time to go through them all, let's just note that as with any tool the question is how it's used. Sometimes a song may even benefit from eschewing an additional verse. Further, even the ostensibly musically unsophisticated proto-garage band, the Ramones, used a so-called 'truck driver's gear change' modulation in "I Wanna Be Sedated". Again, the question is how and to what effect it's used.)

[39]It's my understanding that Elvis Presley was determined to record his own rendition of "I Will Always Love You", but his manager at the last minute demanded Parton hand over 50% of all the song royalties if Presley sang it—claiming (probably legitimately) that this was the deal they made on EVERY song Presley recorded and released, as an Elvis record would almost guarantee the sale of lotsa copies and so

lotsa royalties. It's to Parton's credit she refused the avaricious business entreaty—and serendipitously for her it eventually resulted in gaining her much more money from the song, certainly. But it is unfortunate that Presley didn't record it anyway, as one must expect his generally peerless ability to precisely and effectively navigate between bombast on one side and commonplace on the other would likely have delivered a spectacularly, definitively affecting rendition. Alas, we'll never know.

Chapter Twenty-One

Yes, Yes, We Too Are All So Very Sorry You Weren't Born on a Mississippi Cotton Plantation

Acting is the expression of a neurotic and insincere impulse. Quitting acting, that's the sign of maturity. — Marlon Brando

Anecdote #1: I remember an edition of *Fresh Air*, the NPR interview show, some years ago in which the host, Terry Gross, interviewed John Fogerty of the band Creedence Clearwater Revival. When Gross asked Fogerty to simply say the words "turning" and "burning"—key words in the chorus of his song "Proud Mary"—he answered something like the following: "Uh, uh—turning and burning. But, but—when I sing, it just comes out 'toynin' and 'boynin'. I don't know why; it just naturally comes out that way!"

I'm so glad to have 'loyned' that, John—I used to think you were just a parading poseur, but you've really 'oyned' my respect.

(What? Oh, that. Well, ya see, John, when I *talk* I say "learned" and "earned". But when I *write*, it just comes out "loyned" and "oyned". Honest. I don't know why; it just naturally comes out that way!)[40]

★

Anecdote #2: A few years back a good friend sent me a link to a song performed by a then emerging act with which I was unfamiliar called Alabama Shakes. I clicked to it and endured no more than 30 seconds before reaching my limit with the florid travesty. That it turns out the lead vocalist is herself reportedly half-African American does nothing, of course, to license her blatant and ignorant de facto contempt for the rural black culture she pretends to represent and personify with her cavalierly disrespectful burlesque. She has a capable voice; it would be nice to experience it without the jejune plaster of condescension. Perhaps she's even a good songwriter, but I may never know.

★

Popular song performance allows—indeed, seems to actively encourage and reward—the most baldly contrived and manufactured personas, inauthentic representations, and counterfeit conceits; all the while pompously dissembling as exactly the opposite. It's another measure of the innate and insecure poverty of so much in the discipline that acts (lead singers in particular) regularly seek to obscure their authentic selves behind concocted masks and fabricated vocal 'characters'—and that news media and public are so often acquiescent to, at worst eager collaborators in, the wholesale and demeaning charade.

The tendency in the vocal presentation is perhaps most apparent when a traditional blues song comes into play—suddenly the most erudite, educated and cosmopolitan performer will affect a slurring delivery and over-the-top accent he or she thinks is required to render justice to, or at least to properly perform, the song. "I jes' be a-singin' dis heah song so's y'all ken be a-enjoyin' muh truthful poh' boy se'f up heah on duh stage—ya gots me?" or some similarly grating act.

Earlier I predicted that a hundred years from now awards and awards shows will be viewed as a quaint and treacly hallmark of our times. A second prediction I'll make here is that in the not too distant future the kind of condescending and heavy-handed vocal mannerisms exhibited by so many performers today—especially when appropriating presumed rural black dialect—will be viewed with the same distaste and disgust with which we presently adjudge performing in blackface.

From Tom Waits' (and one-time inamorata Rickie Lee Jones') slurring barfly fabrications, to the gravelly inarticulations of Van Morrison and, to a lesser extent, Randy Newman, to the outright racist "I jes' be a uneducated plantation share cropper" (or more currently, "Suburbanite-Wants-to-be-a-Ghetto-Gangsta") crap of so many blues players and rappers, to the contrived 'good ole country boy' twangs of Dwight Yoakam and (occasionally and incredibly) even middle-class bred Englishman Mick Jagger(!), the weirdness infects just about all branches of popular song performance.

Singing *in* character is one thing—with a song in which the writing is openly invested *in* a specific characterization and scenario (cf. musical theater, or the occasional Randy Newman effort or similar). In just about any other circumstance—and particularly with a song that merits serious attention—it's simple egotism, and it's ultimately *inimical* to producing the desired effect. It demeans the songwriting.

Eschewing such bald contrivances also ultimately imparts *greater* legitimacy and authority to the effort—the irritating vocal forgery is forsworn in favor of a more persuasive authenticity. Over the years, my 'go to' examples to illustrate the point have varied, but consider the effortless and generally unaffected singing of folkies Doc Watson and Gordon Lightfoot; or rockers including Joey Ramone and Jim Morrison—and of course there's many others current or past who could be likewise cited. And look, isn't the advice always given to a performer insecure about how he or she'll be received, "Just trust what you're singing and be yourself!"?

A good song—and that's what we're concerned with here—doesn't need, and shouldn't have inflicted on it, a singer's vaunting impostures.

[40]For the record, no, Fogerty wasn't "Born on the Bayou", but in cosmopolitan Berkeley, California, and raised in the comfortable suburb of El Cerrito, a few miles north. And singing that song and others in his œuvre without the irritatingly fraudulent vocal contrivances would not diminish their impact. He's not a bad songwriter.

Chapter Twenty-Two

Art School Confidential[41]

What all the posturing results in is a vast detachment and cynicism
on the part of the performers, since it's impossible to have respect for an
audience that'll take just about anything you care to dish out.
— Lester Bangs

Now let's talk about playing dress-up.
Because ever-newer blasts of promotional cacophony are constantly assaulting our ears, with the hustlers hoping this time, *finally*, something will get our attention, the rest of us become simply The Gullible
Marketplace. The act attempts try after try, experimenting sequentially
with wholly new manufactures of song orchestration and production—
but much, *much* more often—of simply costuming and 'image'.

The regularly lodged license for all such manufactures, however, is
one we dismissed earlier: no they're not entertainers, after all....

They're Artists!

We're told the commercially successful act—the Britney Spears, David Bowie, Björk, Madonna or (insert-name-here)—is 'reinventing itself',
with the procession of consecutive 're-inventions' presented, simply
through dress-up, as a sure sign of the act's Continuing Cultural Importance and Artistic Bona Fides. (In country music, the Dauntingly Difficult Decision in this area is perhaps limited to just whether one should
start wearing, stop wearing, or start wearing again...a cowboy hat.) Of
course, most of the 're-invention', and I'll put that spurious term in
quotes every time I use it here, is solely that uncomfortably tenuous and
self-conscious costume change—entirely dispossessed of considered insight or cultural relevance beyond the most superficial. "Ziggy Stardust",
anyone?[42]

Alternatively, for the as yet unheralded act, the rebrandings serve as a door opening device; a serial set of calling cards on industrial and public awareness, in desperate hopes that sooner or later one of the constructions commercially clicks. I mean, dammit, what do we have to DO to become Big Stars, after all!?!? We can be just as weird as they are!

As for the songs themselves—what it's supposed to be all about, no?—novelty and production receive far more attention than the actual writing and composing.

The cart has come completely off the rails and wildly careened about ten miles downhill; while the horse looks down on it all in bewildered consternation. It's art school run amok. Signifiers sans signal.

And while there's nothing intrinsically disqualifying in preposterous and desperate attempts at being noticed, the begged question is how much such flatulent affectations ultimately undercut any claim to genuine significance. After all, if you wander into the room or on stage, in serious demeanor, wearing flowerpots on your head—or arriving in a fiberglass 'egg' and smugly introducing yourself as 'Lady Gaga' or some such[43]—there's a strong likelihood what you have to say will be as equally pre-fabricated, shallow, and bereft of authenticity. Cheap show-biz contrivances, dumbed-down schlock, and 'artsy' empty posing are the primary gambits of the vacant wannabe and the cynical sales rep.

Sure, we all dress our best and put on an act—well, put our best foot forward, certainly—when trying to impress. And yes, a large part of show business is most assuredly just trying to make an impression; to 'get in the door'. But significant content invariably requires *time* to germinate, gestate, and effectively complete—a process not normally embraced by the impatient and fame-obsessed.[44]

So to the art school crowd[45], either literally or affectively, so determined to appear—desperate to somehow, somehow *be*—'cutting edge', even (cough, cough) 'dangerous'(!), I relate this lovely and properly deflationary reckoning from French symbolist poet Paul Valéry, over a century ago:

> *Everything changes. Everything changes—except, that is, the avant-garde.*

★

Far better to take the time and produce the sweat to perhaps end up offering actual substance in the material being delivered—the songs—than in yet more studied imbecilic behavior, pretentious posturing, and wacky wardrobe.

Popular song is not alone, of course, but more than any other area of show business and the performing arts it encourages, celebrates—even consecrates—the most cynically ersatz; impression over expression. And it's yet another symptom and product of the emptiness and transience of so much that's presented.

Substance in what's being submitted, on the other hand, doesn't require shrouding in counterfeit conceits.

[41]This chapter's heading taken from the title of the spot-on four-page graphic novel by Daniel Clowes (subsequently adapted by him into a screenplay, with the resultant film directed by Terry Zwigoff).

[42]Let's be absolutely clear about this and similarly vapid and uninhabited 'characters' portentously trotted out as if such sanctimonious games of dress-up bear any resemblance to something deserving consideration. A character is an _entirety_; not just a pretty frock and a blank stare pasted on a human frame belching out non sequitur song lyrics. That kind of artless display is, rather, empty peacockery.

[43]Or, similarly, if vainglory results in naming the band "fun.". (sic—and yes, _with_ that all-important period!) or his or her single self "tUnE-yArDs" (sic), "Will.I.Am" (sic)—or any one of the myriad comparable other monikers rampantly infecting rap, hip-hop and heavy metal in particular, but permutating throughout popular music—one can't help but wonder if these folks simply have too much time on their hands. Here's a suggestion: instead of trying to impress us with the awe-inspiringly courageous disregard for prevailing orthography, spend the time rewriting some of the songs being churned out. Eh?

[44]Words of advice: when asked what someone wants to be or do, be wary if he or she immediately responds, "I want to be famous!" As should be clear by now, such primary objective, while not definitively inimical to creative ability, is usually an egotistically counterproductive diversion from it.

[45]I myself went to both the San Francisco Art Institute and the California College of Arts and Crafts (now California College of the Arts), and kinda experienced what I address here. Art schools are a great environment in which to experiment, play and have fun; rarely availing milieux in which to create actual art or challenge current convention.

Chapter Twenty-Three

Dance? Okay fine. Dance!
Now go away.

If anything, a lot of electronic dance music is stuff that hardly anyone listens to at home. It's really only heard when people are out at a club. — David Byrne

Where lyric writing is subjectively weakest—in which sub-streams of popular songwriting one finds the least craft and inspiration—is open to debate and personal bias as well as disciplined study, of course. As generalizations, a run-of-the-mill Nashville audience might find rap songs worthless; a Broadway audience might dismiss songs coming from the punk sphere—and so on. We each have our personal prejudices, predilections and enculturated expectations—even though, as addressed in Chapter Fifteen, it's important to fight over-generalized antipathies.

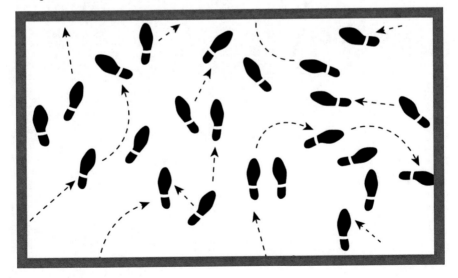

But I expect most would agree that songs intended primarily for dancing—from fiddle tunes to disco to electronic dance music—might be kinda leniently excused from criticism of inconsequence or plain inanity in what's being sung above the pounding beat and repetitive foot-friendly syncopations. There may be an overarching point advanced via the vocals in the occasional dance number—if so, and if it's accomplished exceptionally well, then that's certainly praiseworthy—but what's actually being said, and how inventively, is really quite beside the primary point, no? Let's dance....

Chapter Twenty-Four

It's All Greek—French, Swahili, Latin, Klingon—to Me

How little do they see what really is, who frame their hasty judgment upon that which seems. — Daniel Webster

Popular music with lyrics in a language the listener doesn't understand obviously renders those lyrics and the vocal presentation of them as a solely musical experience—quite literally just another instrument in the musical mix, certainly devoid of precisely discernible content or message—and so typically outside the scope of our task here.

Excusez-moi. Je suis tellement désolé....

★

However, a pertinent and entirely mitigating aspect of that ostensibly 'solely musical experience' occurs when a) songs are translated into and performed in English, or b) when performer(s) and audiences wish to *know* if what they're experiencing in the original non-English language—what's being said—is or is not due their attention.

In other words, when intelligent performers and listeners decide ignorance is *not* bliss.

It's a topic perhaps most readily apparent in textbook display when discussing opera arias, but it's obviously also pertinent when looking at popular songs that may or may not be freighted with lyrics not rising to the same level of accomplishment evinced in the accompanying music.

Most of the popularly familiar operatic arias were written in languages other than English, and so yes, one fluent only in English appreciates them as aural applications, along with any quite incidental performance dramatics a singer may be able to impart to perhaps suggest an emotional disposition.[46] Were they sung having been competently translated into English, however—so available to us as information as well as melody—one would likely conclude far too many of those actual lyrics are overwrought, frivolous, or even nonsensical (outside of the whole from which they've been excised, at any rate).[47]

But those great arias customarily get a public pass—just like those contemporary popular songs in languages not understood; or those ethereal new-age songs written in completely counterfeit 'languages' and generally drowned in reverb and chorusing, which attempt a bald endrun around the idea of communication altogether.

When the argument that 'it's the music that counts', is used in defense of lyrics which *are* comprehended, however—or known through printed translation—we're being *directed* to ignore the obvious facts we honestly, intelligently recognize, and focus entirely on what remains. We're being asked to play dumb; instructed to *be* dumb in considerations of the whole song—in a musical variation of "Ignore that man behind the curtain!", or maybe "Who're you gonna trust, me or your lying ears?"

"The music is what counts" implies a correlate "The lyrics simply do not matter"—synergetic propositions that are often pretty much required when involved in appreciation of opera.

★

*It's the lyrics that make a song, although the tune, of course,
is what makes it last.* — Irving Berlin

A song with which readers are surely familiar is "Time To Say Goodbye" ("Con te partirò"; by Francesco Sartori and Lucio Quarantotto) best known in a recording by Andrea Bocelli and Sarah Brightman. It's a striking, even sumptuous musical composition, with an effectively enticing title—so a solid impulse and a grand setting—leading the innocent listener to presume the rest of the lyrics must be worthy of the surroundings.

But the undeniable compositional accomplishment here is cheapened beyond intelligent redemption by lyrics that are plain babble, in the original Italian *or* English translation.[48] The magnitude of the travesty—the disparity of achievement between the composition of the music and the writing of the lyrics (i.e. the execution of the song's fundamental pretext)—is such that it actually goes beyond exposing the lyricist to ridicule; it sadly begs questioning the integrity and the intelligence of *everyone* involved. It's that bad. (And don't make the mistake of blaming the translation below, thinking others might be better. They aren't. The song really is that bad.)

> When I am alone I sit and dream,
> And when I dream the words are missing.
> Yes, I know that in a room so full of light
> That all the light is missing.
> But I don't see you with me, with me.
> Close up the windows, bring the sun to my room
> Through the door you've opened.
> Close inside of me the light that you see
> That you met in the darkness.
>
> Time to say goodbye.
> Horizons are never far
> Would I have to find them alone—
> Without true light of my own with you.
> I will go on ships over seas
> That I now know.
> No, no, they don't exist anymore.
> It's time to say goodbye[49, 50].......—

We might note in passing that disco diva Donna Summer rewrote the song (also in English), renamed "I Will Go With You" and recorded it as a dance number in 1999. Her rewrite is at best barely serviceable, but it's still a significant improvement over the original fustian silliness.[51]

If the musical composition is good, as Berlin asserts in the epigraph above, it is what will last, yes — as the language evolves and idioms fade, cultural references modify, and actual meanings change.[52] One makes a grave misjudgment, however, in advancing, say, "Time to Say Goodbye" similarly to how one might champion Giacomo Puccini's "Nessun Dorma" (lyrics by Giuseppi Adami and Renato Simoni), aside from any simple musical comparison which may attempt to equate the accomplishments or to disparage one in favor of another. (I don't think Puccini has anything to worry about here; but again, music is secondary to what we're addressing at this point.) There *is* a difference in both provenances and missions of the two songs and their lyrics. One is from almost a hundred years ago, in Italian; part of a musical theatrical creation, and so an excerpt from a complete, much larger, story. The other, coincidentally also in Italian, is simply an ambitious pop song. And while the best known contemporary performance of "Nessun Dorma" is probably by Luciano Pavarotti—and his diction was famously precise and intelligible, so the lyrics clearly understood by Italian speakers—those lyrics are, while without question over-ripe, part of the through-line of the story in which they reside. They're certainly something of a test, yes—to those fluent in Italian, anyway—but they do make sense within the context they serve. To the rest of us, they're just part of the musical soundscape. On the other hand, "Time to Say Goodbye" is patently ridiculous—*and* serves no direct greater purpose extrinsically which might frame and justify (or at least intellectually somewhat ameliorate) some of its immediately obvious feeble-mindedness.

So do those great arias from the past merit slight indulgence—de facto 'grandfathering in'? Unfortunately, that's quite possible, if based on the simple fact it's effectively unavoidable. But the same should not apply to works in the contemporary world—be they popular songs or arias in brand new operas. Poor writing does not deserve endorsement; and good music should be neither an excuse nor a justification for drivel.

[46]In opera, an 'aria' is a veritable song, wedged in between the sections of generally musically rambling speech called 'recitative'.

[47]Interestingly, the English National Opera—to name one of a few major organizations hewing to this practice—*only* presents works which originated in other languages when they have been translated into English. One wonders how much the music—universally acknowledged as the primary component in an operatic production—is diminished when audiences are suddenly exposed to the meanings of the lyrics in their favorite works. One also wonders whether the use of projected supertitles—simultaneous translations generally displayed on a screen above or below the proscenium—is in the end all that constructive an aid to engineering appreciation of an opera in question. Does it ultimately help if the audience knows what's being sung?

[48]A recent piece addressing the matter: "What are the lyrics to 'Time to Say Goodbye'—and do they make any sense?", ClassicFM, 4/5/2018, http://www.classicfm.com/artists/andrea-bocelli/time-to-say-goodbye-translation/ (web search terms: Classic FM - lyricsTime Goodbye)

[49]"Time to Say Goodbye" ("Con te partirò") copyright 1995 by Francesco Sartori and Lucio Quarantotto. Quoted here as permitted within the Fair Use provisions of 17 U.S.C.§107.

[50]These lyrics are *so* confused that it was difficult to even confidently parse them in the attempt to place helpful punctuations.

[51] https://www.lyricsondemand.com/d/donnasummerlyrics/iwillgowithyoucontepartirol yrics.html (web search terms: Lyrics Demand - Donna Summer Go With You)

[52]Similarly, here's one of countless articles about the lost references in Shakespeare's works: *The Atlantic*, 3/2/2016, "Such Ado: The Fight for Shakespeare's Puns", by Megan Garver. https://www.theatlantic.com/entertainment/archive/2016/03/loves-labours-found-saving-shakespeares-puns/471786/ (web search terms: Fight Shakespeare's Puns)

Chapter Twenty-Five

Country Music is "~~Three Chords and the Truth~~" Computerized Drums, a Catering Truck, and a Smirk

I enjoy the videos with the sound off, where you can look at the belly buttons and everything. Some really pretty girls; but I don't know about the music. — Merle Haggard

Today's Tin Pan Alley is Nashville, a songwriting factory town if ever there was one, and the songs derived therefrom essentially a highly lacquered and polished Southern-accented analogue to the mechanical rock band noise found in any bar down at the beach. Country music's well lubricated industrial muscle mostly churns out commodified rubbish that's a distant, cynical, and cluelessly incompatible simulacrum of its long forgotten white proletarian antecedents.

And the marketing of all that debris exacerbates the wholesale poverty of the genre. A performance by one of the practiced Nashville machine acts can be rather indistinguishable from a two-hour beer commercial, presented with all the oily glibness found at a convention of real estate agents.

Further, and as is unfortunately quite readily apparent, the sociopolitical foundation of current country music is a hardcore conservative-to-outright-fascist politics married to the basest and smarmiest retailing cynicism. Even the most circumspect and judiciously politically progressive or intellectually mindful songwriting and/or presentation presents a tangible challenge to parochial Nashville's reigning reactionary mandarins—predictably resulting in the dumbest and shallowest dissimulations imaginable. Even the slightest 'mis-step' can invite career homicide (cf.

the Dixie Chicks), while welcomed with raucous cheers and open arms is retrograde sexism, moronic braggadocio, calculated religiosity, and sanctimonious flag waving. Find an old pickup truck, sign on practiced video girls, affect a deeper, more 'manly' baritone growl—then perhaps add in some cutaways to dogs, beer bar tableaux and pseudo-'down home' paraphernalia; dress the sets with patriotic props and working class marginalia—and rush the aggregate disheveled mess of footage to the editors to cobble together yet another video version of the Same Old Same Old.

The one true and unassailable *positive* about Nashville and country songs, however—and a critically important aspect we'll return to later—is that the words in a country song are always clearly delivered, for easy and full comprehension. This isn't just a vestige of Tin Pan Alley; it goes way back—past the songs composed by Schubert and Beethoven; past the troubadours Blondel and Bernart de Ventadorn; deep into history, surely—to the first vocal recitals that were accompanied by Neanderthals pounding rocks and sticks together. While the overwhelming vast majority of country song lyrics that *are* so clearly delivered and comprehended is hack work, the undiminishing might of Nashville songwriting and country radio is testament to the importance of language and direct communication. And it's a tangible rejection of the oft-promoted thesis that melody is the most important part of a popular song. (We'll examine this dichotomy more fully in Part 4.)

Basic Nashville songwriting practice is to take one and only one passably interesting, novel, or even penetrating statement or phrase—a key line, most often the whole or part of the ultimate song title—surround it with as many 'hooky' performance and production decorations as can be devised—and move on to the next effort. That's simply The Way Things Are Done in a factory churning out product. (There've been other factories, large and small, in the Tin Pan Alley commercial tradition, of course—it's not fair to single out Nashville as anything anomalous. Think of the heyday of Motown Records, perhaps, or the Gold Star Studios world of Phil Spector, et al, for just two examples. Without too much of a stretch, we might also even cite the Albert Grossman dominated Greenwich Village folk scene of the late 1950s and early 1960s. In Chapters Fifty-Two and Fifty-Three we'll briefly touch on other current 'crank-'em-out sweatshops' as well.) And despite the crass avarice and lowest-common-denominator thinking that sooner or later commands in just about *every* such situation, it is possible, on rarest occasion—so even in Nashville—to find the occasional admirable work that's somehow birthed amidst all the malodorous effluvia pumping out.

As to the oft-repeated lauding of the level of musicianship in Nashville, that isn't exactly incorrect—it most generally simply mistakes technical facility as an end rather than a means. There most certainly are crowds of great *players* in the bars, clubs, and recording studios there—as there also are working in the bars, clubs, and recording studios in other major centers. As we'll further advance in Chapter Fifty-Four, instrumental virtuosity and musical knowledge will always be impressive, yes—even stunningly helpful—but they ultimately have very little to do with composing a lasting melody or writing a great song.

If there's any helpful lessons to be actually learned from the low rent productions pumped out of contemporary Nashville and environs, it's primarily just the most basic and rudimentary practices of simple song structure—as noted above, today's country music is the wayward scion of Tin Pan Alley and its historical conventions. Absolutely, unequivocally, valuable knowledge, to be sure—and a great starting point—but in the end only the most elementary starting point.

And later, as noted above, we'll even look at a few songs originating in the country music world that transcend the regular cynical foolishness of the genre.

Chapter Twenty-Six

Country's Brainier Half-Sibling: Americana

After they have been reassured and have lost their fear, they are so art-less and so free with all they possess, that no one would believe it with-out having seen it. — Christopher Columbus

While I'm having some fun above—the explorer was talking about innocent natives he intruded upon after landing on Hispaniola, after all—he may've well been describing today's Americana music sce-ne, because that's where all the oh-so-sensitive-and-sincere-singer-song-writers have settled in. It's been written that "it takes an Americana song five minutes to say what a country song says in three". Whether a legiti-mate comparison or not, it's indicative of the cognate and inferential rela-tionship of Americana to country. While country is freighted with hot air, however, Americana is the land of solipsism run amok—a national open mic night. (Also notable, in passing, is that like country music it's an al-most entirely Caucasian world, except for the occasional 'guest spot'.)

But of primary relevance here, it's a genre in which words—again, as in Nashville country—are generally of paramount significance. And it's currently also the musical marketing category (which is how it was origi-nated) perhaps most likely to produce material of lasting significance—this because Americana acts generally produce songs in which the words are presented for clear intelligibility, as noted, but which also often aspire to thoughtful and perceptive presentation and reception. Whether such is actually achieved or not is another matter, of course, and the unfortunate cancerous blight of inarticulate 'Poetic Lyrics' makes regular appearance in Americana songwriting—a natural tendency, perhaps, given the wide critical approbation given to that stuff.

The relationship of Americana acts to country—the Americana Music Association is even headquartered in Nashville and hands out its own annual awards there—serves as something of a brake on the creative freedom from industrial concerns and blandishments that greater severance might encourage. As it is, there's a constant pull and frequent crossover from one brand to the other. A song that appears on the Americana music charts can concurrently appear, without much fuss, on the country music charts. Further and after all, if the songwriters right next door are making Big Bucks writing asinine 'bro country' garbage while you're a starving *La Bohème* Americana artiste, the temptation to finally buy a nicer used car can easily be an understandable if unfortunate enticement to enthusiastically begging your way into that foulest of déclassé souqs: Nashville Country Music.

The Americana label has even been the kinda latter day 'retirement home' for Johnny Cash, Merle Haggard, Emmylou Harris, Willie Nelson and others when newer, fresher meat (and ever more cynically imbecilic songwriting) is being mainlined by Nashville. They're effectively 'sent back down to the commercial minor leagues'—country's essential assessment of Americana—substantiating that it is country music *itself* that has devolved and depleted so appreciably over past decades. The current meretricious miasma of industrial Nashville's reigning country music bozos and bozettes is not at all an evolving continuation, but rather an *outright rejection*, of the traditional higher aspirations of the form itself in favor of its more menial representations.

Chapter Twenty-Seven

Tradition, Permanence, and Illusions of Same

*I thought the blues was a simple 12-bar format and it's like a jam—
we just improvise. Sonny Boy Williamson kicked the shit out of that
for me. He said "We're gonna do 'Nine Below Zero'" and I thought
well fine—it's a blues! My assumption was you just tell me the key and
the tempo and I'll make it up. So I started, and he virtually whacked
me round the head and said, "No, it starts with this!", and he sang the
opening motif to me—and then there's a drum part, and then this
happens, and so on; it was all very carefully and specifically constructed.
I realized, suddenly, the blues isn't an interchangeable jam at all—each
song is very formally composed.*[53] — Eric Clapton

*A folk song does not exist in any of its variants, but rather in the ag-
gregate of its variants.* — John Lomax

Discussing traditional songs is obviously appropriate here because so
many such songs are recorded and performed right alongside material from contemporary songwriters, and so deserve to be not simply
ignored, exempted—or worse, patronized. These are not museum pieces:
precious, frozen, sanctified. Yet traditional songs present some unique
considerations concerning lyrical content.

First up is that the songwriters—well, loosely, at least until the mid-
nineteenth century—are usually unknown, the song's specific origins lost
in time. This makes the song malleable, even amorphous; finding a 'textbook version' becomes impossible—there *are* no textbook versions. As

soon as a song or a specific line is taken apart, analyzed and re-assembled, one can stumble on a slightly divergent version of the song or line elsewhere that undermines any conclusions at which one may have just arrived. As John Lomax intimates above, a traditional song is a kind of stew, out of which each ladling can bring forth slightly (or wholly) different tastes and textures. So while one's attempted rewrite of, say, "Heartbreak Hotel" might be immediately recognized as counterfeit, a previously unfamiliar insertion into a traditional song—or a new and novel inversion or revision—could easily be (or if entirely fabricated, be duplicitously ascribed to) legitimate cultural anthropological research and exploitation.

Second is that actual folk songs (and of course I include blues here) are almost invariably derived from a working class environment and so tend to eschew intricate constructions—the poetry in traditional songs tends to be a direct, moralistic, or aphoristic presentation, naturally devoid of formal literary aspirations or allusions, yet with sometimes striking metaphors. (The melodic compositions are invariably repetitive, and based around simple harmonic structures—serving primarily as a bed for the lyrics, though allowing for occasional musical flurries and even expansive elaborations, but within the established strict framework.)

And third is that what I'll call 'mainstream traditional songs'—folk and blues songs that are in today's common canon—have already essentially gone through a curatorial process: the discarding, polishing and replacement of words, lines, entire formulations and ideas that, for one reason or another, were judged ineffective or of lesser resonance before the presently dominant construction. There's a de facto curatorial reason this traditional song, in this generalized construction—and not that song or version over there—is regularly performed and recorded.

Which brings up another point I want to make here, implied by the above—and one that may disturb, even offend, the easily upset fragile rigidities of so many adherents and purveyors of folk, bluegrass, old-time, blues, and other traditional forms: *not all traditional songs are well-written, well-crafted or even musically interesting offerings.* Just because it was born in the cotton fields or the coal mines, in the Appalachian hollows or on great wooden sailing ships—or was originally recorded in the back woods and released on 78 rpm record—does *not* mean the song is musically and/or lyrically at all meritorious, or even significant. Sure, it may be of unquestionable interest culturally and historically, but it's not necessarily accomplished or laudable intrinsically.

More to the point, it is absolutely proper to note lapses in the song-writing if and when they occur—and where possible, to address and possibly favorably address those lapses. The danger, of course, is when such efforts yield a song version stripped of any real relationship beyond the most superficial to its heritage. We do owe something in service of historical fidelity.

Often of great help in arriving at a coherent edition, and again as alluded to in the statement by John Lomax above, is that a traditional song can bring along with it something like a gigantic bibliography, offering a potentially rich source for ideas, nuanced alternate lyrical realizations, different interpretations, and divergent melodies for the song.

★

I occasionally do blue collar union work in the Hollywood studios, where what's usually blasting out of radios and internet connections— even despite the exponentially expanded listening options available (albeit unfortunately also rip-offs of songwriters) like Spotify, Pandora and similar—is the same fucking fifty or so nominal 'classic rock' songs, over and Over and OVER again, ad-god-damn-nauseam. Yet one day recently, while working with some guys as sick as I of the expected rote playlist, I suddenly heard the first few notes of a song and performance I instantly recognized from many, many years before: one of the guys had somehow brought up "Lula Walls" (sometimes called "Lulu Walls"), by A.P. (Alvin Pleasant) Carter and recorded by The Carter Family in 1928.[54] The tide of memories that flooded over me brought actual tears to my eyes, such was both the complete and utter unexpectedness of it in the present circumstance and the length of time since I'd last heard the song—a perfect illustration of the power of nostalgia. In fact I'd learned and played "Lula Walls" as a teenager growing up in the Deep South.

But despite the power with which the song entered my hearing that morning, looking at it with dispassion yields a piece of writing that, with the sole exception of the two word description of the titular character preceding mention of her name in the chorus, is about as routine as one might possibly devise. (I'm aware that unlike most we've so far discussed, songs in this chapter may not be known to most readers. If that's the case, I suggest taking a moment to locate versions and hear them.)

> One evening getting dark we first met at the park,
> A-sittin' by the fountain all alone.
> I lifted up my hat and then began to chat;
> She said she'd 'low me to see her at her home.

> chorus:
> Such a star I've never seen;
> She's as pretty as a queen;
> She's as perfect as an angel from above.
> If she'd only be my wife
> I'd live happy all my life,
> With that aggravating beauty Lula Walls.

> If she was only mine, I would build a house so fine,
> And around it so many fences tall.
> It would make me jealous free that no one else but me
> Could gaze upon that beauty Lula Walls.

> chorus repeat

> One evening getting late I met her at the gate
> I asked her if she'd wed me in the fall.
> She only turned away and nothing would she say;
> That aggravating beauty Lula Walls.

> chorus repeat[55]

Folks, this is really just platitudinous vapidity. The *only* interesting thought or experience in the entire song is the idea of a beautiful woman being an aggravation—not easily courted by the singer. An "aggravating beauty"—I'll buy that idea and treatment. But now DO something with it. Because everything else here—all the adulations and all the mises en scene presented—are empty clichés, vacant of insight or interest; with the rhymes arriving with all the delightful subtlety of a Sherman Tank. In short, "Lula Walls" is a fair example of what *today's* country songwriting continues to spew onto the American public: one serviceable notion— surrounded and smothered by innocuous bromides and padding.

However, there is something notably different.

The original Carter Family was a clear and wholesome representation of the heart and aspirations of working class rural white America in the early twentieth century—an important and innocently unaffected act whose recorded performances stand the test of time. But as one of the two generally recognized major founding acts of today's country music (the other being Jimmie Rodgers, "The Singing Brakeman"—and we might even add a third, Uncle Dave Macon) the songwriting constructions that in *their* hands delivered generally genuine and innocent, if unsophisticated, paeans have devolved into the hack and cynical manufactures vomited out of today's Nashville. So as noted earlier and to repeat, rather than move above and beyond its antecedents, today's country music burrows ever further beneath them.

★

Yet, to be precise, even the Carter Family doesn't represent—their songs aren't fully quintessential of—strictly traditional music, insofar as much of their material was either written ground-up or near ground-up (primarily by A.P. Carter). The remainder was primarily songs derived from commercially created pieces (most often parlor songs) that wended their way into isolated rural areas via informal person-to-person transmission, in a songwriting version of the children's game of Telephone—such as, archetypically, the well-known "Wildwood Flower", the wayward descendant of 1860's "I'll Twine Mid the Ringlets" by J.P. Webster and Maud Irving.

So let's briefly discuss a song that is *incontestably* a traditional song; authors unknown, but there were surely scores of them—arguably hundreds—spread over several centuries on at least two and possibly three continents. There's not even a certain title for the song, though, through the general democratic curatorial process mentioned above, most people today know it as "The Cuckoo".

As preceding sentences should understandably prepare us to accept, there's a zillion variations: in what verses to include (of the perhaps thirty or so documented. Fifty? A hundred?...), in whatever order (if any) they properly appear, in what each individual line might convey—*and possibly in what each and every individual word should be*. Here's the basics of the version I've played now and then over the years.[56]

Oh, the cuckoo, she's a pretty bird,
An' she warbles when she flies.
She'll never holler "cu-ckoo"
'Til the fourth day of July.

Jack o' Diamonds, Jack o' Diamonds,
I know you from of old.
You robbed my poor pockets
Of their silver and their gold.

I've played cards in England;
I've played cards in Spain.
An' I'll bet you ten dollars
I'll beat you next game.

I'm gonna build me a log cabin
On a mountain so high,
So I can see my baby
When she goes walkin' by.

Yeah, the cuckoo, she's a pretty bird,
An' she warbles when she flies.
She'll never holler "cu-ckoo"
'Til the fourth day of July.

My own practice, when dealing with—when looking to take on and possibly performing—a traditional song is to look at what's in the stewpot; to look around for as many flavors or 'collectable elements' (verses, basically, but significant variants of those verses as well) as may be available and then to determine carefully which ones work together best in my own recipe for the dish. In the above "Cuckoo" I use just four verses—from the perhaps 20 or so I've encountered here and there over the years—with one, what we'll here call the 'title verse', used to bookend the others; to open and close the song. Nothing at *all* unique here, except perhaps the very limited number of verses I incorporate.

My reason for that severe limitation is that this song, like so many traditional songs (again, including blues songs) can quickly deteriorate into a dish with too many flavors, I feel—so many disconnected verses (read: ideas) that it becomes more an incongruous litany of disparate complaints or uncoordinated observations, or a mix of both, than a truly cohesive whole.

A traditional song tends to be constituted of simple and straight-forward building blocks. But simple *doesn't* mean simplistic—it can also be an adjective used to otherwise properly describe elegance and power, both of which there is a lot in a good traditional song. (And yes, there's also often a lot of dross.) To my ears, even with verses of roughly uniform eloquence, just pumping out verse after disconnected verse *diminishes* the overall impact—there's a strong suggestion of "throwing in the kitchen sink". A writerly schizophrenia. Verses in a traditional song can be so lean and potent that it can be like pouring way too much gunpowder into a canon if you stuff everything you have into the song. Where there's a wish to lengthen the song for time, my choice, almost always, is to call on the instrumental accompaniment, or to possibly designate one specific verse as a de facto chorus and re-insert it more than once into the proceedings. Again, neither solution is at all unusual.

In my rendition of "The Cuckoo", we have, along with the title verse, two of the remaining three concerning gambling, with the final one concerning admiration for a particular woman—so just two primary propositions, wrapped in a somewhat amorphous but engaging bracket. For dancing and similar—where words are of secondary importance and as much as anything else serve to simply break up the monotony—throwing everything ya got into the stew is fine, naturally. We sometimes have a real surfeit of those great, but conceptually entirely independent, ideas and verses—in most cases it's of little consequence when out on the dance floor, so no problem. But to my ears, for literate presentation—for there to be an actual reason for these words to be *listened* to, and not just danced to—there should be a continuity either obviously delineated or clearly implied. More than one general theme is fine, I think—two certainly, and possibly even three. But careful! This is a form in which less *is* more.

Later, we'll look at another traditional song I've played for many years—a basic 12-bar blues—and matters examined here will be looked at from another angle.

The objective, when one assembles a traditional song—and 'assembles' is a good way to put it—should be to seek concordances, continuities, and complementary angles when possible, and to massage and mold them into that coherent presentation that lets the listener know there's *more* here than just a heap of words from all over with no armature, no reason for internal association other than an indeterminate and confused historicity.

As briefly mentioned in footnote 37, earlier, Dolly Parton did—intelligently, capably did—exactly what's described here to "The House of The Rising Sun" in preparation for her own recorded performance of it. She presumably spread out the extant available verses on her desk, studied that material and physically re-arranged the pieces and parts, and added in her own slight editions. (But caveat emptor: The musical accompaniment and production on her recording of the song is just plain wretched—a reminder of how vapid Nashville-oriented production can be, as insipid back in the '80s as now. Her construction of the lyrics, however, is great—as is her singing, naturally. But the rest? Well, consider yourself warned.)

Traditional songs require the same thought and precision in construction—or again, in assembling—as a song written ground-up, but with the critical and pivotal *additional* requirement that the song eventually presented be properly, intelligently consistent with historical antecedents. As noted elsewhere, I think it's part of the proper respect we owe past generations, and a reflection of our own self-respect.

[53] *Mojo*, 3/2/2013, "Eric Clapton: My Life in the Yardbirds, Cream and Beyond", interviewed by Michael Simmons.

[54] I later learned it was one of the set painters—a New Yorker born in Puerto Rico—who knew, very much liked, and had specifically typed "Carter Family" into the internet connection; a rewarding exemplar illustration of the wonderful and unexpected mélange of cultures and ethnicities that comprises America. It made me smile broadly.

[55] Lula Walls", copyright 1928 by A.P. Carter. Quoted here as permitted within the Fair Use provisions of 17 U.S.C.§107.

[56] Probably taken mostly from Clarence Ashley's early-to-mid twentieth century version, as recorded by Alan Lomax in 1961.

Chapter Twenty-Eight

The Disarmingly Enabling Inscience of Rap and Hip-Hop

Words are, of course, the most powerful drug used by mankind.
— Rudyard Kipling

I accept the argument that even describing rap and hip-hop as popular song may somewhat miss the mark, insofar as there's a strong propensity in the form to virtually *bury* any music in a flood of words and booming beat. There are major rap stars, surely, who couldn't knowledgeably play Note One on an actual musical instrument, or creditably sing Note One without going through auto-tune.

But again, at this point we're still addressing the lyrics side of songwriting. (We'll get to musical composition later on, promise.) And this is a genre in which words—*and what is being said*, certainly—is the whole ballgame, or the preponderance of it. However, unfortunately—and given the inherent emphasis on the lyrics here, possibly even more noxiously than in other forms—most of what's being said is utterly worthless. In its worst manifestations it's censurably repulsive, posturing garbage; wrapped in an annoyingly ludicrous sneer.

Ninety-five percent of this stuff is just plain foul-smelling Rap Crap. Swinish stupidity, swathed in ludicrous hot air.

What is incontestably *noteworthy* and *positive* however, is how within rap the lexical constructions and rhymes can veer so far, far away from the expected standard. Rap has arguably accelerated the acceptance of unusual constructions and imperfect rhyme in popular songwriting. (But its employment still remains most widely acclaimed, probably, in the poems of nineteenth century poet and mousy homebody, Emily Dickinson—tell that to the neighborhood wannabe gangsta.)

At one time rhyme in a song had an important technical function along with the desire for pleasing sonority—to aid simple understanding of the words being sung. Before phonographic reproduction, before electronic amplification, mere comprehension of generally unfamiliar material was a significant hurdle, and rhyme was a fundamental tool in overcoming it. But there are only so many perfect rhymes available for any word, obviously leading to overuse and eventual cliché.

The freedom that not being tied to conventional constructions and actual or even near rhyme allows is invigorating to popular songwriting. We're all tired of 'kissing/missing', 'love/above', 'chance/dance/romance' and other obvious combinations—though this *isn't* to say even the most hackneyed rhyme can't work within a fitting context (read: worthwhile surrounding information) and with helpful vocal delivery (such as, again, the singer arriving on the obvious rhyme well before the note upon which it would naturally fall). No, not being constrained by conventional practices in rhyme isn't new, but in rap, almost as a rule, we're wandering in the Wild West of Whatever Works—conventional expectations in rhyme, meter, and overall structure generally be damned.[57]

Effective writing in rap—and here I'm gonna jump right on the bandwagon the reader surely anticipates—is currently perhaps best evinced in the stage musical, *Hamilton*, by Lin-Manuel Miranda, and in his preceding effort, *In the Heights*.[58]

When information is coming in rapidly, relentlessly—thoughtfully—occasional lapses in craft can perhaps be forgiven, are perhaps even effectively hidden, because the very next idea comes right on its heels without allowing the listener the opportunity to analyze or reflect: the general notion is enough. Contrast this with the first song we looked at, "American Pie"—where the failures aren't obscured by adjacent brilliance or even adjacent pertinent information. In contradistinction, Miranda's work generally provides a lot to consider throughout; most of it presented with respect for our intelligence, unafraid and able to reach us using a rich vocabulary. (There's also very little purposely obfuscating dialect or patois, either inherent in the lyrics or affected in the delivery, something that often debilitates rap.)

By the way, the massive mainstream (generally well-educated, moneyed, primarily Caucasian) audience for *Hamilton*—for writing which is a product of rap sensibilities—is an illustration of the point made in Chapter Fifteen: it's not the form that matters, it's the execution.

As concerns the generally rapid-fire delivery in rap, writing adagio to perform prestissimo—if I can put it that way—is a simple enough endeavor. Right, ya just speed everything up beyond what might reasonably be expected, given the difficulty of the words and of the information conveyed, when in performance. The easiest of parlor tricks. However, *without* consistent actual worthwhile substance being present in that torrent of words—because some of it, and it'll be a different part for each individual auditor, *will* be fully comprehended—the song is exposed as but verbosity for verbosity's sake. Miranda's efforts regularly deliver, but the vast insufferable majority of rap and rap-influenced songs don't even come close.

Whatever the generally low quality of the writing in rap and hip-hop, the freedom the form brings to popular songwriting itself is refreshing and liberating. We *are* all tired of 'kissing/missing', 'love/above', 'chance/dance/ romance' — and 'moon/June/spoon' — no?

[57]As for the delivery—the actual rapping—there've always been popular songs that weren't truly 'sung'. A talking blues (first appearing in a song entitled just that, "Talking Blues", by Chris Bouchillon, in 1926) and a patter song (Gilbert & Sullivan did them brilliantly in the late nineteenth century) are just two examples; (as is the vocal technique called 'sprechstimme' in an operatic context). But that aspect of rap is irrelevant to this treatise.

[58]Way off topic here, but both shows do suffer on stage, from the directoral freneticism so common in contemporary musical theater—choreography largely lacking raison d'être or interest; marshaled throughout in the counterproductive and desperate panic to KEEP-EVERYTHING-MOVING-MOVING-MOVING-DAMMIT-DAMMIT-DAMMIT-PEOPLE-WILL-GET-BORED-AND-FALL-ASLEEP-IF-WE-DON'T!!—but that's still one more topic for another essay one day.

Chapter Twenty-Nine

Come to the Cabaret, Old Chum

Give my regards to Broadway! — George M. Cohan

Where one tends to find the most cultivated musicianship—trained musical skills, if not necessarily composing genius or even flair—can unfortunately tend to haul along with it the most pronounced class hauteur. As the chapter head indicates, I'm addressing cabaret, Broadway, and attendant genres. But as with the affectations in country, rap, hard rock and elsewhere, it's imperative to examine the actual writing and composing independent of it, and to take and use what positive lessons we can find.

And there's occasionally some really great writing and composing found in this sometimes most conservative of arenas. Contemporary and recent songwriters whose work comes immediately to mind include Stephen Sondheim, Tim Rice, Howard Ashman, Robert Lopez, Hal David, William Finn, and others. Musical theater—a successful stage musical—requires songs that are sung in character, and that regularly results in a song that may be well-written, but performed outside the show for which it's designed may seem somewhat eccentric (e.g., "Don't Cry For Me Argentina", "One Night in Bangkok").

Working the same side of the street as contemporary Broadway and cabaret are songs in the so-called Great American Songbook—the evergreen 'standards'.[59] Even when the writing and composing are beyond reproach and may still feel current despite having been written countless decades ago, it can be admittedly difficult to find a way to present them freshly. But if it can be done with "The House of the Rising Sun", as noted earlier, it can conceivably be done with songs by Noel Coward, Jerome Kern and the Gershwin brothers as well.

Note, I'm not talking about the tendency for an act in rock, country or wherever to completely avoid association with these songs due to worry about "not being 'authentic' and properly 'anti-establishment'"—*until*, that is, a career is on the skids and there's nowhere else to turn. Suddenly it's time to 're-invent'—and we're told the act secretly loved, Loved, LOVED Rodgers and Hammerstein all along! Wow, really? And even though they're bringing nothing new to the material, they *are* dressed in formalwear now—so please buy this album, okay? (cf. Rod Stewart)

As with material in any realm, it's a matter of how the material is addressed; the intelligence and application brought to bear. And also as with material in any other realm, there's a whole lotta drivel here as well.

But what I think is a particular strength in musical theater—and this gets to the aspect I wish to emphasize in this chapter—derives from the fact that the most important element in making a musical work is neither the lyrics *nor* the music, but what's called the 'book', the story. There remains a place for reflection and commentary (and so, incidentally, a song that is more easily lifted from the show to make a viable stand-alone single), but elsewhere what's most effective is what's called an 'extended musical scene', which can last much longer than a traditional song. The length isn't achieved by simply repeating a 3-4 minute predictable song-form bed ad infinitum, but by expanding it, contracting it, *and diverging entirely* from it—including sometimes combining two songs or musical expositions into a larger cohesive whole—in what can feel like a free-form exploration, maintaining consonance with and support for what's happening in the lyrics, those lyrics that abet the progress of the story.

Stellar examples include the so-called "Bench Scene" from *Carousel*, "Color and Light" from *Sunday in the Park with George*, "Prologue" from *Into the Woods,* and "All-American Prophet" from *The Book of Mormon*.[60] We're cut loose from the expected song-form and taken for a flight, taken for a spin, the direction and length of which are primarily determined by the requirements of the lyrical objectives. The music and structure are effectively subordinated to and focused on conveying important, necessary exposition—fundamental information.

---

[59]I've written at some length on my antipathy for that snidely elitist and exclusionary designation, The Great American Songbook, in the liner notes book for an album by the often exceptional Frank Lindamood called *Songs from the OTHER Great American Songbook*, which I also produced. https://www.franklindamood.com/new-release-songs-from-the-other-great-american-songbook (Web search: Frank Lindamood)

[60]*Carousel* by Richard Rodgers and Oscar Hammerstein, *Sunday in the Park with George* and *Into the Woods* both by Stephen Sondheim and James Lapine, *The Book of Mormon* by Trey Parker, Robert Lopez, and Matt Stone.

Chapter Thirty

Stuck Under a Stack of Marshall Amplifiers

Take care of the sense. The sounds will take care of themselves.
— Lewis Carroll

Probably more than in any other place in popular music, (aside from strictly dance music, as alluded to earlier) hard rock songs live or die by the riff—the endlessly repeated musical phrase that surrounds and permeates the song. But that's a musical factor, so we'll get to it later on.

As concerns what is actually said in a hard rock song, I think we can offer as a fair generalization (but generalization nonetheless) that, "The harder the rock, the less easily decipherable the point of it all". Or how 'bout a cheap shot version of that? "The heavier the metal, the lighter the mental." (Digressive rumination: I'm always somewhat amused by the posturing of so much in heavy metal, insofar as it attempts to fuse the rather antithetical sensibilities of Pre-Raphaelite esthetics and future dystopian fantasy. I guess one *can* manufacture a synthesis, but ya really sorta hafta go one way or the other, dontcha?)

Anyway, let's quickly look at a couple of extremely well-known hard rock songs, examples in which many or most of the lyrics *are* readily discernible, even if the context and objectives aren't necessarily understandable, and continuity and consistency appear to be entirely alien concepts.

It may be claimed—well, in fact there most certainly *are* lots of zealously advanced competing claims about the specifics—that Queen's "Bohemian Rhapsody" (lyrics by Freddie Mercury) or Led Zeppelin's "Stairway to Heaven" (lyrics by Robert Plant) imparts this or that Deep and Universal Message, for instance.

But all the actual pertinent testimonies point in the exact opposite direction.

Here's Queen's guitarist Brian May:

> "So what is 'Bohemian Rhapsody' about? Well, I don't think we'll ever know...I think it's best to leave it with a question mark hanging in the air."[61]

And here's Led Zeppelin's Robert Plant:

> "Depending on what day it is, I still interpret 'Stairway' differently each time—and I wrote it...I'm still trying to work out what I was talking about. Everyone is!"[62]

Zeppelin's guitarist Jimmy Page chimes in:

> "The wonderful thing about 'Stairway' is the fact that just about everybody has got their own individual interpretation to it...Over the years, people have come to me with all manner of stories about what it meant...."[63]

Finding rock songwriters who admit having no idea in hell what they're actually 'saying' ain't hard, unfortunately. But even if it were, the songs speak for themselves—or rather, all too often *don't* speak for themselves, and that's the unfunny joke. Here's Noel Gallagher of Oasis, concerning his massive commercial hit, "Don't Look Back in Anger":

> "I get the odd night when I'm halfway through it, and I say to myself, 'I still don't know what these words mean!' I'm thinking 'What the fuck?'...And all these kids will be singing it at the top of their voices with all their arms around each other and I kind of feel like stopping and going, 'Look, can somebody help me out here? Am I missing something?'"[64]

What's really sad about all the above statements is that there's little embarrassment or disappointment evinced by any of the speakers. They may be bemused, but if anything they're on balance *proud* of not communicating—or to be more precise, of aggressively blasting out songs that they know effectively say *nothing*. If there's any message or information in the communication between songwriter and auditor—better:

in the *intersection* of songwriter and auditor—it's entirely a construction of the auditor's imagination, imputations, and subjective psychological preferences. It isn't really communication at all.

Am I implying that all hard rock songs that have an unexpected or unusual lyrical content are lesser works that fail as communicative efforts? Not at all. Of course not.

A strong counter example to impress that is another song readers have certainly heard countless times over the years, the Who's "I Can See For Miles" (written and composed by Pete Townsend)—which I expect just about anyone could also fairly characterize as a full-on oddball conception, no? Someone claiming to literally see for miles and miles? How is a metaphor like that born? But it 100% works. Superbly done: a clear, consistent, distinct point of view—and unabashedly idiosyncratic, certainly—that still communicates precisely what the songwriter intended.

And—surprise!—as we'll see later, a song like "I Can See For Miles" is much better written, much more *poetic*, if you will, than so many other songs which are critically praised as actual 'poetry'.

That "Bohemian Rhapsody" and "Stairway to Heaven" satisfy uncritical audiences is primarily a testament to the musical composition and structure. As noted, we're given little more than pretentious pomposities and silliness—not much coherent information is imparted; even less is worth retaining. But the *construction* created for the musical delivery of all that lyrical nonsense is far removed from any conventional song format. In fact, the two songs resemble, more than anything else, those extended musical scenes from a West End or Broadway show that I described in the preceding chapter.

Let's pause for a moment here to consider that surely unexpected consonance.

Neither "Rhapsody" nor "Stairway" is at all predictable structurally or musically from moment to moment, and each traverses a lot of changing, shifting ground. We have no idea where they're going next, and so we're swept along on an unusual musical journey, just as in an extended musical scene in a well-written Broadway or West End musical.

But after it's all over, wouldn't it have been rewarding to know that in this case the excursion had actually been *worth* our damned time and attention?

[61]*Queen: Greatest Video Hits DVD*, 2002.
[62]London press conference, 9/20/2012.
[63]*Fresh Air,* 6/2/2003.
[64]ContactMusic.com; 8/12/2005.

MANIFESTO

PART THREE: Lyrics
— THE GOOD, THE BAD & THE UGLY —

We'll now finally start to swing back to songwriting specifics. Unfortunately, however, there's still one more Big Negative to confront, and so we'll start Part Three with that, get it over with, and move forward—first into aspects both practical and theoretical. Then we'll examine several well-known songs—examples of both good and bad songwriting—in light of what's been exposed.

Chapter Thirty-One

Ethics? In SONGWRITING ITSELF...?!? or "Scumbags and Lowlifes and Crooks, Oh My!"

Just because someone's a musician, I don't say he's cleansed and holy. You got some dirty people in all walks of life. Look at all the things the politicians and people like that have to cover up and sweep under the rug—why in hell would a musician be any better?
— Johnny Shines

Ready for an indignant digression here? Yeah, we've been digressing throughout—as promised (threatened?)—but this time we're addressing a particularly serious matter.

The chapter took a lot of time to put together, and to a reader who might think I must've secretly enjoyed it due to the obvious amount of research required, *let me be absolutely clear that is <u>not</u> the case*. And I'm irritated about two aspects of it all: 1) the facts themselves, and 2) the time and work required away from the primary focus of this effort to properly establish them for a reader who may be ignorant of them—and then to write it up.

Because we come now to the practice of ripping off songwriting credits, and some of the biggest names in popular music have done it, with greater or lesser degrees of dishonesty and success—Johnny Cash, Paul Simon, Brian Wilson, Yusuf Islam/Cat Stevens, and Led Zeppelin among them.[65] (Once again, I'll focus here on older acts and songs, as most readers will have at least passing familiarity with them.)

But probably the most feverish pirate of all, over the years, has been Bob Dylan. Which is doubly unfortunate, because it'd be cleaner, less encumbered, were we able to limit our look at his work strictly *to* that work. But even before getting to that, there's this subordinate but pervasive aspect to address. And as he's without question the current lion of popular songwriting, to leave it unattended would be a dereliction—and imply de facto apologia for a very despicable practice; one perfectly illustrative of the current critical unseriousness regularly encountered in popular music.

★

Bob Dylan is an admitted plagiarist. He is a thief. A crook. When confronted, he claims he's simply 'using the folk process', which—according to him—has *always* permitted stealing work created by someone else.

That is just plain untrue, and I'll explain why.

'The folk process' is in fact primarily a convenient academic characterization for the evolution of songs, the specific provenance and evolution of which is unclear, unknown. Full stop.

Over decades or even centuries in the pre-industrial world, a song would naturally and inexorably change and calve new versions as it was transmitted, usually orally, from one performer to another, one generation to the next—often incorporating bits and pieces from elsewhere into the continuously evolving admixture the song had become. "I'll Twine Mid the Ringlets" evolving into "Wildwood Flower", noted earlier, is an example of this mechanism. The so-called folk process is an after-the-fact label for that untraceable and highly individualized process, and nothing more. It is definitely *not* a license for self-entitled multimillionaires, or anyone else, to knowingly steal the work of others, all the while claiming they're just "aw, shucks" simple, innocent balladeers.

Dylan's documented history of larceny dates from late adolescence[66] but continued into his recording career, perhaps most notably early-on with his claim of authorship of "Corrina, Corrina", a song very much still under the 1929 copyright (renewed in 1957) of by-then destitute blues singer Bo Chatmon. Dylan's career had already taken off, with money starting to roll in; Chatmon died a couple of years later, in abject poverty.

And far, far beyond what anyone else has done in popular songwriting, he's ripped off *countless* traditional melodies for his 'original songs'. His "Masters of War" IS "Nottamun Town", "Blowin' in the Wind" IS "No More Auction Block", "With God On Our Side" IS "The Patriot Game", "Restless Farewell" IS "The Parting Glass", "Bob Dylan's Dream" IS "Lord Franklin's Lament", "Farewell, Angelina" IS "Farewell to Tarwathie"—and the list quite literally does go on and On and <u>ON</u>; one stolen melody after another, often along with the lyrical blueprint as well. To put the industrial-strength piracy into perspective, it's akin to rapaciously plundering archeological sites, demolishing ancient graveyards with a bulldozer—and is in fact *contemptuous* and *destructive* of folk music, history and culture. To be clear, Dylan Incorporated isn't the only pop music entertainment vandal—in his case, a costumed-in-denim 'folk singer'—to strip mine traditional tunes for greedy profit; he's just the most ruthless, spineless, and prosperous.

We'll more directly address matters on the music side of songwriting later, however.

But as concerns lyrics, Dylan's imperious plagiarism of the poetry of Henry Timrod and the copyrighted work of Junichi Saga is undisputed. And when exposed and confronted, he defends himself by claiming he's perfectly innocent, adding—and here's the fun part—that anyone who doesn't accept that is an "evil motherfucker!".[67]

(While our primary subject here is obviously songwriting, it may be worth also noting that Dylan can't even indulge in his hobby of painting pictures—paintings then sold for many thousands of bucks—without stealing.[68] And his 2004 book, *Chronicles: Volume I* is packed to the rafters with outright plagiarized material.[69] There's a history of blatant criminality by design here, not isolated, possibly blameless inadvertencies.)

A simple truth should come to the fore: Plagiarism wants you *not* to know or recognize the original, wowed by what you've just encountered, crediting it to the immediate purveyor; whereas allusion wants you to *know*—or be newly-informed via proper citation—of the original and be pleased by the concordance. To predacious Bob, those who aren't deceived or acquiescent to his larcenies are, to repeat, "evil motherfuckers".

Finally, and quite telling—critically telling—is that despite the claim his own self-entitled thefts are harmless and firmly 'within the folk process', Dylan's on constant vigil when he's on the other side.[70, 71] His pugnacious Beverly Hills attorneys are ready to pounce on adventitious trespassers when his songs are even remotely threatened with the possibility of copyright infringement, to squeeze as much money as possible from them—those other people now using Dylan's, ahem, um, 'folk process'.

You can't have it both ways.

By the way, though Dylan asserts he's simply following in the tradition of his hero, Woody Guthrie, that's another lie. Guthrie's outlook and practice were pretty far removed from Dylan's. He regularly and notably even used an *anti*-copyright notice—including this one, on his best-known effort, no less, "This Land is Your Land":

> *This song is Copyrighted in U.S., under Seal of Copyright #154085, for a period of 28 years, and anybody caught singin it without our permission, will be mighty good friends of ourn, cause we don't give a dern. Publish it. Write it. Sing it. Swing to it. Yodel it. We wrote it, that's all we wanted to do.*

Could anyone ever even *imagine* Dylan doing similar?

Yet Guthrie did use melodies from popular songs of his era. "This Land is Your Land" is taken from The Carter Family's "When the World's On Fire", for instance (and perhaps their "Little Darlin' Pal of Mine" as well—it's an extremely common chord progression and simple melody)[72] and there's no telling what he might have done if presented with the option of 'graduating' to Dylan's level of wholesale grand larceny. But the ongoing *social consciousness* and commitment to the *politics* of his work was clearly primary, and the songs themselves even sometimes deliberately transient. There was no big money nor lasting large commercial imprint to be obtained. Guthrie's songs were generally intended, first and foremost, to mobilize and celebrate working class pride, empowerment and social progress. Dylan's thefts, in contradistinction, are designed to advance his cupidity and personal agenda, almost entirely bereft of larger consideration.[73]

With Guthrie, one gets a class-conscious message; with Dylan, the message is Bob—perhaps why even his songs that address issues generally strike as ill-fitting and shallow. Guthrie's work embraced political righteous indignation; Dylan's trumpets self-righteous celebrity entitlement. Neither was/is a truly great writer, but I'll take Guthrie's assertively egalitarian worldview over Dylan's arrogantly selfish vacancy any day.

★

Good artists borrow; great artists steal.

The above bit of fatuous casuistry, in various permutations attributed to various sources over past decades, has been tossed out, cavalierly, as some kind of twisted, indisputable defense for plagiarism, especially including Dylan's, by his admirers.[74] "Good artists borrow; great artists steal"? If we compliantly agree to the notion, perhaps Dylan's apologists will have to agree in return—based on that formula—that the Greatest Popular Music Artist of the Past Half-Century certainly *isn't* their Bob at all...but surely Andrew Lloyd Webber.[75] Willing to go there, Dylanoids?

Yet let's take the above a little further, because I'd like to offer my own

revision of that persistent, despicable "Good artists borrow; great artists steal" sophism.

If one isn't simply duplicating but truly expanding upon something that was written by someone else before him or her, then the use can be possibly justified, both morally and artistically. To me, it doesn't matter whence an idea or even a locution or insight derives—if it works in a *compelling* and *original* realization. However, *and in each and every case,* if the 'borrowing'—the unauthorized appropriation, really—is significant, then sourcing IS ABSOLUTELY REQUIRED. Naturally. And why not? I mean what's lost in doing so?

Looked at from the other side, is anything—anything beyond the obvious moral imperative—*gained* through attribution? The answer is yes. Absolutely. The borrower, if his or her usage augments and expands on the original, is now firmly part of the artistic chain, the cultural continuum, attempting respectful commune with the greats and near-greats.

So here's my revision:

> *Great artists borrow; careerist incompetents steal.*

Another 'defense' of Bob's reprehensible thieveries (and by extension, presumably of Led Zeppelin's and of any other of pop music's willfully contemptuous plagiarisms as well) comes to us from Princeton University's Sean Wilentz, yet one more pathetically loopy Dylan hobbyist, who fawningly gushes, "Art is different—especially the kind Dylan creates!"[76] (Wilentz gives himself the title of—and again, I'm not making this up—"Historian-in-Residence at the Bob Dylan Web Site". Honest. Superfans

who can't just <u>be</u> their celebrity heroes—oh, the unfairness of it all—will so often easily manufacture some inflated parasitic role, to then become slavishly, um, 'connected' to them. So here: a bubbleheaded volunteer "Historian-in-Residence"...for multinational conglomerate Sony Music Corporation's web site. Dear God save us.)

Except for the fact that the 'art' Dylan 'creates' makes him and his record company millions and millions of dollars, I'm not sure I see any 'difference'. An across-the-board license to steal, though, like that unctuously trumpeted by Professor Wilentz, is certainly rather breathtaking.

And as noted, it's not at all clear if *all* art is 'different' in Wilentz's asinine argument—meaning maybe he and others like him are okay with *anyone* and *everyone* plagiarizing, so long as their songs pass some kinda 'art test'. But what would that be? If they're played on the radio? If the act has big piles of money? Good lawyers? They smile a lot? Tough call.

Hey, I've got it! Perhaps (as would seem to be the line advocated by inflamed Dylanoids like Wilentz) Bob alone should be exempt and allowed to pillage, rip off, and ransack—because he's Just So Very Special. Fine. No, perfect! In fact, we should presumably all *encourage* Dylan to steal—wildly applaud and genuflect each time he does, and then tell all the victims, and anyone else scrupulous and respectful of American cultural history, to go fuck themselves....

Seriously, theft is theft, no? Maybe the sheltered Wilentz has never heard of the artists Andy Warhol, Shepard Fairey, and Jeff Koons? Or of George Harrison of the Beatles? Or of any of the other songwriters mentioned at the beginning of this chapter—and of all the money they've had to pay out in court judgments and settlements, all because no, art is *not* 'different'. (No word yet from dutiful sycophants like Wilentz on Dylan's plagiarized oil paintings or book, and if they're also, uh, 'different'.)

And just think about it for a moment. When some backwoods banjo player a hundred years ago commandeered a piece of music or a line of lyrics to perform at the Saturday night barn dance, there really was 'no harm, no foul'—nothing of seminal cultural consequence, certainly, or even minor financial displacement. The same latitude might properly apply today in most contexts that are similarly inconsequential or informal. The situation is of more concern, though still only marginally, with Guthrie's generally fleeting appropriations. When Dylan steals, however, we've reached intensive scorched-earth industrialized rapacity. If the material is still under copyright, it takes income from his victims and stuffs it very firmly into his own pockets. That's clear. It also, *much more damagingly*, quite literally claims their creative work *isn't* theirs at all, but his! He created it. Bob Dylan Wrote This, dammit!—no matter who actually did. Even when he loots material that's fallen out of copyright, he *still* attempts to hide and deny his thefts—viciously attacking those who object. "Pay no attention to that man behind the curtain!", screams the imposter.

And so I'll repeat the distinction made earlier: Plagiarism wants you *not* to know the original, whereas allusion wants you to know.[77]

Finally, we come to the "Aw, Good Old Frolicsome Bob Sure Is A Lovable Li'l Scamp, Ain't He?" purported 'defense'—usually incorporating an ostensibly exculpating 'He's just a magpie!' characterization. Dylan is not a 'magpie'—a bird known (incorrectly, a recent study indicates) for its determined pilferage of shiny objects. He's a human being. (Hey, cute little hamsters often eat their young. So—just wondering here—if Dylan was discovered Jeffrey Daumer-izing his own kids, would obsequious fans rush to forgive him as, say, a 'lovably roguish hamster'? Eh? Yes, there's a difference between thievery and cannibalism. There's also a difference between thievery and honesty—and there's *no* excuse for exonerating determined, lowlife villainy with smug distractions.)

In any other discipline, an arrogant racketeer like Dylan is shamed and shunned—usually with devastating career repercussions. That he simply steamrolls on, entirely unaffected, is yet another emblematic illustration of the current malignant dereliction infecting of so much popular music criticism, and the contemporary disposable nature of popular songs generally. If Dylan is or was ahead of his time in any serious capacity, it may simply be that his greedy dishonesty is a perfect representation for the present diseased Trump Era. After all, if he can get away with plagiarism, it really does effectively license everyone to do the same.

★

What this all does, bottom line—even beyond the wholesale destruction of cultural patrimony and the personal, professional, and creative damage to the direct victims—is accentuate and exacerbate the two most pandemically deleterious predispositions in the popular music social contract. The first is the contempt for art and audiences by the successful act, which operates with impunity. (The contempt for morality and law are just symptoms.) The second is the cognitive dissonance engaged in by the audience—enthusiastic, knee-jerk fans—that eagerly, robotically manufactures eye-rollingly warped excuses and alibis for criminality.

"Professional fans'—enthusiasts who are critics and academics, and who would vehemently, vigorously condemn and completely ostracize a fellow writer who plagiarizes—suddenly discover, fabricate and obediently champion delusional contortions and exonerating rationales for the celebrity act that does the very same thing. Ordinary fans, who at home would immediately call the police if they saw a thief rip off something from a neighbor's front porch, shrug their shoulders and smile with bemused submission when their pop hero effectively does the exact same thing. The critic, academic and average fan have willfully forged a demeaning and repugnant alliance with corruption. And the act laughs all the way to the bank—or the bank and the Nobel Prize.[78]

Back on the music side of matters for a moment, for a look at how to *ethically* make use of a traditional or other already existing melody in a new song, see Chapter Fifty-Four.

One final caveat before we continue, however inconvenient—even unpleasant—it may be. General dishonesty, thievery—and just about any other vices—does *not* preclude the possibility of creative talent also being in residence. Agreed? I stress once again that we must divorce *all* extraneous considerations when we address actual work itself—and lamentably for those who may find refuge in a fanciful Perfect World Populated by Perfect Artists, ethical behavior or the lack thereof is yet another superfluous matter. Our 'go-to' proof might even be the rather unassailable genius of sculptor Michelangelo, who began his career as an actual art forger.[79, 80] Surely, few would deny the brilliance in so much of his work.

[65]Paul Simon's "American Tune" uses an uncredited melody—rather, a melody dishonestly credited to him—which is actually "O Sacred Head, Now Wounded", a hymn composed by Hans Leo Hassler around 1600. Johnny Cash outright stole "Folsom Prison Blues"—words *and* music—from "Crescent City Blues", written in 1953 by Gordon Jenkins. Yusuf Islam/Cat Stevens took writing and composing credit for "Morning Has Broken", which is another church hymn, this one with lyrics written in 1931 by Eleanor Farjeon, to a melody from a Christmas carol called "Child in the Manger". Brian Wilson stole Chuck Berry's "Sweet Little Sixteen" for "Surfin' USA". None of these facts are contested. And here's a list of Led Zeppelin's many, many rip-offs: https://en.wikipedia.org/wiki/List_of_Led_Zeppelin_songs_written_or_inspired_by_others (web search terms: Zeppelin songs inspired others Wiki) along with some informal side-by-side audio comparisons: https://www.youtube.com/watch?v=o8VG80RxDMw (YouTube title search: Howard Stern Truth Behind Led Zeppelin Part 2)

[66]Passing off a 1959 song written by Hank Snow, called "Little Buddy", as an original poem for publication: http://www.rollingstone.com/music/news/handwritten-poem-by-teenage-bob-dylan-up-for-auction-20090519 (web search terms: Poem Teenage Dylan Auction)

[67] *Rolling Stone*, 9/27/2012, interview by Mikal Gilmore, titled, "Bob Dylan Unleashed":
Before we end the conversation, I want to ask about the controversy over your quotations in your songs from the works of other writers, such as Japanese author Junichi Saga's *Confessions of a Yakuza*, and the Civil War poetry of Henry Timrod. Some critics say that you didn't cite your sources clearly. Yet in folk and jazz, quotation is a rich and enriching tradition. What's your response to those kinds of charges?

"Oh, yeah, in folk and jazz, quotation is a rich and enriching tradition. That certainly is true. It's true for everybody, but me. I mean, everyone else can do it but not me. There are different rules for me. And as far as Henry Timrod is concerned, have you even heard of him? Who's been reading him lately? And who's pushed him to the forefront? Who's been making you read him? And ask his descendants what they think of the hoopla. And if you think it's so easy to quote him and it can help your work, do it yourself and see how far you can get. Wussies and pussies complain about that stuff. It's an old thing—it's part of the tradition. It goes way back. These are the same people that tried to pin the name Judas on me. Judas, the most hated name in human history! If you think you've been called a bad name, try to work your way out from under that. Yeah, and for what? For playing an electric guitar? As if that is in some kind of way equitable to betraying our Lord and delivering him up to be crucified. All those evil motherfuckers can rot in hell."

Seriously?

"I'm working within my art form. It's that simple. I work within the rules and limitations of it. There are authoritarian figures that can explain that kind of art form better to you than I can. It's called songwriting. It has to do with melody and rhythm, and then after that, anything goes. You make everything yours. We all do it." [Uh, Bob? No, we don't. — MK]

[68] "Bob Dylan in Plagiarism Row Over Paintings", Sean Michaels, *The Guardian*, 9/28/2011: https://www.theguardian.com/music/2011/sep/28/bob-dylan-paintings (web search terms: Dylan plagiarism row paintings)

[69] "Bob Dylan's 'Da Vinci Code' Cracked in New Book", Marc Hogan, *Spin*, 5/19/2014: https://www.spin.com/2014/05/bob-dylan-da-vinci-code-chronicles-memoir-dylanologists-plagiarism/ (web search terms: Dylan's Da Vinci Cracked Book)

[70] CBSNews Interactive 9/13/2012, by Lauren Moraski, titled "Dylan Calls Plagiarism Accusers 'Wussies'":
Meanwhile, Dylan himself has been caught up in lawsuit involving use of his name. In 1994, he filed a trademark infringement lawsuit against Apple, asking for a court order to keep the computer giant from using his name. There are also reports Dylan reached an out-of-court settlement in 1995 with Hootie & the Blowfish over the band's hit song 'Only Wanna Be With You.' Dylan reportedly claimed frontman Darius Rucker borrowed some of his lyrics in the track.

[71] *Los Angeles Times*; 6/26/1988, by Patrick Goldstein, titled "Rod Stewart Sounds an Echo of Dylan":
"The song, 'Forever Young', is very much Rod's song," explained his manager, Arnold Stiefel. "When we were putting the album together, someone

pointed out that there was a Dylan song with the same title, so we listened to the two songs. And it would be fair to say that while the melody and the music are not at all the same, the *idea* is similar." Saying he was concerned, Stiefel immediately sent the song to Dylan, asking whether he had a problem with it. "His attorney relayed the message that he had no problem with the song—but he did want to participate in the ownership." So Dylan will get a 50-50 split of all the royalties.

[72]The gravity of what we're addressing in this chapter surely militates against inserting a light-hearted diversion at this point, but for some later fun concerning "This Land Is Your Land", see Chapter Forty-Two and its accessory footnote 102.

[73]We should probably note that Dylan's net worth—I just checked—is estimated to be a hundred and eighty million dollars.

[74]No, Picasso never said that, nor did Stravinsky, nor Eliot, nor Faulkner—it's as bogus as a quote as it is as a defense.

[75]For a quick audio survey of many melodies Lloyd Webber seems to have, um, "recomposed": https://www.youtube.com/watch?v=4eMf_smG4Uk. (YouTube title search: Is Andrew Lloyd Webber a Plagiarist?)

[76]*Reuters Entertainment News*, 9/12/2012, interviewed by Chris Francescani. https://www.reuters.com/article/uk-bobdylan-plagiarism/bob-dylan-says-plagiarism-charges-made-by-wussies-and-pussies-idUKBRE88C00F20120913 (web search terms: Reuters Dylan wussies)

[77]This is actually a quote from our favorite Dylanoid, Chris Ricks, who (laughably but naturally) after offering this concise differentiation scurries back into the Twilight Zone of Cognitive Dissonance, defending his heartthrob hero in perfectly ridiculous Wilentzian fashion as 'special!', 'different!', etc, etc.

[78]Despite the seriousness of this chapter, I'm laughing out loud in mockery as I add this footnote. Today, June 13, 2017—just a couple of days after writing for this section was completed—we learn that Dylan even plagiarized his NOBEL PRIZE ACCEPTANCE SPEECH! The Nobel doofuses (doofi?) deserve contempt and ridicule as much as does Dylan. And just consider for a moment: if presented with a complete list of *every single possible situation in life* in which one might plagiarize, wouldn't the speech accepting the Nobel Prize—in Literature(!)—be THE most unlikely, THE most sacrosanct? The entire blundering circus of the 2016 Nobel Lit Prize is both ludicrous and outright repulsive. http://www.slate.com/articles/arts/culturebox/2017/06/did_bob_dylan_take_from_sparknotes_for_his_nobel_lecture.html (web search terms: Slate - Freewheelin' Dylan)

And yet, Dylan's most slavishly adoring fans, critics and academics fiercely defend him—complicitly place him *above* criticism for even this most garishly crude dishonesty. https://worldnews.easybranches.com/entertainment/tv-web/academics-defend-bob-dylan-s-plagiarism-as-a-post-modern-work-of-art-174007 (web search terms: Academics Defend Dylan Post Modern Art)

[79]Artsy.net, 8/10/2016, "The Forgery That Earned Michelangelo His First Roman Patron", by Nora Landes. https://www.artsy.net/article/artsy-editorial-how-michelangelo-got-his-start-by-forging-antiquities (web search terms: Forgery Michelangelo Patron)

[80]It might also be noted that Michelangelo didn't continue onward, *building an entire career* on being a crook—er, I mean being a 'magpie'.

Chapter Thirty-Two

The Twentieth Century Ended Almost Two Decades Ago

Great art speaks a language that every intelligent person can understand. Modernism speaks a different language.
— Marshall McLuhan

I sometimes speculate that the lack of direction and articulation found in so many critically and popularly acclaimed songs of the past several decades may just be a product and illustration of the final throes of literary modernism—modernism having finally wound and found its way down into popular songwriting, taken refuge there, and refusing to die a long-overdue and honorable death.

One can read a modernist masterpiece, say Joyce's *Ulysses* or Eliot's *The Waste Land*, and marvel at the brilliant execution and impressive eclecticism, but it's hard to avoid admitting the going can be quite a slog—as much an exercise in admiring and solving a demanding word puzzle as in potentially finding passing enlightenment or insight. Modernism opened culture to parading psychological depth front and center, though of course it's always been evident in creative works, implied and necessary. As interior came to eclipse exterior, obscuration rebuffing revelation, it came to provide literary critics and college English departments so much raw material to explore, interpret, and expound upon that we've dutifully allowed much of what literature traditionally can and should readily deliver as almost a matter of course (story, character, direct impact) to become peripheral and discounted—even dishonored—as somehow inconsequential and superficial. Instead, a work becomes a game of intellectual hide-and-seek, an elitist competition of academic enterprise ever more removed from quotidian appreciation and application—or *ready* quotidian appreciation and application, surely.

While there is some discernment in Eliot's dictum, "Genuine poetry can communicate before it is understood", total subscription to the implied derogation of a work that *can* be immediately assimilated—it's presumably not "genuine poetry"—exacerbates the problem. A poem—song, story, novel—that we judge to be impressive should arguably do more than simply intellectually stun. It should viscerally *involve*, reveal and communicate—or it is, really, not much more than a parlor trick, albeit even a possibly commanding one. I don't want to pick too much on Tom Eliot, but here's another critical prescription of his that's only partly correct—in this case he was speaking about theater, but that obviously doesn't confine the purview: "A play should give you something to think about. When I see a play and understand it the first time, then I know it can't be much good."

Well again, yes—and no. An easy inference (and in respect to Eliot, possibly unintentional by him, but if so the fault in the glibness of his statement) is that comprehending a work in any immediate manner means the work is, *necessarily*, devoid of deeper strata. And while that's of course ludicrous, it enjoys wide de facto cultural currency in modernist thinking: the explanation of an artwork is even more important than the artwork itself (cf. conceptual art and latter remanifestations). Repeating: the explanation of a work of art is more important—lasting, substantiating, worthy—than the work itself.

No.

What such thinking does in passing is generally cow an insecure populace into entirely subjugating their own intelligence and perception to the judgment of expert opinion; expert opinion that is absolutely culturally invaluable, of course. But it might be more productively and deferentially applied to complement and expand upon—to increase—intelligently received appreciation, rather than demand appreciation be based *entirely* on subliminal analysis and understanding, the gaining of which is found primarily and conveniently within the remove of, and by, that scholarly elite; and that only works requiring such expert exegeses can be truly adjudged to be culturally valuable.

It's wonderful to be introduced to aspects of creative innovation and achievement to which one was previously ignorant, but such can quite properly be in addition to—indeed, can be even justifiably *peripheral* to(!)—immediate perceptive cognition or intuition of legitimate artistic accomplishment. And of course, informed criticism can also perform the valuable subordinate functions of providing context, noting similarities and differences from related efforts, exposing derivative work that's being passed off as innovative—even introducing questions about the fundamental validity of that initial intuitively, intellectually, or emotionally derived positive reaction.

But immediacy *devoid* of intensifying substrata can most certainly provide wisdom or provoke introspection—a punch to the gut is exactly what economy and precision in language allows. And happily, one often finds that when such is encountered, the elegant disclosure or observation actually isn't barren of secondary and tertiary overtones after all. Such is the serendipitous beauty—the definitive character—of eloquence.

To be clear, in songwriting I'm differentiating between Hallmark Card kitsch (think not only of Dylan's execrable "Forever Young" but also of his "Masters of War" or "Lay, Lady Lay", both of which we'll also briefly examine later)—filled with pedestrian clichés and buzzwords easily assimilated and easily discarded—and powerful and reverberating ideas, also immediately recognized, such as those we'll note later when discussing Kris Kristofferson's "Me and Bobby McGee".

On the other side, while entirely subterranean consistencies in an effort of ostensibly more serious invention can end up being of great intellectual reward (and a lot of fun), the work in question can remain essentially lacking in emotional satisfaction and/or resonance: barren, hollow. And it's the *combination* of the intellectual and the emotional that provides lasting plangence, no? We are, each of us, both thinkers <u>and</u> lovers.

The Modernist Art Establishment—what we might call the 'Clement Greenberg School' of criticism—has given us a bankrupt esthetics, the eventual exact *opposite* of what it presumed to champion, insofar as 'avant-garde or 'high art' itself very quickly devolved into an overwhelming supply of works that were simply de facto decoration (i.e., yes, *actual* kitsch).[81] And it effectively assigned the pivotal task of determining *not only* ultimate merit but even of decoding, mediating, and delivering superficial content to denizens and habitués of the faculty lounge: 'the academy'—again, in direct opposition to its original posited aims.

Literary modernism, similarly—as it burrowed and percolated down into popular songwriting—unfortunately licensed a whole lot of over-reaching blather. Blather that's been postured—and surprisingly, often generally submissively received—as profound; eschewing the basic human aspiration for and appreciation of eloquence (which I'll define as the marriage of precision and imagination) in favor of a thudding obscurantism, or simple smoke, mirrors, and bluster (e.g., the preponderance of Dylan's œuvre), be it derived inadvertently via ineptitude, deliberately from pretense, or indifferently through sheer self-indulgence and torpor.

One cause for this has been wide-spread academic over-subscription to the 'Intentional Fallacy', a literary modernist conceit that it is a 'critical fallacy' to consider authorial intent when analyzing a work of art.

Yes, to a point. But as I've written elsewhere before, the reductio ad absurdum distillation of this would necessarily be to seriously, studiously critique a 'painting'…done by a chimpanzee…entirely on its 'esthetic accomplishments'. Or the 'poem' that chimp taps out on a keyboard.

And as it is to the critic and the academic, inarticulate songwriting is a perfect gift—wrapped in gaudy paper with a big shiny bow—to obsessed fans eager to smoke out, stumble upon, or scare up the most clandestine and convoluted explanations, references and direct personal messages from the lyricist to themselves and the world. Rigorous clarity and coherence in a song obviously doesn't offer as fertile a field for such ruminations by the amateur modernist—or critic or academic—who perforce revels, even wallows, in the gyrations of the chaotic and inarticulate.

But the twentieth century—with its valuable, distinctive (if often erratic) cultural accomplishments—ended a long time ago, eh? We got it, right?

As stated at the top of this chapter, I'm really just speculating on a very large and general cultural question here, but the take does seem to me to be a reasonable assessment of the situation. Yet if precisely accurate or not, I think in 2019 there's no reason for the fancies, attitudes, and enculturated hallmarks of modernism—or their simulacrums, 'cause it's one or the other that's metastasized here—to continue dominant in serious songwriting, an art and craft in which, contrarily, spare precision and a direct comprehension are pivotally important. Time to move on.

[81] cf. "Avant-Garde and Kitsch", Clement Greenberg, *Partisan Review*, Fall 1939. (It's hard to pin down, but this historically pivotal piece has also been reported to have actually been co-authored by Greenberg and *Partisan Review* editor Dwight Macdonald, rather than by Greenberg alone.)

Chapter Thirty-Three

The Insolvency of 'Po-Mo'

The tyranny of postmodernism wears people down with boredom and semi-literate prose. — Christopher Hitchens

Following as we do on a brief look at the deleterious impact of modernism on popular song, and even granting that the premise of the previous chapter was perhaps as much inquiry as argument, how about a quick commentary on its bastard—better, wayward—progeny: post-modernism? Any imprint on contemporary songwriting?

Let's ponder a moment....

(I originally thought to label this Chapter Thirty-Two A—rather than Chapter Thirty-Three—because to my thinking post-modernism really isn't even a distinct progressive evolutionary stage in critical thinking at all, but rather simply the grasping-at-any-fucking-available-straws last gasps of modernism itself—superannuated modernism recklessly troweling on way too much makeup.)

Probably the essential component of 'po-mo criticism'—the primary (though not the only) real-world impact of post-modernism's application on popular song—is an over-reticence to actually critique; an intellectual insecurity founded on understandable contemporary practical political considerations, focused sensitivities, and simple self-awarenesses by which previous generations were typically at best only lightly touched. Modernist criticism felt its way gingerly through historical haze with an often progressive, Marxist-aligned sensibility; po-mo critical judgments implode into impotent irrelevance. The admirable if easily misguided wish to fully culturally and/or psychologically empathize and respectfully defer (or, in many cases, to simply be in the fellowship that 'gets it') breeds an unholy capitulation towards work that is often, in fact and by *any* unencumbered analysis, inferior—even wholly vacant beyond the merest slip of its igniting precept. In the po-mo world, 'irony' and (effectively anti-cultural) intellectual timidity finesse all aspiration to objective reality—because a key tenet in post-modernist analyses is that there can *never* be 'objective reality' (Oh, sure, I agree, in the abstract—but then why even try, eh? Waddaya say let's just all go home early.)

The praiseworthy *progressive* effect of po-mo is a definitely heightened sensitivity to the eccentric, the idiosyncratic, the culturally 'other', and the economically (and hence, politically) disadvantaged. On balance, unquestionably good; it's about damn time. The collateral *negative* effect, however, is divorce from rigorous intellectual esthetic responsibility—which, sadly and critically, but necessarily, also inadvertently abets the ugly and potent outright destructive impulses rife within basest capitalist (and so-called 'libertarian') calculations. It can sometimes help racist, sexist, self-entitled scumbag reactionaries sound, at least superficially, sane and measured in comparison.

When we encounter an intelligent pop music review or criticism that gets too heavily into the (so to speak) 'anthropological legitimacy' of the act in question—concurrently paying only scant attention to, effectively making excuses for, or wildly over-praising, the work that the act in fact produces—we're probably being treated to the contravening paternalist manifestations of laissez-faire post-modern critical ideation.

★

Another grand bit of mischief that's a product of post-modernist thinking is a de facto smartier-pants-than-thou awed indulgence of 'appropriation'—plagiarism—under the guise of 'taking artistic possession' or 're-ordering an existing creation' and by so doing ostensibly 'creating a New Work of Art'. All the quotation marks in the preceding sentence should indicate my contempt for most (albeit not all) such claims.

And for an example of this kind of flailing academic/critical idiocy, I suggest consulting the references cited in footnote 77 on page 133.

While creative efforts have occasionally, throughout the ages, quoted from or paid homage to previous works in passing, those 'hat tips', critically, *rarely ever put the extract at the intellectual or emotional center* of the proclaimed New Work. But even when it's taken that far—such as with Andy Warhol's Campbell Soup and Brillo pieces—it's done with *deliberate* blatancy; the 're-working' is obvious, owned, and may legitimately address the intellectual-cultural questions at hand. It also tends, understandably, to lose a great deal of whatever potency may have been initially derived subsequent to that first encounter. We quickly get it. This is generally the opposite of the effect induced by entirely original creations, from which—if the work is masterful in most or every sense, that is—repeated exposure expands our appreciations.

A genuine homage or quotation is usually (albeit certainly not always) somewhat extraneous to the primary task at hand in the creative enterprise. I'm reminded of Jean-Luc Goddard's tiger-feeding scene in *Bande à Part*, a direct nod to his good friend Claude Chabrol's then upcoming film, *Le Tigre Aime la Chair Fraîche* (*The Tiger Likes Fresh Meat*). In *Bande à Part*, the female lead takes a steak from her refrigerator, walks outside and feeds it to a tiger in a traveling circus camped nearby; then continues on her way. It's an *entirely* unnecessary—but quick, and definitely amusing—tangent from the progress of the film, and so, yes, a hat tip, a bow to a respected colleague and his work. Also specifically note that Goddard *didn't* simply re-stage—steal—a central story Chabrol had shot, make it pivotal in his own film, then feign beleaguered innocence.

What we regularly encounter in songwriting, however, is broad and outright theft—carefully hidden, if possible—but critically *exonerated*, when discovered, as some kinda 'delightfully post-modern appropriation', as noted earlier when discussing the wholesale and largely artless plagiarisms by Led Zeppelin, Dylan, and others. (Fanboys in academia might sometimes label it 'intertextuality'—this yet another bit of lit crit exuberance; one irretrievably squishy, flamboyantly licensing, and too easily irresponsibly applied.) And, of course, they're rarely (if ever) innocently 'tipping their hat' to a friend or influence; they're determinedly burglarizing, with armies of lawyers to help them get away with it. The disburdening notion that it's all just post-modernism applied to songwriting is an insult to intelligence, an abomination.

★

Aside: I may be off here, but I wonder if much—or at least some?—of the critical footwork accrediting po-mo creative theft doesn't innocently derive from a rough fraternal similarity in outlook or 'mission' between post-modernist practitioner and critic or academic, at least insofar as both the usurper (invidiously or innocently) and the ethically honorable critic are dealing with extant creations, attempting to *add* to primary creative work that was 80% or so antecedently attained. And with that ground already so well explored by Duchamp, Jarry, Tzara, and confrères now over a century ago, so much current or recent work is really quite derivative; postured, conceptually old hat. In any event, a post-modern 'recontextualization'—or a critic's enlightened critical exegesis—as legitimately worthy as either may even be, generally comes long after the real heavy lifting has been done; and so the conversation between post-modernist and critic is going to be on matters safely familiar to each.

It's a forum—a playing field—in which both critic *and* practitioner happily invoke the mannered and emotionally distancing lexicon (and essentially conservative thinking, obviously) of academic formalism. Not necessarily an enlightening exchange—and indeed, even regressive; a bit institutionally authoritarian.

Chapter Thirty-Four

Song Lyrics vs. Poems (and Essays, Novels, Stories, Fairy Tales, Jokes, and Comic Books)

A difference between poetry and lyrics is that lyrics sort of fade into the background. Music straightjackets a poem and prevents it from breathing on its own, whereas it liberates a lyric. Poetry doesn't need music; lyrics do. — Stephen Sondheim

A discussion that can quickly get deep into the woods and choked by the weeds is defining the difference between a song and a poem. Yes, one has music attached to it and the other doesn't; yes, one is primarily heard and the other primarily read. But I maintain those differences, and others so thoughtfully delineated by intelligent and perceptive people like Steve Sondheim, above, are actually incidental and after-the-fact.

The determining element *isn't* prescriptive or proscriptive at all, but *affective*. If it works with music—if it is of a piece in presentation—then it is, obviously, a convincing song lyric, no matter what the initial impetus, intention, or cultivation of the written lines. Period.

And I don't at all mind being that simple about it; if it seems glib, or like an evasion or cop-out, it's not. Yet to engage the matter more definitively, let's wander about a little.

A song needs to be wholly intelligible on first hearing—if not every word and line, certainly enough to induce confidence in the listener that the song merits his or her attention. What music (all of it: melody, rhythm, time signature, arrangement, orchestration and so on) and performance (including production) allow is the ability to highlight parts of the written presentation that merit particular focus, and to hide—underplay, audibly obfuscate—those facets which are of lesser moment or craft. I've already gone through aspects of this earlier, especially concerning live performance.

But you're still only going to hear the song on its own terms: how it's performed, either live or in a recording. Reading a poem obviously allows stopping, going backwards and forwards, re-reading sections on the fly and at whim, digressively researching allusions as they appear, etc.

The fact is that any differentiation between a song lyric and a poem or other written communication—*other than the ex post facto subjective determination of simply whether it works or not*—is subordinate, all the way down to the most mechanical considerations. It's not required that the lines of a song rhyme—occasional well-known songs have no rhyming at all.[82] It's not necessary that a song have a repeated chorus. There is no written-in-stone law requiring a song to last at least, or no more than, any specified length of time. Words in a song *can* be just as obscure or specialized as those found in the densest poem, if employed skillfully. ALL that matters is whether those words work within the musical setting.

Some years ago, Randy Newman wrote a song called "A Few Words in Defense of Our Country"—which doesn't so much resemble a standard song at all as it does a dramatic monolog with musical underscoring. I'm neither champion nor detractor of the piece itself, but note it as an example of the relaxed frontier between what is and isn't culturally accepted, *defined*, as a serviceable, workable song.

Would one, for instance—could one—attempt to set an entire short story to music and thereby create a long song from it? Theoretically, why not? What is an opera or a sung-through musical but pretty much exactly that? And what about a poem read to musical accompaniment—is it now, in fact, a song? How about song lyrics appearing in printed form—are they then, suddenly, no longer a song but a poem? Or how about a song delivered without actual singing but simply spoken? Think way back, to Richard Harris' vocal delivery of Jimmy Webb's "MacArthur Park"—or most rap songs. Might they be more properly called recorded poetry readings, even though accompanied by music?

Yes, I'm quite aware all these rhetorical questions are *very* facile, but the point of them isn't.

The considerations that come into play are particular to the specific written lines themselves, and how they can be effectively communicated with music. (Just a gut feeling here, but I expect the Newman effort noted above, prose-like and conversational that it is, might come off as a bit pompous and disjointed if truly sung, and would need to be significantly rewritten to work effectively that way. But that's just a gut feeling, and I may be wrong.)

So, like the Newman effort—or a poetry reading with musical accompaniment—could we simply read, say, O. Henry's short story, "The Gift of the Magi", as is, to a specifically composed (or even appropriated) underscoring, and *call* it a song—albeit a long one, certainly—without being dismissed?

I don't think so, but not because it's an impossibility—rather, for practical reasons relating to the specific story.

Adapting a work that *already exists* into a song is a different exercise from creating a musical piece ground-up, after all. Absolute word-for-word fidelity to the source necessarily becomes secondary, but fidelity to direction and meaning properly remains primary—or what's the point? So while taking an extant story—our "The Gift of the Magi", for example—and setting it, *word-for-word*, might be an interesting experiment, it's admittedly extremely unlikely to result in a successful song—or opera, musical, or oratorio.

To make it work, we'd first off surely want to edit it for brevity in our adaptation. I expect we'd probably also consider writing it as a duet of two first-person accounts, so the thinking and motivations of the two characters would be revealed directly as the story progresses. (The short story is written entirely in third person—the story is told *to* us.) And we might consider adding what would become essentially a refrain or short repeating chorus section—perhaps as 'Greek chorus commentary' on the world in which the story is set, to serve as a punctuation of the sections of the story-song as the whole develops. I'm not married to any of these notions—they're just suggestions and possibilities—and it's all admittedly digressive, yet I think helpful.

Similar analytical thinking—analytical guessing, really—goes into setting a poem to music, and continues our walk around the question.

146 | WORDS AND MUSIC INTO THE FUTURE

Undoubtedly one of the first major poets whose work a songwriter might categorically *avoid* trying to appropriate, thinking the poems 'unadaptable into song' would be T.S. Eliot, no? Read his best-known pieces, and as a songwriter you're faced with a prickly forest of tangled words, references and disconnected voices. How do ya musicalize that?!? And yet, what about all those songs in the musical *Cats*? So again, it's not the source material, it's the *marriage* and adaptation—the completed execution—that determines whether there is a workable song.

I do doubt many songs from *Cats* are truly capable of standing alone outside the context of that overblown theatrical juggernaut, however. The only thing from it one ever hears performed elsewhere is "Memory", the song in the show *least* tethered to Eliot's whimsical poems in his *Old Possum's Book of Practical Cats*. This despite the fact *Cats* is one of the two or three most commercially successful stage musicals of all time, and so all the songs at least somewhat familiar.

Yet we must admit that the rest of the numbers in the musical *are* his poems, adapted into songs, eh?

And so what, exactly *is* the difference between poem and song lyric?

In most cases in which a poem is adapted into a song, there are adjustments—read: changes—made to the text. The challenge is to do so with such finesse and attention that the editorial work is seamless; of commensurate accomplishment as the original poem—not a bastardization (simply bloating with transient filler, or eviscerating with crippling cuts). If it is done well and displays proper adherence to the original, only a listener most intimately familiar with the poem might detect the alterations, and in that case one hopes the music is a further positive application, a legitimate justification, for the altered work.[83] If it is, we ultimately discover that the poem, having been faithfully adapted and scored, has acquitted itself quite well as a song lyric. Voilà.

It's interesting that when things go in the other direction, however— when song lyrics are printed—there's rarely any adjustment made for their new appearance as de facto poetry. They show up simply as a verbatim transcript of what is sung, generally punctuated solely by occasional commas at the end of lines, as if they really *are* finished poems and have been all along. I think what we're doing with this, culturally, is effectively acknowledging that song lyrics aren't meant to be read at all.

This is only a visual record and nothing more: simple reportage allowing for the audio presentation to be more easily followed.

★

Okay, I admit it. All we've done here is simply dance around the question—'dance around it' because informal conjecture is really all that's expedient. In the end—as I posited from the very beginning—the pivotal question is simply and solely how the words we've appropriated or assembled work in the musical setting, as a song.

So let me close with an observation from the painter Georges Braque: "Once an object has been incorporated into a picture it accepts a new destiny." Yes. The same with a poem—with *any* prior construction of language—used in a song. The only issue is whether it *does*, in fact, accept that destiny. Other distinctions between forms are interesting, certainly, but extraneous; merely an academic exercise.

[82] For example, "Moonlight in Vermont" (written by John Blackburn and Karl Suessdorf), "Fields of Gold" (Sting), "America" (Paul Simon), "Across the Universe" (John Lennon), "Lady" (Lionel Richie), "Frank Mills" (James Rado, Gerome Ragni, Galt MacDermot), and many, many more.

[83] On one of my albums I adapted into song a poem written in 1899 by William Butler Yeats. And yes, I most certainly (brazenly?) added words here and there to his quite well-known poem. But I've yet to encounter even one listener, including English professors who teach Yeats, who's objected to the emendations—or who even seemed to recognize they were there—which perhaps indicates the effort was properly respectful of the source material and esthetically successful. I hope that's the case.

Chapter Thirty-Five

"But It's Poetry!"—
Refuge for the Inarticulate

David Bowie's songs <u>should</u> be about nothing, because it allows them to be about everything! — Ben Greenman[84]

But building on forward from the previous chapter, 'poetry' is a word, like 'artist' earlier, that we need to de-fang and redefine—well, no, not 'redefine', but shake some sense into when it's used in discussions about songwriting.

Because when a song doesn't make ready sense—isn't straightforward and articulate—someone's bound to come along to helpfully explain "That's because it's poetry!" The assertive subtext to the claim is that poetry, *by definition*, is supposed to mean writing that is arcane, recondite, desultory, or convoluted.

As we noted earlier, this refuge is largely a bastard byproduct of literary modernism, which revels in the esoteric. We're effectively expected to concede to the songwriter, accepting without doubt that he, she, or they know *exactly* what they're doing; his, her, or their work has been completed, and now it's <u>our</u> job to figure it all out. If we can't do so, it's probably because we fail to grasp the intricacies and depth of the writing. Surely the writer has succeeded; apparently we have failed.

Communication—the precise, elegant, and economical use of words to convey a clear intent, message and direction—is implicated as being inessential, subordinate, even definitive of *inferior* songwriting.

Compounding the problem is that calling a song lyric 'poetry', along with excusing opaqueness, is also supposed to imply elevation. Poetry is asserted to be, also by definition, *better* than song lyrics—an exalted form to which songwriting aspires.

So we essentially have a frenzied five-step process:

Step One: The song doesn't make sense.

Step Two: That's because it's poetry.

Step Three: Poetry is a higher form of language. Ipso facto, this song is actually a *better*-written song.

Step Four: Because it *is* 'a better-written song', it most certainly *does* make perfect, elegant, eloquent sense. We must just find the key to interpret it properly. And when we do we'll recognize it does accomplish that—even if our solution is labyrinthine, confused, or entirely unmoored from what's written. We visited an example of delusional 'explanations' attempting to justify outright ineptitude earlier, with "The Night They Drove Old Dixie Down". But that song is actually a very straight-forward effort—it's not at all from the 'Poetic Lyrics' school. Here the moronic and obstinately contorted 'interpretations' run completely unchecked.

And Step Five: Now that we've wholly fabricated a scaffold upon which to hang this danged maundering babble—er, I mean 'found the golden thread and beautiful tapestry hidden within this patently sublime work'—we can proclaim our job done as well.

And yes, I'm obviously being curmudgeonly and simplistic here, but there's enough truth to warrant further investigation.

And the idiotic quote concerning David Bowie's songs, used as the epigraph above, is an almost perfect and emblematic distillation of the problem. We've actually reached the point where imprecision and confused histrionics aren't merely shrugged off—or even supposedly justified via convoluted wild-assed interpretations, as I've just illustrated—but celebrated as luminous accomplishment in and of themselves.

> *"Random collections of words become poetry when they are given meaning. If it means something to a large number of people, then it is a good poem."*[85]

The above is an uncredited statement on a comment board that I encountered while preparing this chapter. 'Gibberish as genius', basically—

and sadly, it's a belief that's actually rather accepted in the intellectually insecure times in which we live, leading us in the absolutely wrong direction. Even academics and critics would likely have to agree, as total subscription to such thinking essentially obviates the need for their analyses.

Yes, of course, something that reaches into a collective consciousness is prevailing communication. Such is the raison d'être of the most basic employments of language—in road signs, recipes, cliché social greetings, and so forth. But imputed substance—'meaning' in calculated opposition to societal consensus, entirely and individually subjectively manufactured from unstructured and nebulous verbiage *and even if widely indulged*—is just wishful thinking. Words have meaning.

On the other hand, using plain-spoken language to effectively convey, clearly and concisely, a *greater* directive or observation—using language that is elegant, economical, and eloquent—is fundamentally what the word 'poetry' was created to describe, no?

We've all seen the occasional article asserting that song lyrics are The New Poetry, or The People's Poetry, or similar. Sometimes it's just plain 'patronizing the plebes'—willfully confusing emptiness for authenticity, and paternally applauding. (See Chapter Thirty-Three on post-modern criticism, above.)

But much more often the piece goes in the other direction, of course. It's that 'Poetry-With-A-Capital-P' has been, up to recently and this article alerting us to the change, a higher art than song lyrics—but now, suddenly, some song lyrics *are* poetry. They have Achieved Ascendency into the Numinous Higher Realm.

Such opinion pieces have been appearing for decades—you've seen them and so have I. The article will likely follow the lede by citing the unusual subject of a specific song in particular—or even an eccentric rhyme in a specific song—and assert that one or other (or both) requires us to therefore recognize the probable legitimacy of the basic argument. It'll go on to support the notion by citing these and those other lyric lines, in this or that other song, to further validate the supposed depth that's now being achieved: it's poetry.

The big Achilles Heel of these articles is that left entirely unaddressed is any a priori qualitative statement on poetry itself—recognition that there is such a thing as *bad* poems; *poorly* written versification; doggerel.

If dispensing with qualitative judgments in both spheres, one could credibly assert that song lyrics have *always* been poetry, no? And so what?

So here again, we're faced with two compounding and equally meretricious tendencies. The first is the compliant lionization of something posited to be Poetry as therefore intrinsically admirable. The second is that because song lyrics—some song lyrics—are Poetry, those now thus-cloaked lyrics are also necessarily worthy and deserving of great respect.

First off, folks, there's a whole lot of bad poetry out there—essentially trivial information, lacking potentially salvaging intelligence and devoid of command in language, available and delivered to us categorized as poems. (I'm not arguing here whether something qualifies as a Poem; rather whether something qualifies as Worthy of Our Time.) What's regularly encountered in recent years, particularly, is a free verse dispatch of a minor observation or interpersonal transaction, reported in mundane manner, and presented as poetry—typographically 'versified'—without much apparent attempt at attaining elegance in the exposition. It's writing that properly qualifies as 'prosaic' in more ways than one. I don't mean to be too hard on casual reflection—or what might be called 'dinner party anecdotes'—but so much really is just slender ephemera. Formatting it for the page to 'sorta look like a poem' and calling it poetry doesn't make it significant—and even if it *is* potentially revelatory, that formatting obviously wouldn't necessarily mean it's significant *and* well-written.

Coming at things from the other direction, presenting something that arguably does display flashes of mastery in use of language doesn't suddenly make the *heart* of that effort significant either. Style is not substance—and it's a slippery academic slope into ultimate irrelevance when style becomes the primary focus of attention with substance effectively an afterthought.

In songwriting, similarly, just because it has a title, melody, and gets sung in public doesn't mean it's good writing and/or otherwise significant either—especially if the lyrics do not clearly convey recognizable, definitive, *and resonant* information. In the introductory chapters of this book we looked at some songs that were examples of bad writing, and if we were to call them poetry, that wouldn't suddenly make them *good* writing either.

Of course none of the preceding addresses 'word salad poetry'—those disjointed word jumbles often found in free verse efforts and pseudo-Beat poems—and in songwriting products like Lennon's "Come Together" or so many of those Bowie songs, Dylan songs, and similar.

The argument is often promoted that, by definition, poetry is less concerned with *what* is said than *how* it it is said—an argument that, when taken to reductio ad absurdum lengths and wholly transferred to popular song, is advanced as validation (or at minimum, license) for what might otherwise be properly characterized as directionless ramblings or outright incoherence. So let's clean that up a bit. Both disciplines, poetry and song, should obviously be concerned with how something is said. But as has been argued here all along, when presentation—even a masterfully executed writerly application—is disconnected from, unconcerned with, substantiality, even to the point of near-total eclipse, what we really have is at best impressive amusement, light entertainment, fugitive distraction.

If we're talking about serious work, how something is said *is* subsidiary—in song *or* in poetry; just as, for example, how a vocalist may act out a song is subsidiary to what that song actually says, or how a well-metered line may be sonorously pleasing in a poem but impertinent to the essence of that poem. Presentation—performance and production in songs, how a poem sounds or looks in poetry; as opposed to what either is saying—is most often, *and should almost always be*, secondary to the words and the inciting ideas that presumably provide reason for those words in the first place.

Inarticulate convolutions are not what defines poetry. Rambling imprecision—no matter how pleasingly mellifluous the sequence of words—isn't really poetic at all. It's the *exact opposite* of poetic—and of what comprises good poetry, and good songwriting. And keep in mind throughout this examination that song lyrics have the *profound* additional advantages of music and production—extremely powerful 'bells and whistles' to help them along.

In songwriting, especially—because songs appear in specific time (as opposed to poetry on the page, which allows one to luxuriate in reflection and study)—plain speaking is not only *not* inimical to depth, it's mandated and *facilitates* depth. It's when clear and precise language introduces ideas, expressions, insights, or even jokes that are revelatory that use of the adjective 'poetic', when describing a song, is properly warranted. (And yes, jokes—wit and wordplay—specifically included.) That's why, for instance, some great blues and folk songs can be rightly called poetic; while so many celebrated popular songs, awash in turbulence and diffusion, are simply twaddle—confused twaddle.

So let's be wary of the magisterial and misbegotten characterization of a song as 'poetry', and celebrate writing that is elegant, economical, eloquent—writing that is truly *poetic* in that it summons, reveals, and steers our thoughts into new appreciations, considerations, and reconsiderations without first requiring us to cobble together a wholly unlikely, individualized, and fanciful 'interpretation'. The songwriter's job is to *communicate*—and to do so lucidly and productively.

[84]*The New Yorker*, 1/9/2016, "The Beautiful Meaninglessness of David Bowie", by Ben Greenman.
[85]https://en.wikipedia.org/wiki/Talk%3APoetry%2FArchive_1.

Chapter Thirty-Six

Sincerity Isn't Depth

"Remind me again, what's wrong with Dave Matthews?"
"Basically everything, except technical proficiency," Walter said.
"Right."
"But maybe especially the banality of the lyrics. 'Gotta be free, so free,
yeah, yeah, yeah. Can't live without my freedom, yeah, yeah.'
That's pretty much every song."
— Jonathan Franzen[86]

A song can come to us wrapped in gorgeous melody, sitting in a groove that's absolutely irresistible, sung in perfect six-part harmony by A Choir of God's Angels Flown in from Heaven—but if all we're gonna get from the effort is routine inanities or incoherent pomposities, who really cares?

Sincerity is not depth.

While we each surely invest deeply in the overarching ambitions, deep disappointments, joyful accomplishments, major incidents, or unusual sightings we've ourselves experienced—or that someone we *personally know* has experienced—those sentiments are not necessarily gonna be worth many other people's time. We all got lots goin' on, pal! Love ya—really do—but gotta run....

If—and a big 'if' it is, too—the lessons realized from those events can bring new understanding, awareness, or even laughter to people *not* intimately involved, *and* they can be presented in language and manner that demands legitimate attention, then they may perhaps merit conveying to others in song.

Otherwise, however, best to limit reporting on those life-changing experiences to Mom. Or to a best friend, therapist, drinking pal, psychiatrist, parole officer, town gossip, cell mate, campaign manager, or significant other. The rest of us probably aren't really interested—or even all that curious, frankly. No one is being done a favor by having emotional or intellectual banalities written up and sung to them in an original song—and it's the height of egotism to presume differently.

Sure, I'm possibly *much* too severe here. But a song is a monolog, after all—a lecture, a speech, an incursion, a very one-sided event. It's a literal demand that other people passively listen to what the songwriter or performer has to say—and then applaud it all at the end.

And we each *do* have something to say, naturally. But in truth, we *don't* often have something to say that's worth hearing presented in an extended monolog.

Showmanship certainly helps. It diverts, distracts, enables and can even dazzle; yet no matter how accomplished, showmanship is ultimately just packaging.

I don't really think we need to expand on the subject any further here, so let's move on. But because we've noted it earlier—concerning the insufferably cloying and inconsequential "Forever Young"—and because of its unequivocal importance, let's move on after repeating the admonition yet one more time:

Sincerity Is Not Depth.

[86]*Freedom* by Jonathan Franzen. (New York: Farrar, Straus and Giroux, 2010), 145

Chapter Thirty-Seven

The Kids Are Alright!

*Until the rise of American advertising, it never occurred
to anyone anywhere in the world that the teenager was
captive in a hostile world of adults.*
— Gore Vidal

An ostensibly axiomatic argument regularly trotted out in defense of inconsequence, of fatuousness, in popular songs—particularly rock songs—is that they're so often Written By And/Or Meant For Young People. And therefore, case closed.

I reject both the formulation and the principle. Unless we're talking about literal pre-school age children here (say, six year olds and younger), the assertion is plain old adult condescension writ large—and, more pertinently and poisonously, a bogus justification for second-rate work.

In many areas of entertainment, the wise direction given is to 'treat young people as you would adults—they don't need to be talked down to'. In popular songwriting however, limited vocabularies, lack of actual wit, repulsive misogyny, repetitive vapidities, and preposterous swagger are de rigueur features, defended with a shrug as inherent in the form—just a part of the 'world of youth culture'—and then marketed *to* younger people with unrelenting freight-train determination.

I don't buy it. In truth, the cultural dialectic has never been literally one of youth versus age, but rather of intelligence versus stupidity; creative inspiration and revolution facing off against convention and atrophy.

No doubt that maturation, simple lengthened existence in the culture and society—more years on Earth—allows each of us to become more confident in our intuitions and intelligence, refine our sensibilities, and grow out of the more self-absorbed and insecure vestiges of youth.

And that's exactly what transpired in my own evolved reactions to songs and acts pushed on me by the record industry early on, as recounted earlier in Chapter Four.

I think we can make a fair assertion that smart kids generally can and do appreciate what smart grown-ups appreciate; and dumb adults champion the same crap that dumb kids champion. There are superficial generational differences—in slang vocabularies and technical jargon, for instance—but they are, indeed, generally unimportant. And there'll always be youthful assertions of independence from, and so a collateral postured antipathy towards, art found meritorious by one's immediate antecedents. But such proves to be more posture than actuality.

Let's pause just a second to allow the late critic Lester Bangs to offer some insight on the true and much, *much* larger imperative at work here:

> *The essential misapprehension about popular music is that it is anything other than a totally capitalistic enterprise. It has absolutely nothing to do with anything except making money and getting rich.*[87]

Yes, of course. The low-rent cynicism and marketing calculations of the recording/broadcasting industry exploits and profits quite mightily from the dumbing down of popular music; with that dumbing down is used as a wedge to separate and isolate an entire continually incipient (and so understandably insecure) market: teenagers and younger adults who're told this is *their* music, these are *their* songs; songs they should all rally 'round —and <u>BUY</u>! A further aspect of that schema is the concomitant focus on fast turnaround, production, and marketing—quicker and bigger pay-offs—in opposition to substantive statement and actual cultural advance. After all, once the general formulas have been mastered, and an entire ever-replenishing sub-population indoctrinated with and enlisted in a generational 'us vs them' dogma, it's not difficult to manufacture yet more and more disposable reinforcing foolishness—and successively interchangeable acts performing it—for that targeted demographic. The money keeps rolling in.

But corporate popular music and its indie counterparts are very much *not* a place in which to seek true revolutionary (read: anti-authoritarian, pro-humanist, anti-capitalist) heroes.[88]

Posturing? Yes, Yes, YES. Tons and tons of it!

Actuality? Not much.

Let's also note that while it's obvious that new eyes can bring reappraisal and innovation to any entrenched endeavor, this has nothing to do with some imagined and strictly confined 'youth vs age' contest. Those 'new eyes' can just as easily be those of actors arriving from outside the locally prevailing culture generally, simply from participants already within the majority population newly introduced to the discipline itself—or even derive, albeit with extreme rarity, from an experienced inside practitioner's Damascus Road conversion.

So <u>now</u>...case closed.

[87]*All You Need Is Love: The Story of Popular Music* by Tony Palmer (New York: Grossman Publishers/Viking Press, 1976), 287

[88]Much of their manager Malcolm McLaren's tedious machinations aside, the Sex Pistols' persistent intense slugfests with the record industry and attendant media— through even to their outright (and one must presume sincere) contempt for the band's attempted usurpation by the sanctimonious Rock and Roll Hall of Fame decades after their international rise—is an admittedly very-far-from-perfect yet high-profile illustration of what *actual* confrontation with the establishment begets.

Chapter Thirty-Eight

La-Da-Da / Na-Na-Na / Lie-La-Lie / Sha-La-Ti-Da

If time be of all things the most precious, wasting it must be the greatest profligacy. — Benjamin Franklin

As we begin turning our attention back to analyzing specific song examples, a quick look at what's technically termed 'non-lexical vocables' is in order. As the chapter subhead above indicates, non-lexical vocables (we'll abbreviate them as NLVs) are vocal sounds of all types that aren't actual words—so not just 'La-La-La', but the comparable nonsense syllables found famously (or sometimes infamously) in the long fade-out of Paul McCartney's "Hey Jude", the chorus of Paul Simon's "The Boxer"; throughout Lady Gaga's idiotic "Bad Romance"; in scat singing, whistling, cowboy yodeling, cheap Disney flummery like "Zip-a-Dee-Doo-Dah" and "Chim-Chim-Cher-ee"—even a throw-away sigh, growl or similar—and so on. In some sub-genres of popular song they're a major, even definitive, component (e.g., doo-wop; or again, yodeling in cowboy songs).

There are so many different possibilities for use of such sounds in a song that I hesitate to make a blanket assessment—this is an area in which there are going to be wide variations in employment and significant exceptions in value of that employment. An act like the Swingle Singers, for instance, or Bobby McFerrin, exist as marvelous exemplars of what the human voice can do when invoked solely as a musical instrument bereft of responsibility to convey shaded rhetorical objectives.

In countless traditional songs the entire refrain or entire chorus is nothing but NLVs; and there are whole genres of songs, in cultures spread around the world, constructed of essentially nothing but NLVs. They will serve a percussive, punctuating, or intentionally lyrically unimportant space-filling function.

New-age music songs may sometimes employ a complete palette of NLVs, but in the calculated attempt to mimic real language—albeit 'language' that obviously no one listening can understand a single word of. This kind of thing is also most notably sometimes heard in commercials and film scores.

Given all the above, however, some general observations are surely appropriate here. And I think, while being open to multiple exceptions, we can offer that rarely—very rarely—can NLVs be justified within a song the remainder of which is presented as a serious effort at linguistic communication. A little of this thing goes a long, long way.

I expect that's because using the human voice in service of absolutely and assertively *not* transmitting identifiable information can seem to be a) a cavalier disregard by the songwriter for the effort at communication generally, and/or b) an admission that the songwriter was simply phoning it in at this juncture, treading water, resigned to being drained of ideas with space yet to fill, and/or c) a signal to listeners that the words in this song—in this part of it, certainly, but possibly *all the rest of it as well*— really aren't that important. Though perhaps seeming innocuous, NLVs can be a virulent menace to a serious effort. A failure of songwriting.

Johnny Cash's "I Walk the Line" is a perhaps particularly noteworthy exception here. Before starting in on each verse, he hums the single note on which the first word of that verse begins, for several beats. Because the novelty is so underplayed it avoids being an intrusion on the substance of the song and becomes, instead, a unique and engaging appliance. Rare.

On the other hand, yes, occasionally a guttural wail or similar may be a legitimately indicated cri de cœur in the context of a song that deals, for example, with profound emotional distress or longing; a sigh can affirm a wistful resignation, longing, or remembrance; and etcetera.

I addressed the absurd use of NLVs in the chorus of "The Night They Drove Old Dixie Down" earlier. And while Van Morrison's "Brown Eyed Girl" is unlikely to leap into mind were we asked to suggest a 'serious song', he at least sets up—legitimizes—his 'Sha-la-la-las' in his chorus there; deploying his NLVs as stand-ins for (presumably forgotten?) actual lyrics within the context of the song, or as the self-aware youthful nonsense they otherwise are:

> Do you remember when we used to sing
> "Sha la la la la la la la la la la dee da"?
> Just like that:
> "Sha la la la la la la la la la la dee da;
> La dee dah."[89]

So while Morrison may somewhat justify his chorus here, to my ears the song still drops several levels in accomplishment with the descent into nonsense vocables. And as we'll see in a later chapter, even ostensibly validating NLVs by slyly introducing them en masse as a long coda just to fill out the time and to perhaps beg contemplation of preceding information—or as a kinda 'universal song code', the precise lyrics of which are immaterial—does not, ipso facto, support using them.

This stuff is like playing with fire.

[89]"Brown Eyed Girl", copyright 1967 by Van Morrison. Quoted here as permitted within the Fair Use provisions of 17 U.S.C.§107.

Chapter Thirty-Nine

So is 'The Folk Process' An Expired Mechanism?

It is only with the heart that one can see rightly; what is essential is invisible to the eye. — Antoine de Saint-Exupéry

To answer the question above: no, 'The Folk Process', certainly in its loosest and most general connotations, isn't an expired mechanism; not at all. Songs do change—all the time. Every time a new act covers a song the argument can be made that a de facto (if not literal) contemporary manifestation of the folk process is taking place—the new rendition is a continuation of the creation of the song (though the harness and restraint of enforceable copyright restricts most changes to being superficial.)

But a more strictly defined folk process also continues, even in this age of the internet with all its offered accesses and protections. I've been part of it myself, and perhaps you have as well.

For example, here's a song written by Furry Lewis, which he record-ed in 1928.[90] It's the first song I ever learned to play (although then in a very, *very* simplified form, naturally) called "I Will Turn Your Money Green", also sometimes known as "Follow Me Baby", or by the title I learned it as, "Rockefeller Blues".

When I was in Missouri, they would not let me be.
When I was in Missouri, they would not let me be.
Wouldn't rest content till I came to Tennessee.

If you follow me baby; I'll turn your money green.
If you follow me baby; I'll turn your money green.
I show you more money than Rockefeller's ever seen.
If the river was whiskey and baby I was a duck,

If the river was whiskey and baby I was a duck,
I'd dive to the bottom, Lord, and I'd never come up.

Lord the woman I hate, I see her every day.
Lord the woman I hate, I see her every day.
But the woman I love—she's so far away.

Talk about sweetheart; I declare I'm a honest man.
Talk about sweetheart; I declare I'm a honest man.
Give my woman so many dollars, it broke her apron string.

All she give me was trouble; trouble all the time.
All she give me was trouble; trouble all the time.
I been troubled so long that trouble don't worry my mind.

I been down so long it seems like up to me.
I been down so long it seems like up to me.
The woman I love; she done quit poor me.

What's the need of me hollering; what's the need of me crying?
What's the need of me hollering; what's the need of me crying?
The woman I love, she don't pay me no mind.[91]

I learned the song from Jacksonville, Florida, blues player M.L. Riley, who got it directly from Furry Lewis years previously. I didn't hear Lewis' own rendition of the song until many, *many* years later—and by then the song I was performing, musically, was about ten light-years removed from his original. The lyrics—while still certainly recognizable—had also evolved. There were entire verses I had never heard—and others I'd heard when learning the song so long ago, but decided not to incorporate and subsequently just forgot. The lyrics and the order in which I presently perform the song go like this:

Follow me baby; I'll turn your money green.
Follow me baby; I'll turn your money green.
I'll give you more money than them Rockefellers ever seen.

People in Missouri, they sure are down on me.
People in Missouri, they sure are down on me.
Guess I shoulda stayed home in Tennessee.

I been down so long it looks like up to me.
I been down so long it looks like up to me.
So I'll head back on home to Tennessee.

Follow me baby; I'll turn your money green.
Follow me baby; I'll turn your money green.
I'll give you more money than them Rockefellers ever seen.[91]

This is obviously a reduced rendition—a simpler song—than what Furry Lewis performed (or what M.L. Riley probably taught me). And I honestly can't recall how I got to where I am with the song today: the twists, turns, and inadvertent variations that got set in concrete—until the next inadvertent variation, and so on.

You may also note that it structurally resembles my version of "The Cuckoo", mentioned earlier—'title verse' first and last; with three verses in between them in "The Cuckoo", two in "Rockefeller Blues". (In both songs, I also add in instrumental sections—instrumental verses and improvised bridges.)

And while I would've been far too insecure and innocent to say so then, the fact of the matter is that even at the time I must have felt there were too many elements—verses with quite disparate, unconnected concerns—to easily hold together within a cohesive song. And so I took what I particularly liked and could scavenge to make, in my view, a workable lyrical whole. (Going for 'serious' meant I had to sadly eschew the thoroughly entertaining 'If the river was whiskey and I was a duck' verse, but so be it.)

Rigid folk purists may claim at this point, with supreme indignation, that Lewis' song was already a delightful, cohesive whole—and who the hell was I to promiscuously tamper with it!

But any such preconceptions on the matter are simply wrong—and wrong-headed. Furry Lewis' original work is enjoyable, engaging and an important piece of American folk culture. He wrote and composed some good stuff in the song. But there is *no* obligation to simply mimic his arrangement, to sing all the verses he sang, or to do them in the same order.

On the musical side, and as noted above, while still a basic 12-bar blues construction, the song I've played over the years began to differ from Furry Lewis' composition from the outset—then simply due to my newness to the guitar—and it continued *and continues* to diverge and evolve as years pass, having less and less resemblance to his original.

But of course I always credit the song to Furry Lewis, no matter how far it's journeyed.

And *that*, friends, is the real 'folk process' at work.

[90]Walter "Furry" Lewis (1893–1981) was a singular fellow. Musician by night, when the irregular opportunity arose; professional street sweeper for the City of Memphis by day—as he was damned well intent on never being completely broke, and absolutely determined to get a pension when he reached retirement age. Joni Mitchell wrote a song about him called "Furry Sings the Blues"—and while most folks might've been touched, even proud, to have a song written about them lauding their abilities, it got Lewis angry, as he didn't like someone making money using his name without getting a share.

[91]"I Will Turn Your Money Green", copyright 1928 by Furry Lewis. Quoted here as permitted within the Fair Use provisions of 17 U.S.C.§107.

Chapter Forty

Lessons from Browne's "These Days" and Kristofferson's "Me and Bobby McGee"—Both Positive and Negative

Trifles make perfection, and perfection is no trifle.
— Michelangelo Buonarroti

Now, finally, let's get back to examining some examples of both good and bad songwriting. We'll begin with two songs—and again, songs surely known to most readers—each of which demonstrates both exemplary and mediocre work in the very same piece.

★

One of Jackson Browne's signature efforts, a song he reportedly wrote while still a teenager(!), called "These Days", is particularly interesting in that it contains an example of outright lyrical brilliance—but directly adjacent to an example of self-satisfied cleverness—a feeble and lead-footed *masquerade* of brilliance.

Of notable interest here is that Browne has himself changed the lyrics to this song several times in subsequent years—presumably aware of its deficiencies and attempting to arrive at a more coherent effort.

Here's the song—in its entirety. Lyrics later tossed by him are crossed out; and new, additional or replacement lines are underscored:

I've been out walkin';
I don't do too much talkin' these days.
These days—
These days I seem to think a lot
About the things that I forgot to do for you;
And all the times I had the chance to.

~~I stopped my ramblin'.~~
~~I don't do too much gamblin' these days.~~
~~These days~~
~~These days I seem to think about~~
~~How all the changes came about my way;~~
~~And I wonder if I'll see another highway~~

And I had a lover.
I don't think I'll risk another these days—
These days.
And if I seem to be afraid
To live the life that I have made in song,
Well it's just 'cause I've been losing so long.

~~Well I'll stop my dreamin';~~
~~I don't do too much schemin' these days.~~
<u>I'll keep on moving;</u>
<u>Things are bound to be improving these days.</u>
These days—
These days I'll sit on cornerstones
And count the time in quartertones to ten, my friend.
Please don't confront me with my failures
I had not forgotten them.[92, 93]

The rhyme scheme that Browne built for himself, with its interior rhymes and enjambments—in a song that attempts to be a soul-searching recitation—is perhaps a bit antithetical to that grasp for sincerity, a little too structurally sophisticated. (Again, however, one might remember, kindly, that he was just a teenager when he wrote the first version—and like all of us at that age he evinced the tendency of trying a little too hard to impress.) Maintaining a tight, demanding rhyme scheme, without causing eye-rolling in an audience by simply 'going for whatever rhymes' can sometimes be a difficult task.

It's the final four lines I'd like to quickly focus on here—maybe look them over again. The first two of the four are, indeed, of the eye-rolling variety. Sure, 'quartertones' and 'cornerstones' obviously rhyme, but it's an utterly meaningless goulash of words. You only "count the time in quartertones", Jackson? (What does that even mean?) "Sitting on corner-stones"? (What does THAT mean as well—and how, exactly do you do it? A cornerstone is a foundation stone—so with a wall of bricks already sitting on it. And you apparently *only* sit on 'cornerstones', yes? No? Why specify them?) And what importance or pertinence does counting "to ten" have to do with anything—beyond the mechanical (in that it arbitrarily sets up the slant-rhyme of the word "them" which ends the next line)? Gimme a break. This is cleverness for its own sake—cleverness without justification. The added "my friend"—as contrasted to the "for you" at the same point in the first verse, which does contribute value there—adds nothing here; and because it adds nothing smacks, really, of a too-easy grasp to simply chalk up one more rhyme, just for the hell of it. (But I'll admit, sympathetically, this can be a hard temptation to re-sist—especially in a song like this, so interlaced with rhyme. And Browne himself reportedly sometimes drops both of those appendages, perhaps recognizing that dropping the "for you" leaves a knowing passage there; while the "my friend" is just gratuitous.)

The two lines following, however—the final two lines of the song—are of an entirely different magnitude of proficiency. "Don't confront me with my failures; I had not forgotten them" is simply dazzling stuff—reaching deep into each of us who hears it. I want to go further here, to highlight the powerful self-reproach he brings forward. Were I to have written it, I'm sure I'd have written "Don't remind me of my fail-ures..."—so 'remind' instead of 'confront'; and a much less effective or efficient use of language than what Browne comes up with. Why? Well, the reference to memory is nailed just a few words later, with 'forgot-ten'—so using 'remind' here is a waste of two syllables in his set-up to what concludes both this verse and the whole song—syllables that he instead brilliantly allocates to the word 'confront', which adds to the line the implication of uncertain, unsettled, contestation.

What we have are two textbook lessons in those four lines—one on exactly what *not* to do, immediately followed by one displaying what a flash of real brilliance can deliver. Whether one buys the finished song or not—and I'm ambivalent, beyond simply gagging at the 'cornerstones / quartertones' house of cards—there was effort put into it. Good that he discarded the original second verse—which was pretty much just aimless prattle—but the remaining now-second verse still strikes me as less than optimal. Perhaps I'm too demanding. But I also suggest the song's final line would be improved slightly by replacing "I had" with "I've". It would a) sing a bit better, and b) make the statement more immediate.

Yet those final two lines remain unequivocally terrific, and the whole song a certainly uneven, though tolerable, piece—particularly given the structural confines he set for himself.

★

Kris Kristofferson's "Me and Bobby McGee" is another song in which one finds some outstanding statements—lyric lines which make the listener cock his or her head in startled appreciation.

The song[94]:

Busted flat in Baton Rouge, and headin' for the trains,
Feelin' nearly faded as my jeans.
Bobby thumbed a diesel down just before it rained,
Took us all the way to New Orleans.
Took my harpoon out of my dirty red bandana
And was blowin' sad while Bobby sang the blues.
With them windshield wipers slappin' time and
Bobby clappin' hands we finally sang up every song that driver knew.

chorus 1:
Freedom's just another word for nothin' left to lose,
And nothin' ain't worth nothin', but it's free.
Feelin' good was easy, Lord, when Bobby sang the blues,
Feelin' good was good enough for me—
Good enough for me and Bobby McGee.

From the coal mines of Kentucky to the California sun,
Bobby shared the secrets of my soul.
Standin' right beside me through everythin' I done,
Every night she kept me from the cold.
Then somewhere near Salinas, Lord, I let her slip away—
Lookin' for the home I hope she'll find.
And I'd trade all my tomorrows for a single yesterday,
Holdin' Bobby's body close to mine.

chorus 2:
> Freedom's just another word for nothin' left to lose,
> Nothin' left is all she left for me.
> Feelin' good was easy, Lord, when Bobby sang the blues,
> Buddy that was good enough for me—
> Good enough for me and Bobby McGee.[95]

Wistful sentiment aside—and I think Kristofferson got most all the immediate resonance into the song that he could've wanted—there are components of it that are rather simple, achieved without much difficulty. When a place name is used in a song, unless the place has a specific necessary reason to be cited, it's usually invoked simply to rhyme another word—the word the lyricist is covetously aiming to use—to be rhymed, in other words, so that the desired important thought can be delivered. Alternatively, sometimes it's just another 'bit of color' to add into the lyrics, and it's chosen primarily for its romance, or even simply its sonority. So the lines with Baton Rouge, New Orleans, Kentucky, Salinas—even California, though this last proper noun serves the additional value of being an adjective to 'sun'—are all pretty easily arrived at. (He could just as readily have written, for example, "From the mines of Pennsylvania [or 'the canyons of Manhattan'] to the Arizona [or Tijuana, maybe?] sun..."—there's lots that could competently fill out this space. But his primary objective was to set up the stronger "Standin' right beside me through everythin' I done, and every night she kept me from the cold.")

The above observations are secondary, however, and obviously also open to debate, one by one. What is primary, and incontestably impressive, is the chorus. "Freedom's just another word for nothing left to lose"—immediately followed by "nothin' ain't worth nothin' but it's free"—a quick and powerful one-two punch straight to the gut. The points he's making come across immediately, but the lines are so evocative that they deserve—demand—being repeated to oneself over and over again long after the song has ended. This is great songwriting. And yes, truly *poetic*.

Kris, you've done some good work. If you can't or don't want to add yet more colorful story or another layer of consequence to the song, let's just stop here.

Because, as we all know, what happens now is that we're suddenly flung into the dreadfully affected and over-the-top 'la-la-la-la-la-la-la-la-la!' substitute for an actual third verse, which Janis Joplin belches out in the best-known edition of the song, and whose bombast everyone since seems to mimic. Yikes. (In her possible defense[?], it just follows the template provided by the very first recorded performance of it, by Roger Miller, though *much* less histrionically.) And, naturally—in Joplin's version, certainly—it turns the song into a flippant sing-along mockery.

The whole NLV third verse contrivance—when it's overdone, as it almost *always* is—tells us the preceding picaresque travelogue and the moving emotional reflections were all really just a lightweight song; a pop ditty. It essentially gives us a big fat middle finger for being so gullible, for believing in what we've just heard. Nothing to see here—move along, dummies, nothing to take seriously or to heart. La-la-la-la-la….

Kristofferson himself didn't first record the song until a year after Miller, and I wasn't able to ascertain if he himself regularly stretched things out with the whole verse of NLVs *before* it got to Miller for that first recording. I mean did he walk around town, pitching the song to various music publishers and recording companies, with 'la-la-la' literally written on the lead sheets? So where the now de rigeur performance appendage to the song originated is unknown to me. It does need to be noted, however, that Kristofferson *did* apply that third verse of NLVs on his own recording of the song when that finally came out. But—and here's the pivotal consideration—he did so with profound understatement, similar to Johnny Cash's understated use of NLVs in "I Walk the Line". The long NLV tag in Kristofferson's *own* hands is precise, reflective; not at all histrionic and pompous. Listen to *his* version of the song to get the most from it.

I expect a songwriter with Kristofferson's genuine gifts—not a lot of his stuff is great, but when he's on, he is ON—could write an *actual* third verse to this song and hit the whole thing outa the park. But it was written at a time when Nashville country songs were, in my memory certainly, getting shorter and shorter—shorter even than the 2:45 or so median length then current in radio-friendly pop and rock songs—and so one often encountered country radio songs of 'two verses with the chorus after each, and out'. (Yet hold on a second; if even mainstream Nashville performer Roger Miller sang that third verse of non-lexical vocables, there must have been a general 'industrial preference' for this song to be longer, no? Why isn't it? Because there's generally an abnegation of responsibility when the only alternative considered—well, the one arrived at—is 'la-la-la-la-la'.)

How should one deal with a song that feels—or even inarguably *is*— 'too short' for the magnitude of the ideas and presentation so far provided, and would be disserviced by tacking on a lot of nonsense? Simple, really. There are two primary components of a song: the lyrics and the melody—the music. Going out of "Me and Bobby McGee" instrumentally would have been an easy, secure—and generally satisfying— culmination to some brilliant songwriting. And whether one agrees about that choice or not, it certainly beats the hell outa having the up-to-this-point reflective raconteur go into the usual and shamelessly clownish 'la-la-la-la-la's. Yes, Kristofferson, in his own rendition, gets away with it— but once again, *that's because he carefully, deliberately, underplays it.* The difference—the effect *he* achieves by taking the conceit way down—is stunning.

But another, much, *much* better suggestion is to insert an additional verse—a new second verse, making the present one third, as that one does serve as a solid summation of precedent events and experiences— that takes a different look at what's available within the established context and content. Perhaps a reflection on the America the two footloose protagonists find before them—an expansive take on the people and land they encounter and from which they learn as they grow and experience? (In such scenario, one might presumably use a rather standard organization of verse 1, verse 2, THEN the chorus, short instrumental bridge, verse 3, repeat chorus and out; and so making a song lasting somewhere around 3:00 to 3:30—without the danger of devolving into sing-along.)

By the way, do note the line Kristofferson changed in his own rendition—the second line in the second pass through the chorus. This was surely something that came to him after Miller and Joplin's recordings, and it's a further polishing of the small gem he's created.

But because nowadays just about everyone who performs the song murders the NLV 'third verse', we end with a piece of really great songwriting, with its horse often shot right out from under it mid-stream when it's performed. One must presume Kristofferson was satisfied with the song we know, but *did* he have an additional verse he for some reason discarded or didn't complete? (In that case, it's time to rewrite it rather than go with less—the great song at this point offers a magnificent opportunity for amplification or augmentation. There's very little chance here of spoiling it with elaboration. We know barely anything, really, about the two protagonists, and our curiosity has been ignited.)

Was it a matter of offhand carelessness? Laziness? Who knows?

[92]Greg Allman, who many years after it was written had a pop hit with the "These Days", changed the last line to "I'm aware of them", which I don't think is as strong as "I had not forgotten them". In the latter, the admission of awareness is there as well—but to my ears with the added implication of these particular failures having produced a still-smarting sting, and lingering regret, that time can't alleviate. "I'm aware of them" strikes as somewhat argumentative, mitigating our sympathy.

[93]"These Days", copyright 1967 by Jackson Browne. Quoted here as permitted within the Fair Use provisions of 17 U.S.C.§107.

[94]The lyrics here are Kristofferson's original lines as I've been able to ascertain them. (The only exception to that may be the second line in the chorus during its second appearance, which I assume came to Kristofferson *after* both Miller's and Joplin's recordings or they would have both surely included it.) Note that Joplin changed a few words in her much better-known recording—to the song's detriment, in my opinion.

[95]"Me and Bobby McGee", copyright 1969 by Kris Kristofferson and Fred Foster. Quoted here as permitted within the Fair Use provisions of 17 U.S.C.§107.

Chapter Forty-One

Well How 'Bout That, Some Country Music IS...

...three chords and the truth! — Harlan Howard

As noted earlier, the One Great Convention that advantages country music over so much in rock and rap is that the lyrics in Nashville songs are intended, and expected by the audience, to be fully, unequivocally comprehended. The writing may be hack work—and just as in rock, rap, pop and whatever else, it most often is—but dammit, yer gonna UNDERSTAND it! 'Poetic Lyrics' rarely appear in a song intended for a country listenership. While it's unusual to encounter country songs that merit legitimate praise, such of course do and have existed. What's interesting is that most of the songs I'll mention below, when they came out, were played on country radio stations and appeared on the country music charts. But today, unless rendered by an already commercially successful act and so benefiting from major industrial push (which in some of the cases below, is exactly what transpired back when as well) would much more reasonably be expected to be considered 'Americana' rather than 'country'. These are songs that aren't yer usual Nashville garbage. I defy anyone with any popular music preferences—heavy metal, Broadway, rap, bluegrass, you-name-it—to not be reached by at least one or more of the following songs, the origins of which are spread out over most of the last century: "Down The Old Road to Home" (songwriter Jimmie Rodgers, 1932), "El Paso" (Marty Robbins, 1959), "California Cotton Fields" (Dallas Frazier and Earl Montgomery, 1969), "The Gambler" (Don Schlitz, 1978), "The Dance" (Tony Arata, 1988), "I Can't Make You Love Me" (Mike Reid and Allen Shamblin, 1991) or "Travelin' Soldier" (Bruce Robison, 1996). These are personal reflections, story-songs, metaphors, socio-political laments, simple soliloquies; but all expertly crafted and with what easily convinces as honest self-awareness. Not one relies on Dylanesque posturing and pseudo-modernist 'it's your job to interpret it and make it make sense' affectations. They are songs, in other words, that among more universal accomplishments should inspire all songwriters to attempt to achieve similar results.

So let's look at a few of those mentioned above. Going through them all would take too much time, and displaying a couple of positive examples is really all that's needed to further the discussion. But no matter how familiar one may be with any or all, I urge readers to give a close listen to each of them once again.

★

The Grateful Dead's Bob Weir often freely reported that "El Paso" was the band's 'most requested song'—a remarkable allowance insofar as while properly emphasizing the strength of the songwriting in "El Paso" it also inadvertently admits to the across-the-board *insignificance* of the band's own ground-up creations, particularly insofar as the rabid audience for this particular act might reasonably have been expected to be more open to the ostensibly 'poetic' lyrics in the band's original material, and to obviously know that material intimately.[96] Further, the Dead's performances of "El Paso" were nothing to brag about—I wasn't able to find an authorized recording, so perhaps click around the net to hear one. So, no, it wasn't the presentation that made it so loved by their audiences. The Dead's "El Paso" was really just Weir doing a creditable open mic night rendition, loosely accompanied by the rest of the band. What makes it work is that it's simply a vividly written song—even stripped of Grady Martin's stunningly nonesuch lead guitar work on Robbins' original recording.

> Out in the West Texas town of El Paso,
> I fell in love with a Mexican girl.
> Nighttime would find me in Rosa's cantina;
> Music would play and Felina would whirl.
>
> Blacker than night were the eyes of Felina;
> Wicked and evil while casting a spell.
> My love was deep for this Mexican maiden;
> I was in love, but in vain I could tell.

One night a wild young cowboy came in—
Wild as the West Texas wind.
Dashing and daring, a drink he was sharing
With wicked Felina, the girl that I loved.

So in anger I challenged his right for the love of this maiden;
Down went his hand for the gun that he wore.
My challenge was answered in less than a heartbeat;
The handsome young stranger lay dead on the floor.

Just for a moment I stood there in silence,
Shocked by the foul evil deed I had done.
Many thoughts raced through my mind as I stood there—
I had but one chance and that was to run.

Out through the back door of Rosa's I ran;
Out where the horses were tied.
I caught a good one, it looked like it could run;
Up on its back and away I did ride—

Just as fast as I could from the West Texas town of El Paso,
Out to the badlands of New Mexico.
Back in El Paso my life would be worthless;
Everything's gone in life; nothing is left.

It's been so long since I've seen the young maiden.
My love is stronger than my fear of death.

I saddled up and away I did go
Riding alone in the dark.
Maybe tomorrow a bullet may find me;
Tonight nothing's worse than this pain in my heart.

And at last here I am on the hill overlooking El Paso;
I can see Rosa's Cantina below.
My love is strong and it pushes me onward;
Down off the hill to Felina I go.

Off to my right I see five mounted cowboys;
Off to my left ride a dozen or more.

Shouting and shooting, I can't let them catch me;
I have to make it to Rosa's back door.

Something is dreadfully wrong, for I feel
A deep burning pain in my side.
Though I am trying to stay in the saddle,
I'm getting weary, unable to ride.

But my love for Felina is strong and I rise where I've fallen;
Though I am weary, I can't stop to rest.
I see the white puff of smoke from the rifle;
I feel the bullet go deep in my chest.

From out of nowhere Felina has found me
Kissing my cheek as she kneels by my side.
Cradled by two loving arms that I'll die for;
One little kiss, then Felina goodbye.[97]

"El Paso" is so well constructed and so well written that there's really very little that can be criticized—it must simply be held up and admired for the radiant work it most certainly is. Especially noteworthy, perhaps, is that the first two-thirds of the song is told in past tense—it's all backstory, not even truly within the otherwise compact timeline of now, as we have no idea how long he's been gone from El Paso. When he returns we're suddenly thrown into the very midst of the real-time cataclysmic climax. And the last line is told—presumably and incredibly, because from where else could it arrive—from beyond the grave! Well, the precise moment of death, anyway—so he's gone but ain't yet buried. (Even the great song, "Green, Green Grass of Home", by Curly Putman in 1964, stops short of actually addressing us from after death—the raconteur there instead singing to us in solemn anticipation of its impending arrival—and I doubt that song could've gotten away with it.) Talk about finality. And is there anyone—any listener—who doesn't buy it?

And, of course, there's the obvious additional uncertainty of whether Felina does actually arrive or if she's the imagined wish fulfillment—the phantasmagoria—of a dying man; in a slant repurchase of Ambrose Bierce's "An Occurrence at Owl Creek Bridge".

Yep, that's all that need be taken apart here, as we respectfully take a few steps back to look and listen. "El Paso" is incontestably brilliant work that will most assuredly stand the test of time.

★

Another great piece of writing—and really quite simple; not at all overly ambitious—is "Down the Old Road to Home", written now almost a century ago:

> Dear, I'm thinking of you while here all alone;
> I'm wishing and longing for you and for home.
> I'd give this whole world if I could only say,
> "I'm climbing that hill, headed that way."

chorus:
> For I'm lonesome and blue for some place to roam;
> And I wish it could be down that old road to home.

> With a troubled mind and a heart full of pain,
> I've searched the whole world for fortune and fame.
> But I'm longing to be with you once again,
> So we could stroll down old memory lane.

chorus repeat

> There's a little red house on top of a hill,
> Not very far from an old syrup mill.
> And I'd give this world if I could only say,
> "I'm climbing that hill, headed that way."

chorus repeat[98]

Jimmie Rodgers' songwriting here, unassuming as it is, captures all that needs be said about being away from home—and, I unhesitatingly assert, it is that unassuming simplicity that touches us. While the writing flirts tenuously close to corny clichés, I think we're inclined to indulge them within the forlorn aspirations and definite overall depth. While I often admire Paul Simon's songwriting, his similarly inclined "Homeward Bound", so much more elevated and precise than Rodgers' effort here, to my ears doesn't reach the same level of emotional pull this simple song awakens—and "Homeward Bound" is by no means insignificant work.

The argument has been presented to me by a correspondent that it is Rodgers' recorded performance that makes the song resonate, not the actual lyrics (which, in the same argument, are overly sentimental and ripe). While there are certainly superior and inferior fits of any specific song to particular performer, I remain unconvinced that a seriously invested rendering of "Down the Old Road to Home", by a capable vocalist, would strike a sophisticated and intelligent listener as false or lesser work. To my ears it's just that good. (In fact, there is one thing that Rodgers adds into his recorded performance—yodeling—that *does* detract from the effort. You have to have some sympathy for him—and he's a creditable yodeler—as yodeling was an identifying commercial trademark of his singing. So he surely felt obligated to include some on nearly every record he made—unfortunately, in this case.)⁹⁹

★

"The Gambler" is an interesting effort that deserves some examination and comment here as well. We may particularly benefit by sharply distancing from the well-known Kenny Rogers rendition. (This may be a good test of how well we've learned to jettison biases based on extraneous considerations, eh?) While he creditably weaves through most of the song in journeyman fashion, Rogers latterly careens off into near pop sing-along caricature. Shades of Joplin's "Me and Bobby McGee".

But Schlitz caught lightning in a bottle using the game of poker as metaphor for great lessons of life; there was so much material to mine and incorporate. And he came through with a great piece of songwriting:

> On a warm summer's evenin',
> On a train bound for nowhere,
> I met up with a gambler;
> We were both too tired to sleep.
> So we took turns a-starin'
> Out the window at the darkness.
> The boredom overtook us,
> And he began to speak.
>
> He said, "Son, I've made a life
> Out of readin' people's faces;
> And knowin' what the cards were

By the way they held their eyes.
So if you don't mind me sayin',
I can see you're out of aces.
For a taste of your whiskey
I'll give you some advice".

So I handed him my bottle,
And he drank down my last swallow.
Then he bummed a cigarette
And then he bummed a light.
And the night got deathly quiet;
And his faced lost all expression;
He said, "If you're gonna play the game, boy
You gotta learn to play it right:

"'Cause every gambler knows
That the secret to survivin'
Is knowin' what to throw away
And knowin' what to keep.
'Cause every hand's a winner,
Just like every hand's a loser;
And the best that you can hope for
Is to die in your sleep.

chorus:
   "You've got to know when to hold 'em.
   Know when to fold 'em.
   Know when to walk away
   And know when to run.
   You never count your money
   When you're sittin' at the table.
   There'll be time enough for countin'
   When the dealin's done."

And when he finished speakin'
He turned back toward the window
He crushed out his cigarette
And faded off to sleep.

And somewhere in the darkness,
The Gambler he broke even.
But in his final words
I found an ace that I could keep.

chorus repeat[100]

If it was Schlitz himself who originated the multiple chorus repetitions that Rogers then later also employed, it's unfortunate and it unnecessarily lessens the preceding effort. A big, happy sing-along after the primary character DIES?!? Was it just to lengthen a great song from 2:45 to 3:30—was that the objective? If so, may I suggest, here again, an instrumental pass or two on that chorus instead?[101]

But, really, for what more could one ask in a song? A good story that comes off as almost a fable of The Old West; a pleasant melody; and not just one, but several well-played observations and insights in a complete and well-rounded presentation. This is work to admire.

I will offer that to me, however, even though the character of The Gambler outright dies in the song story—which one might assert should already put the entire composition into higher relief—his demise comes off as almost offhanded; a negligibility. Whether this reservation is worthy or not, one additional verse still might advantage the effort, or at least wouldn't over-burden the concept: a verse wherein we take yet one more step away from preceding events to paint a larger picture or reflection. Perhaps conjecture by the narrator on the antecedent life of The Gambler—the compromises he must have made, how twists of life may have brought him to what he became, the loves he must have had and now left behind, unknowing. Or perhaps even a partial philosophical *rejection* of The Gambler's imparted wisdom as too reductionist or pat, despite accepting its obvious sagacity. Without taking a lot of time to consider further what such an additional verse might reveal or advance, I can certainly concede my intuition here may just be too demanding, as there's no question Schlitz has done a bang-up job.

★

As noted earlier, it would take too much time to go through all seven examples mentioned here as songs particularly deserving appreciation. But it's necessary in our analytical look at popular songs to include a couple of critical examinations of positive efforts like these, along with the many negative ones we consider. So I again urge readers to take some time with each. Great work deserves recognition and study. Yet great work is *also* not exempt from questions, comments, and critique.

And while these are all country and Americana songs, that shouldn't be construed to imply there's nothing worth praising in rock or other genres. (We've already lauded "I Can See For Miles", for instance.) There's just not enough time to extoll the rare exceptions everywhere.

By the way, later on we'll return to examine one more of these stellar works, "California Cotton Fields", in a slightly different context.

[96]Old joke: "What did the Deadhead say when the drugs finally wore off?" "I don't know—what *did* the Deadhead say when the drugs finally wore off?" "Gosh, actually, this band sucks."

[97]"El Paso", copyright 1959 by Marty Robbins. Quoted here as permitted within the Fair Use provisions of 17 U.S.C.§107.

[98]"Down the Old Road to Home", copyright 1932 by Jimmie Rodgers. Quoted here as permitted within the Fair Use provisions of 17 U.S.C.§107.

[99]Similarly and famously, Western swing band leader Bob Wills apparently felt 'inspired' to doggedly inject his wildly intrusive (albeit also ultimately entertaining, from a strictly performance standpoint) "A-ha!"s and other distracting falsetto interruptions into his band's performances. The tail wags the dog—shtick becomes the identifying showbiz necessity—to the detriment of a serious song. In Wills' case, of course, he was leading a dance band—see the chapter on dance music earlier—so such conceits may be more tolerantly indulged. But I've often wondered if his interpolations didn't really derive, at first anyway, from jealousy; simple fear of being over-shadowed, upstaged, by the vocalist in his band. (It's MY band, dammit, so I'm gonna make sure everyone's CONSTANTLY reminded of that!) Who knows? (See Chapter Fifty-One for a little more on the topic generally.)

[100]"The Gambler", copyright 1976 by Don Schlitz. Quoted here as permitted within the Fair Use provisions of 17 U.S.C.§107.

[101]Yes, I've suggested this same musical solution in similar circumstance earlier as well, for "Me and Bobby McGee". And though the reader may think me simplistic or limited in that consistency, let me again cite Garrison Keillor's work: in this case, a simple but effective production allocation of time in the *A Prairie Home Companion* radio show. Almost always following his "News from Lake Wobegon" recitations—10-15 minutes generally accepted to be the highlight of that two-hour broadcast—there came a strictly instrumental musical interlude; an adagio opportunity for audience reflection on what had just been transmitted; very much as one might encounter in a well-programmed church service following the pastor's homily or sermon. I absolutely believe this was programmed there for similar effect, from similar showbiz experience and awareness. (After all, what is a good—rather, an effective—church service but practiced practical showbiz, eh?) When one has delivered work that allows—if lucky, even requires—thought, the 'tried and true' segue is into a musical, (i.e., a nonverbal) denouement.

Chapter Forty-Two

Quick! Get Me Rewrite!

Art is never finished, only abandoned. — Leonardo da Vinci

A quick look at some key aspects of copyright law is perhaps in order. I've not been sure where to insert this chapter—it's germane though something of a tangent—but here is probably as good a place as any.

First off, on the music side, a melody can be copyrighted, but a chord progression can't. And for those reading who have no musical knowledge, the reason for this is that any number of melodies can be derived and constructed from the exact same chord sequence. A melody is just a single note to the next single note to the next, with the length of the spaces in between; as a chord contains *many* notes and there are *many* ways to get from one note to another to another.

Dolly Parton's "I Will Always Love You", mentioned earlier, has the exact same chord sequence as Elton John's "Crocodile Rock", John Lennon's "Happiness is a Warm Gun", Ben E. King's "Stand By Me"—and zillions more songs. If a chord sequence *could* be copyrighted, very few 1950s pop songs would ever have existed—probably most of 'em would be instantly recognized to be a simple variation on one of just two basic chord structures. Either C-Am-F-G (in this or another key, so more demotically notated as I, vi, IV, V)—which is also the chord progression of all those songs just named above—and the 12-bar blues, in whatever key. So the first songs written in each sequence—copyrighted—would have squelched the thousands or *tens* of thousands of songs that actually followed. Make sense?

Back in Chapter Thirty-One, we briefly noted that Woody Guthrie's "This Land is Your Land" used the very same chord progression as two songs by the Carter Family, "When The World's On Fire" and "Little Darlin' Pal of Mine". But, of course, there are many, many songs using nothing but that exact same chord sequence as well. (The great Mississippi John Hurt didn't record all that many compositions, yet *three* of his songs used it: "Richland Woman Blues", "My Creole Belle", and "All Night Long".) For a light-hearted personal anecdote concerning another, well, 'song' using the progression, see footnote 102 below.[102]

On the lyrics side, writing new lyrics for, or inserting other lyrics into, a copyrighted song, without permission, is called 'creating an unauthorized derivative work', and it's a violation of copyright.

How much one can get away with on either side of the matter— melody or lyrics—is up to the legal system in each and every individual case, of course. What you or I *think* the law allows or prohibits is really just ignorant conjecture—and frankly, even the most capable lawyers are ultimately guessing. (The big difference, obviously—and why they get paid mountains of money—is they have a wealth of training and experience to guide their 'guess'.) What I'm saying here in a rather circuitous way is that first there has to be a lawsuit filed, then it has to be won (or lost) to know if the defendant's work violated copyright (or not). Circumstances are never exactly the same; the law and interpretations of it change over time; judges and juries do not all think alike.

It always surprises me how unaware and frightened—innocently ignorant and afraid—most people are of such matters. Flagrant violations are obvious, of course—and don't think otherwise. But most are just various shades of gray along a continuum, from brightest white to deepest black. And, as noted, copyright actually *changes* over time as new lawsuits are brought and either won or lost, and as new thinking is incorporated into law.

For instance, the "Blurred Lines"/"Got To Give It Up" case of a couple years back may end up opening some interesting flood gates, insofar as what determined the guilty verdict was essentially just the production and influences evinced in the song—genre, style, orchestration, 'sound', 'vibe', 'groove' and etc—as opposed to actual melody or lyrics. An utterly ignorant decision, absolutely—helped by the "Blurred Lines" defendants coming off as arrogantly insufferable idiots—but it *was* the legal decision.

Even the length of copyright itself has changed—greatly expanding in duration. In the United States, it started with the first laws established in 1790, setting copyright at 14 years with an optional renewal of 14 more. Today, it lasts the lifetime of the author plus 70 years thereafter.

Could one bring a successful suit against an act—say a female sing-er—who simply changed the word 'her' in a song to 'him', in order to work better for her gender? Well, first off, as I'm indicating—and this really can't be over-emphasized—*anyone* can be sued for *anything*. But we used the word 'successful' in our question, and so the answer is certainly no, as it's unlikely any damage to the work could be legitimately argued, and so the suit would surely be tossed before even reaching the courtroom.

Yet it most certainly is, very strictly, an alteration of the copyrighted lyrics, no?

I know this may all seem a bit arcane and petty—and you betcha, 'legalistic'—but it very directly impacts even the most innocent of songwriting efforts.

★

True story: I liked the sound of a song I'd heard many years before called "Above and Beyond", recorded and commercially successful by Buck Owens and later by Rodney Crowell. The song came to mind every once in a while over the years, until I eventually worked up a solo acoustic guitar arrangement that seemed to work. But I was always doubtful about the lyrics, which appeared, well, 'unfinished' to me. Here it is—it starts with the chorus:

chorus:
> Oh, I'll give you love
> That's above and beyond the call of lo-o-ove,
> And I'll never ever make you cry.
> Ah yes, I'll give you love
> That's above and beyond the call of lo-o-ove;
> And love's something that money can't buy.

verse one:
> Well a poor boy's chances for a pretty girl's glances
> Are sometimes very few.
> Though I've got no money, if you'll be my honey,
> Here's what I'll offer you:

chorus repeat

verse two:
 We met by chance and I knew at a glance
 That I'd found my destiny.
 Now I want to carry you off and marry you
 If you will agree.

chorus repeat[103]

No, _not_ great art, but a possibly pleasant distraction; a nice melody; filler. I wasn't crazy about the chorus—"I'll give you love that's above and beyond the call of love", with that last (very redundant) word spread over three ascending notes. And I also felt it needed a third verse. So here's the song, as I rewrote it and recorded it on my first album:

verse one (same as original):

chorus (revised):
 I'll give you love
 That's above and beyond everything you've dreamed of,
 And I'll never ever make you cry.
 Yes, I'll give you love
 That's above and beyond everything you've dreamed of,
 And love's something that money can't buy.

verse two (same as original):

chorus repeat

verse three (new):
 I've met lots of girls around this old world,
 And some have given my heart a thrill.
 But I never met one who was half as much fun
 And I reckon I never will.

chorus repeat[103]

Absolutely the same song, yes. And still not 'great art'. But, I also assert, clearly stronger.

Before recording (and in retrospect what was I thinking?!?) I played my rewrite for Buck himself—not realizing how presumptuous the whole endeavor was—naively hoping for a green light. I'm glad he was such an approachable guy, believe me.

His response stays with me still. After about three awkward seconds of dead air, he blurted out, "Well, heck, Michael, that's a better song! That's a better song. Now I can't sing it that way because of what folks expect, but you go right on ahead. Good job!"

This was quickly appended by another bit of dead air and a sudden look of concern. "But you're payin' the royalties, right?!?"

I confirmed the obvious obligation and we both laughed. And, of course, the original copyright hadn't changed at all.

Lesson: what most songwriters worry about are two primary things. First, that any change—big or small, inadvertent or deliberate—isn't an embarrassment (or worse, an outright trashing). And second, equally, that dollars—pounds, euros, rands, clams, simoleons—are properly paid. That obviously doesn't mean one should arrogantly disregard formal responsibilities and proper respect; it means the exact opposite.

Fun addendum: Though "Above and Beyond" was a hit record for both Buck Owens and Rodney Crowell, it was *written* by the great Harlan Howard—meaning Buck's 'authorization' was, frankly, illegitimate.

And so could Harlan Howard have sued me? Sure, if he wanted to. I expect he would have easily prevailed, too, and the judgment so steep I'd still be poor today. How poor? Too poor to even pay attention. (Sorry, old joke—couldn't help myself.)

The bigger you get, the bigger the finances, and the more bellicose the lawyers; the greater the propriety, circumspection, and responsibility that is required—in songwriting as elsewhere throughout life.

★

But of even more pertinence to what we're engaged in here was Owens' truly remarkable willingness—remarkable rare willingness and ability—to recognize better lyrics in a song he had been performing for over two decades. It is almost always *profoundly* difficult for someone, having been exposed to a song for years and years and years, to accept different—yes, even noticeably better—lyrics to it than those that have become known by heart. The challenge to do so will be regularly encountered in the next chapter, which addresses Bob Dylan's songs, and where—as earlier when I've suggested replacing specific words and lines in other songs—we'll be discussing lyrics that are probably known word for word in many readers' memories.

[102]One day when I was still in the South, playin' guitar out on the front porch as the sun settled in for the night, I realized that a commercial jingle then bein' used by Schlitz Beer had the same chord progression as "This Land Is Your Land." The jingle had a different melody—it used alternative notes in those chords—so it could be sung directly counter to, in harmony with, Woody Guthrie's song. Another thought that hit me was that the 200th anniversary of the signing of the American Declaration of Independence was a few years off, so this musta been in the early 1970s. I mulled all that over and came up with what I thought would be my Ticket To Riches.

(You can hear the Schlitz jingle here: https://www.youtube.com/watch?v=qOYLRnuQIQM. (YouTube title search: Schlitz Beer Commercial [1967] Three's a Crowd)

Here's how the chords, melodies, and lyrics all mesh:

```
  C              F                              C
"This land is your land.        This land is my land.
"If you like it light with a big taste too, there's only one brew that will do.
                    G                          C
                    This land was made for you and me!"
When you're out of Schlitz,        you're out of beer!"
```

So anyway, I wrote a letter to the Schlitz Brewing Company in far off Milwaukie, Wisconsin, proposing they prepare an ad campaign that tied their existing jingle and "This Land Is Your Land" together for the impending national celebrations of the Bicentennial. (For one thing, this would obviously make for a smooth, almost seamless, segue from one campaign into the other.) TV commercials could show regular Americans from coast to coast: lobster fishermen, garage mechanics, grade school teachers, working cowboys. And the slogan that would tie everything together at the end, with now all the singers joining in big multi-part harmony, would be—you'll wince at this (as I sheepishly do now), but try to think as an advertising creative director (or as a teenager with too much time on his hands)—"This Beer Was Made for You and Me!" (And hell, didn't Woody stipulate anyone could use the song? 'Course his kids woulda probably come lookin' for me with a shotgun—but I wasn't thinkin' that far ahead....)

A month later Schlitz sent me back an obvious form letter, telling me quite pleasantly, politely—but clearly—to get fuckin' lost. Ah, well.

*

Which reminds me, to stray even farther from what we should be talkin' about—but since we're havin' a little fun along the way—of *another* advertising idea I once had. See, there was a company that made (as I remember it, anyway) the first pocket calculator that could store an actual number in its memory to use in a subsequent calculation. It was a Real Big Deal at the time. The calculator was made by the Wang Computer Company up in Massachusetts.

But their magazine and newspaper ads were about as dull as a legal contract.

So I wrote them as well, with my sure-fire idea to juice up their advertising and get 'em some notice! The idea? A simple slogan—a blaring pitch line—at the top of all those print advertisements. "If You Can't Count It On Your Fingers, Use Your Wang!"

Those folks never even wrote back....

[103]"Above and Beyond", copyright 1960 by Harlan Howard. Quoted here as permitted within the Fair Use provisions of 17 U.S.C.§107.

Chapter Forty-Three

Bob Dylan: Bad Writer, Bad Influence

If we've been bamboozled long enough, we tend to reject any evidence of the bamboozle. We're no longer interested in finding the truth; the bamboozle has captured us. It's simply too painful to acknowledge, even to ourselves, that we've been taken. Once you give a charlatan power over you, you almost never get it back. — Carl Sagan

Despite the heading for this chapter, there's actually a significant aspect of songwriting on which Bob Dylan has had a seminal, positive influence. We'll elaborate on its importance in Chapter Fifty-Six.

But if we want to get firmly into *good* songwriting, we have to get past inexcusably magnified *bad* songwriting, meaning we have to address Dylan's actual work. And the insipid "Forever Young", discussed earlier, is just the tip of the iceberg. In this and the next chapter we'll shovel through some more of his ham-fisted efforts.

First off, however, a digression—in the form of a question: have ya ever heard of Edward Bulwer-Lytton?

Sound at *all* familiar?

Bulwer-Lytton was probably <u>the</u> most famous and successful author of the nineteenth century—his career was truly outsized.[104] He was even offered—get this—the throne of Greece. Yes, if he'd wanted he could have been King Edward I of Greece, with all the rarefied royal exemptions and prerogatives. True. (I assume he turned the gig down 'cause it mighta cramped his style. Edward Bulwer-Lytton lived a LARGE life.) More famous and popularly admired in his time than Charles Dickens, Herman Melville, Leo Tolstoy, or Samuel Clemens (maybe even of all of them combined), today he's mostly known, if at all, as simply the butt of a joke.

Bulwer-Lytton is the author of that now most ridiculed of opening lines, "It was a dark and stormy night...."

Here's another fun look back. In 1890, twenty-plus successful painters in Paris dined together at the home of a high-profile art dealer to debate and consider which artists then working would be considered the greatest a century later.[105] This was the era of Courbet, Renoir, Cézanne, Delacroix, Corot, Manet, Degas, Seurat, Van Gogh, Monet, Toulouse-Lautrec, Gauguin and others whose work we all know and love today. The assembled artists and allied professionals carefully deliberated, and finally decided that THE two great talents of the time—the ones who would remain superstars *far* into the future were—drum roll, please: William-Adolphe Bouguereau and Jean-Louis-Ernest Meissonier! I'm willing to bet it's better than even odds you've never heard of either of 'em.

And how about Louis Spohr? The composer Louis Spohr? Listen to his stuff much? Hum his tunes in the shower? A contemporary and friend of Beethoven, he was by far the more successful of the two. In fact, he was arguably *the* most revered and rewarded composer of the entire nineteenth century.

Earlier I made a couple of predictions about the future—one about singing in affected 'po' folks' accent and one about awards shows: that both will be seen as distasteful examples of the hubris of these times. Another one I'll add here is that a hundred years from now Bob Dylan—like Bulwer-Lytton, Bouguereau, Meissonier, and Spohr today—will be trash-canned by history; seen as a gawky second-rate idiosyncrasy of our epoch. His songs, if remembered at all, will be performed as minor amusements or as oddball museum curiosities. "Wow! People back then thought THIS stuff was good writing?!?"

But obviously, Dylan has had and continues to enjoy a major place in *current* American culture. For those who fancy a pleasant pop tune, but seek more depth than what's found in the rest of the great sea of industrial waste, his stuff offers an academically approved opportunity to 1.) join in the fun, while 2.) additionally maintaining (due to those academic and critical imprimaturs) that one is championing songs that are actually Serious, Substantive Works Of Art.

Unfortunately for that obstinate conceit, the songs are in fact *not* 'serious, substantive works of art'. And he's an embarrassingly inept writer.

Because his songs are regularly verbose—he doesn't use language effectively, but he's not averse to filling up pages and pages—those wishing for more significance than is generally encountered can simply defer to the *quantity* of words, despite that they're so often bunglingly used, and insinuate depth. In fact, this itself is actually a further indictment of the overall quality of writing in popular songs—Dylan's blunderbussing compounds the problem, doing nothing to alleviate it.

And, in the 'credit where due department', there are specific occasional songs in which he does a passably workmanlike job.

But assessing his work requires first slashing away a whole lot of entangled, inessential nonsense—the kind I tried to eradicate in Part One—and the most pernicious of which when discussing Dylan is all the pathetic fan idolatry; the middlebrow babble from brainless boosters. Think 'Kardashians Go To Community College'.

While this chapter was being written, for instance, he was named recipient of the 2016 Nobel Prize in Literature for his collected lyrics. The Nobel folks were obviously seeking celebrity, and presumably thought themselves quite clever and trendy in the matter; but the precarious posturing is at best cynically panting, really almost laughable. (No, *actually* laughable—I did exactly that when I heard the announcement itself. Two of the Great Reasons they venerated him were—get this—"He's a wonderful sampler...[and] he's reinvented himself constantly, creating a new identity over and over!".[106] I think my thoughts on plagiarism—er, sorry, I mean 'sampling'—and on an act 're-inventing itself' are pretty clear.) If they were so determined to hand more money to this or that already rich popular American baby boomer celebrity, why not to Woody Allen for his collected screenplays? Or to Garrison Keillor for his mammoth body of often excellent radio and print work? Or—while he's not American, he's still English-speaking, and certainly successful—the consistently, explosively brilliant playwright Tom Stoppard? Oh, you folks in Stockholm were dead set on an American *songwriter*? Okay, well, ever heard of Stephen Sondheim? All four of them—Allen, Keillor, Stoppard, Sondheim—unquestionably, far, *far* better writers than the haplessly hamstrung Dylan. But they'd hoped for a <u>fun</u> evening, darn it—music and glitz and a big time pop star with whom to hobnob—not like their usual arid bestowals. Unfortunately, Dylan squelched even that by dispatching the always eager Patti Smith—she kinda pop music's 'Sir Edmund Hillary of Social Climbing'—as his surrogate. I honestly expect that in the end the Nobel folks were properly embarrassed, and relieved when the thorough travesty they'd manufactured had begun to pass. If you sidestepped it, perhaps refer back to Chapter Thirteen, on the burlesque of awards.

★

Anecdote #1: Dave Van Ronk, the paterfamilias of the Greenwich Village folk scene in the early 1960s, reportedly enjoyed telling the following story: One late night, Dylan—then crashing at Van Ronk's place—came in holding tight to some papers, lyrics for a new song he'd just written, eager to learn Van Ronk's reaction. The avuncular Van Ronk, apparently always an available and honest critic, handed over the guitar and Dylan played his new composition. Van Ronk then immediately launched into a short battery of questions—obviously not at all impressed. "Bob, it doesn't make any sense. WHAT 'wind'? What are you talking about? What's the point? What 'answers'? 'answers are blowing in the wind'?!?"... Van Ronk apparently liked to tell the story in later years as a self-deprecation, getting a laugh from his audience and enjoying the laugh at his own expense—as "Blowin' in the Wind" was of course successfully marketed to an adolescent generation, brought in a whole lot of money, and attained cultural landmark status. (A key adjective in the preceding sentence is that word 'adolescent', an aspect of popular song marketing addressed back in Chapter Thirty-Seven.)

Yet were we dropping in on that scene this very moment, Van Ronk sitting across from me, I'd step forward, take firm hold of and shake him by his shoulders, look him in the eye, and say, "But Dave! Dave! Hold on! You were right! It IS poorly-written! This IS crap! Trust your gut, dammit—and let go of the self-doubt just because it became a pop hit!"[107]

★

Anecdote #2: Many years ago I came across mention of a Dylan song of which I'd never heard, and that had apparently been a big hit when covered by another performer. I immediately thought, "Wow! Here's a chance to take a look at a piece of his work without being affected by the melody or performance—a song that was popularly successful, in fact. Wonderful! What a great opportunity." I googled the lyrics—the web was already able to deliver useful info like that—and I studied them....

Let's see here.... Well those two lines do (in a way) refer back to this (half-baked) thought over there, yes. Okay. And that entire short verse over there does make intrinsic sense, no question about that. On the other hand, it's got nothing to do with any of the rest of the song. Hmm. And that verse up there seems tossed in from somewhere else entirely, totally disconnected from everything else. The title, the kinda 'point' line, is repeated there and there—that's neither good nor bad, but worth noting that he's at least *trying* to create some persistence, a whole package.... And so forth—I spent serious time with it, back and forth, up and down, trying to find connections and divine objectives, to find this or that particularly satisfying turn of phrase or bit of wisdom, to deduce that overarching intent and direction. It was an interesting, informative exercise. But I came away quite underwhelmed.

A year and a half later, wanting to see if maybe I'd missed something that first time around, I took that same song AGAIN, and went through it all another time, line by line, verse by verse. True. A completely fresh investigation. After all, maybe I had overlooked something important—a pivotal connection, allusion, thematic compass, or piece of sagacity. (I mean he's 'Bob Dylan The Voice of A Generation', right? Or so I was then still with some honest innocence thinking. All the encomiums and tributes really couldn't be misplaced, could they?)

Result? I came to the same conclusion about the song as I had eighteen months earlier: incompetent blather, pedestrian drivel. Exasperating, really, were one to sing it trying to muster conviction. I still haven't heard the song—and melody and performance can certainly make a difference in one's simple unguarded amusement. But those aspects are in fact subsidiary; we are discussing the maintained depth of the writing.

No, I'm not gonna reveal the name of the song here, because the specific piece isn't important. But I suggest you try the experiment yourself. Find a song of his you've never heard, web search and print out the lyrics, and take a long, careful, dispassionate look at it. Don't simply find lines or words that remind you of something else that's been culturally canonized and be satisfied—the dimwitted and superficial Sir Chris Ricks approach to literary criticism—but look for full-scale *ideas*, fleshed out and presented with eloquence. See if you find any. And see if you find some overall consistency and coherence—*without*, that is, resorting

to contorted wishful nonsense in the form of wild-eyed, operatically du-
bious 'explanation'. Good luck.

★

Anecdote #3: A good friend of mine and his band comprised of long-
time professionals, all with hit songs and national tours behind them,
had just completed recording an album. In casual conversation, he mentioned that all the songs on the album were written by different band
members and pairings of band members except one: they were a little
short, so they worked up a Bob Dylan song. "Which one?" I asked. I
thought his shrugging response a perfect comment on Dylan's œuvre:
"Oh…Damn…I can't remember," he laughed, "It doesn't matter." I immediately recognized he was right, of course. He didn't mean to be critical—or even realize the wisdom he'd revealed—but in many ways Bob's
songs really *are* quite negligible, interchangeable. Pop wallpaper. (We'll
get to why that is below.)

★

Language is in decline. Not only has eloquence departed, but simple
direct speech as well—though pomposity and banality have not.
— Edwin Newman

As I noted earlier when discussing "Forever Young", one could really
never credibly put the words 'Bob Dylan' and 'articulate' in the same sentence. The notion is laughable. Elegance, economy, and precision are
quite outside his compass. But that has made his songs, and the sheer
output of them, a great gift to obsessive fans, striving academics, and DIY
pseudo-intellectuals eager to find, analyze, and interpret the purportedly
deep meanings and hidden associations in the wibbling efforts by their
hero—their hero who deftly, and I'd say with good reason, adamantly
refuses seriously discussing them himself.

The upshot of that evasion, of course, is that along with freeing him
from having to explain the flat-footed songs, it concurrently feeds the
hungry cottage industry of self-described 'Dylanologists' that takes on
the burden. And ultimately, abetted by celebrity culture and the low-rent
popular fascination with an unforthcoming (read: 'elusive!', 'mysterious!') luminary, the whole threadbare apparatus lurches onward. A lot of
happy fans fill a lot of contented hours pursuing their all-consuming pas-
time. The single-minded sanctimoniousness of it all is reminiscent of

what you might find with a bunch of old guys in overalls and railroad hats happily playing with model trains down in the basement: obliviously consumed, blindly committed hobbyists—most of whose marriages probably stopped working twenty years ago. When gathered in real-life university-sponsored 'academic Dylan conferences'—Comic-Cons for the frenzied Dylanoid—the reported subtextual objective of every presentation, of every *conversation*, is to be *the* most committed fan, *the* biggest apologist, *the* One Who Loves Bob The Most.

There's a frantic reality-show emptiness and intellectual lethargy common in the Dylan phenomenon, a 'discipline' that finds riches in privation, transcendence in twaddle, substance in vacancy, and most pertinently—and sadly—subjective validation in idolatry.

Bob is productive, no doubt about that. But so what? As noted earlier, simply pumping out product is a mercantile accomplishment, not an artistic one.

When he goes the 'Poetic Lyrics' route, there's a paucity of actual ideas—and those that are extant so maladroitly addressed that you have to throw up your hands in exasperation. (Or, of course, there's always the last gasp option of just exclaiming, "But it's POETRY!"….) Regularly exacerbating the poverty is what I call 'Faux-folk'—the tortured syntax and obtuse inversions that are the imperious (or just incompetent?) written equivalents, really, of the vocalist-pretending-to-have-been-born-on-a-cotton-plantation condescensions exposed earlier.

And when he attempts to use the language efficiently and directly, the klutzy songs invariably waddle along deprived of finesse, bereft of grace, like the aforementioned "Forever Young". Let's look at a few more examples of both breeds.

First up, "Hurricane":

Pistols shots ring out in the bar room night.
Enter Patty Valentine from the upper hall.
She sees the bartender in a pool of blood;
Cries out, "My God, they killed them all!"

Here comes the story of the Hurricane;
The man the authorities came to blame
For something that he never done.

> Put him in a prison cell but one time he coulda been
> The champion of the world![108].......—

We're told in the song, four times, that Reuben "Hurricane" Carter could've been a world champion—it's the ultimate line in that chorus above, which we hear again and again. The rest of the song is a frenetic stitching together of the posited facts of the case, and as such I think it unfair to criticize the rhymes and wording too harshly. After all, Dylan's essentially trying to present a legal case. But even so—and as usual when he attempts to write and speak plainly—what we get is pretty much devoid of anything beyond mediocre, disjointed prose; in this case something reminiscent of a high school book report. (And a high school book report evincing the student didn't actually read the whole book: Carter's 'innocence' was precariously unlikely. More on page 214, footnote 118.)

And does anyone really care—*should* anyone really care—that Carter could have been a world champ? Is that really of any pertinence in arguing for his supposed innocence? To shallow Bob, it sure seems to be.

★

"Masters of War": Talk about ungainly, fatiguing tripe. Even as that insecure, provincial teenager back in the Deep South, I knew this was *far* beneath anything I could allow myself to perform.

> Come you masters of war;
> You that build all the guns;.
> You that build the death planes;
> You that build all the bombs;
> You that hide behind walls;
> You that hide behind desks;
> I just want you to know
> I can see through your masks.
>
> You that never done nothin'
> But build to destroy;
> You play with my world
> Like it's your little toy.
> You put a gun in my hand
> And you hide from my eyes.

And you turn and run farther
When the fast bullets fly[109].......—

And so on.

What can one say about something this leaden, this ponderous? If you'd never heard it, and someone reported it was written by an immigrant student, a brand new arrival into the English-speaking world, you might be impressed with how he or she is progressing in learning the language—but that's about it. And as noted earlier, this was another of Dylan's many outright musical thefts.

As for the lyrics: "death planes"? "fast bullets"? Short on adjectives, are we? That's the best you can do? Even here, using the simplest of one-syllable words, the lack of language skills is glaring. Bob, bullets *always* fly fast; "fast bullets fly" is redundant—shades of "ladder" and "climb" in "Forever Young". How about—and it didn't take hours of thinking—'big' or 'hard' instead of 'fast'? Better, isn't it? Both suggestions are *also* obvious descriptors, yes, though not as obvious *and* redundant as 'fast' is with 'fly'. With 'hard', the negligible loss in alliteration is more than made up in added description—and if we use 'big' we simply trade alliterative words and get greater description. After all, the point is to underscore the sinister destructive power of the weapons, not just fill space.

And "You play with my world", Bob? If one is trying to foment popular antipathy, better would surely be "You play with <u>our</u> world", eh? And "You put guns in <u>our</u> hands and you hide from <u>our</u> eyes"? Ya see, Bob, it's the pivotal, critical difference between "I shall overcome" and "<u>We</u> shall overcome." Or maybe that difference is too subtle for ya?

But this song needs one hell of a lot more help than simply changing the view from first person singular to first person plural and rewriting some lyrics here and there. That's just rearranging deck chairs on Bob's hard-tilting *Titanic*.

"Masters of War" is really just another example illustrating that, as with the preponderance of his efforts, the real underlying 'message' is Dylan's glaringly limited capacities as a writer.

★

Now for some of the 'Poetic Lyrics', for which he's held in such high regard.

And in my research for this manifesto, believe it or not, I actually discovered a long lost part to one of Dylan's most celebrated songs! It's a never before heard verse to his "A Hard Rain's A-Gonna Fall". Here's the first verse of that well-known song:

Oh, where have you been, my blue-eyed son?
And where have you been my darling young one?
I've stumbled on the side of twelve misty mountains,
I've walked and I've crawled on six crooked highways,
I've stepped in the middle of seven sad forests,
I've been out in front of a dozen dead oceans,
I've been ten thousand miles in the mouth of a graveyard.

And it's a hard, it's a hard, it's a hard, it's a hard,
It's a hard rain's a-gonna fall![110]

And here's the unknown, long lost verse I stumbled upon:

Oh, what did you see, my blue-eyed son?
Oh, what did you see, my darling young one?
I saw twelve drummers drummin' and eleven pipers pipin',
I watched ten lords a-leapin' with nine ladies dancin',
There were eight maids a-milkin' and seven swans a-swimmin',
Then six geese a-layin', wearin' five golden rings,
I saw four calling birds and three chirping French hens,
I saw two turtle doves…and a partridge in a pear tree!

And it's a hard, it's a hard, it's a hard, it's a hard,
It's a hard rain's a-gonna fall!

Yes, this 'lost verse' is obviously a joke. It simply came to me that "The Twelve Days of Christmas" perfectly fit the structure and conceits of his "Hard Rain". But Bob's pleasant yet turgidly impotent song is also a joke. And our contribution to it is on the same level of 'poetic brilliance'—offering commensurate 'wisdom'—so fine.

I really don't see the need to take time going through the song line by line. Is "I've been ten thousand miles in the mouth of a graveyard" a lyric that says something profound to you? Without a whole lot of entirely wishful, um, er, 'interpretation'? Sure, it might *sound* kinda substantive;

but that proves to be an illusion and a waste of time when actually considered. Clumsy pretense is clumsy pretense. There's no there there.

Oh, and yes, this is yet another theft—this one plundering a song called "Lord Randall", both the melody *and* the lyrical blueprint.

★

"Mr Tambourine Man": First off, it's hard to "play a song" on a tambourine—requesting, repeatedly, that one do so is a ridiculous stretch. And all the befuddled clutter—the rhyme scheme looking desperately for rhymes—brings us to where, exactly? Is there a point to this song other than the self-absorbed "I like to smoke dope—and the writing in this song kinda proves it in more ways than one"?

> Hey, Mr. Tambourine man, play a song for me.
> I'm not sleepy and there is no place I'm going to.
> Hey, Mr. Tambourine man, play a song for me;
> In the jingle-jangle morning I'll come following you.
>
> Though I know that evening's empire has returned into sand,
> Vanished from my hand,
> Left me blindly here to stand but still not sleeping;
> My weariness amazes me, I'm branded on my feet,
> I have no one to meet,
> And the ancient empty street's too dead for dreaming[111].......—

But let's forbear and indulge. One can argue—and reasonably, too—that the off-beat and amusing "jingle-jangle morning" (a phrase coined by 1950s comedian Lord Buckley) refers back to the sound of a tambourine, or just nicely bookends it. Hell, I'll buy it. Sure. But that's about all, really. And to what end? Cute, but no more. We're just back to the Tambourine Man, for whatever reason he's supposed to be here.[112] "Evening's empire has returned into sand"? "Evening's empire", Bob? That doesn't really tell us anything, does it? "Empire"? A little over-ripe as a metaphor for yesterday, eh? And "into sand"? Why? "Vanished from"—where? "my hand"? Are you kidding me? The events of yesterday, presumably, "vanished from my hand"?

Yes, it really *wants* to be poetry, and it really *does* try—and it all just goes on and on, floundering about, gasping for air, flopping this way and that—in desperate determination to jackhammer this square peg rhyme into that round hole line and get outta there before anyone notices. As 'poetry', pathetic. As a pleasant, radio-friendly pop ditty, sure. It does have that nice tune beneath it.

★

"Chimes of Freedom": Chimes *ring*. Lights flash. But chimes don't flash—unless maybe we're singing about a railroad crossing? But even there, with the two things going at once, it's still the *lights* flashing, and the chimes *ringing*. So Bob, look, no two ways about it: chimes don't flash, okay? No matter how urgently you sing it, and how often you re-peat it, it's *still* stupid. And you've just told us there's no reason we should indulge anything else here—that you're incapable of conveying whatever it is you hope we'll think you're saying (cf. "American Pie").

This is a song that's overflowing with what I call Fortune Cookie Wisdom—and as with other attempts Dylan makes to say something sig-nificant, simply bounces along the surface, avoiding actual engagement. A litany of non-sequiturs, ostensibly ratified by that squishy portentous refrain—those gosh-darn lovably irrepressible 'Flashing Chimes'.

And, once again, another Dylan rip-off—melody and structure—this time of a song called "The Chimes of Trinity".

Go rewrite this, then compose an original melody for it, and maybe come back later, okay?

★

"Subterranean Homesick Blues": yet another trip into cholesterol-rich near-gibberish pawned off as stream-of-consciousness illumination.

> Johnny's in the basement,
> Mixing up the medicine.
> I'm on the pavement,
> Thinking about the government.
> The man in the trench coat—
> Badge out, laid off—
> Says he's got a bad cough;
> Wants to get it paid off.
> Look out kid,
> It's somethin' you did.

God knows when
But you're doin' it again.
You better duck down the alley way,
Lookin' for a new friend.
The man in the coonskin cap
By the big pen
Wants eleven dollar bills
You only got ten[113]........—

This tedious blather—another of the many songs sometimes claimed to be 'the first rap song', by the way—would actually be a fair *counter-example* to good rap writing. It's got some, but very little, coherent information, disarrayed in a preposterously prolix package. "Wants to get his cough paid off."? "The man in the coonskin cap by the big pen wants eleven dollar bills."? Does anyone really care? You can 'interpret' this as well as I, certainly—but can we rather just agree it isn't worth our time?

★

"Lay Lady Lay": Christ, here we go again. "Lay *across* my big brass bed," Bob? "Across"? She's supposed to get comfortable in this scenario, right? (Or is the song not a seduction at all, but just a paean to some strange new variation on the prank of short-sheeting?)

Lay, lady, lay; lay across my big brass bed.
Lay, lady, lay; lay across my big brass bed.
Whatever colors you have in your mind,
I'll show them to you and you'll see them shine.

Lay, lady, lay; lay across my big brass bed.
Stay, lady, stay; stay with your man awhile.
Until the break of day; let me see you make him smile.
His clothes are dirty but his hands are clean,
And you're the best thing that he's ever seen[114]........—

We're back to a 'Bob Dylan trying to talk straight' song once again—with all the lead-footed straining and battering ram subtleties this provides. "Whatever colors you have in your mind, I'll show them to you and you'll see them shine"? Sex as a Sherwin-Williams sample wheel. "You'll see them shine" actually makes me groan. (But maybe he's just continuing the dumb metaphor. So, gloss tints? Day-Glo?) "Let me see you make him smile"? Him? So you're now suddenly gonna talk about yourself in third person? You want to watch her make *him* smile. Why? Are we being coy? Cute? Don't have the commitment—or maybe the vocabulary—to continue beseeching directly?

As it is with poignancy, romantic seduction is much beyond his grasp. And we'll briefly discuss his outright contempt for women generally in a following chapter.

★

"The Times They Are A-Changin'": Here's a song that's not aging gracefully. But it's got my all-time Number One Favorite Dylan Faux-folk Line: "The loser now will be later to win." So ludicrously mangled that it's hard to not just bursting into loud laughter. "The loser now will be later to win." I love it! And on a lesser level there's also "the wheel's still in spin"—which probably means the 'wash' and 'rinse' cycles are done.

But seriously, yes, times change. For some reason, I don't find that all too insightful. Bob's severe thematic limitations—the closest he can come to direction is haphazardly piling up a big list of dissipated, perfunctory remonstrations—is on full display here. And the primary line, "The times, they are a-changin'"—yet more Faux-folk fatuity—*is* rather precious, don't ya think?

> Come gather 'round people
> Wherever you roam,
> And admit that the waters
> Around you have grown.
> And accept it that soon
> You'll be drenched to the bone.
> If your time to you
> Is worth savin',
> Then you better start swimmin'
> Or you'll sink like a stone,
> For the times they are a-changin'![115].......—

"Come gather 'round people"—okay, so we're all here in this place, we're being asked to close ranks and listen. Sure thing. "Wherever you roam"—no wait, he must be speaking to us by radio or some such. So we're *not* all here in this spot. Ah, well then let's all huddle around our radios in each of our communities. An awkwardly lunging false start, but go ahead, Bob.

"And admit that the waters around you have grown." Perhaps better than "admit" would be "accept", but maybe I'm quibbling.

And of course if we do use "accept", then we surely shouldn't immediately use it again in the next line, as he does. But that's not a major obstacle. Perhaps "realize"—enunciated as two syllables in keeping with the Faux-folk affectation—might work even better than "accept", as it additionally highlights that the singer is, indeed, warning us of something of which we may not have been aware. So "And realize the waters around you have grown." He's bringing us new information. It's also both more sonorous and elides across the notes much better than the three staccato syllables of "admit that". We could even go with "And see that the waters around you have grown." Again, he alerts us—so it would definitely be an improvement over "admit".

But what the hell; let's just stay with it anyway—stay with his "and admit that the waters around you have grown"—and move on.

"And accept it that soon you'll be drenched to the bone." Drenched to the bone? The point of the verse here, as specified in the previous line and nailed in subsequent lines, is that it's a rising flood we're facing. "Drenched to the bone" is a phrase much more suitable—generally applicable—to addressing the effects of a rainstorm, or maybe a water-balloon fight. An apocalyptic flood is a whole different ballgame. Rain can be part of it, of course, but it's certainly quite secondary. How about "And accept it that soon you'll be drowning alone", or some variation on that statement. As usual, I don't assert this is the best we can do—good writing takes time, and plenty of other available ideas and rhyming words exist with which to work here—but it's certainly a lot closer, a better fit, to the overall intent. "Or you'll sink like a stone" later nails that very idea—so let's allow it to do that. "Drenched to the bone" is really kind of weak; a waste of space and a misdirection. (But, by the way, "you'll sink like a stone", his clincher line here, is actually *also* half-assed. It implies that people are now—*have already been*—swimming but then couldn't keep going for one reason or another. Not that they stayed put while the waters got steadily higher around them—the scenario he's been setting up. You have the immediate choice of swimming or sinking—which is what he's presenting—if you get tossed into *already* deep water.)

A chorus—in this case more accurately a refrain line—of such simplicity as the one here can most certainly work, though, so in itself this isn't a problem, and despite even the cutesy syntax. Hell, give us some depth elsewhere and it's fine; don't get me wrong. But to do so, here again, the ideas *between* the repeated maxim should give real, thoughtful insights—the refrain then providing a summation or direction derived, clearly, from those collected reports. What we get here instead are blocks of generalities, clumsily recounted, saying nothing at all penetrating or even coherently assertive—culminating in that vacuous pronouncement.

It's all kinda reminiscent of the mild, inoffensive act of some hack toupée-wearing Borscht Belt comedian: poke saccharine fun at usual targets, keep it moving, and Do Not Offend. If you're a hardcore right-winger, for instance, is there *anything* said in the said in the song (other than, possibly, the single "your sons and your daughters are beyond your command" line) that you can't happily sign on to? Think about it. Dylan even licensed the song to one of the Big Five banks in Canada to use in TV commercials. And why not? An anthem of progressivism this song certainly ain't. An astute commentary on life and societal evolutions this song really isn't either. A pretentious, portentous but unremarkable ramble it most definitely *is*. Times change. Yes they do.

★

We've just given some quick looks at a few of his best-known, most prized efforts. But enough here. I don't have the patience to spend time enduring—and then rewriting—every fucking clumsy, half-baked song Bob Dylan has disgorged. So let's end this Parade of Invalids with a song that's such spasmodic piffle we can just let it 'speak' for itself: his well-known "You Ain't Goin' Nowhere"…

Clouds so swift,
Rain won't lift;
Gate won't close,
Railings froze.
Get your mind off wintertime
You ain't goin' nowhere.

chorus:

    Whoo-ee! Ride me high.
    Tomorrow's the day
    My bride's gonna come.
    Oh, oh, are we gonna fly
    Down in the easy chair!

    I don't care
    How many letters they sent;
    Morning came and morning went.
    Pick up your money
    And pack up your tent;
    You ain't goin' nowhere.

chorus repeat

    Buy me a flute
    And a gun that shoots
    Tailgates and substitutes.
    Strap yourself
    To the tree with roots;
    You ain't goin' nowhere.

chorus repeat

    Genghis Khan,
    He could not keep
    All his kings
    Supplied with sleep.
    We'll climb that hill no matter how steep,
    When we get up to it.

chorus repeat[116]

Truly embarrassing. "Genghis Khan, he could not keep all his kings supplied with sleep." "Buy me a flute and a gun that shoots tailgates and substitutes." "Whoo-ee! Ride me high. Tomorrow's the day my bride's gonna come. Oh, oh, are we gonna fly down in the easy chair!"

Yes, yes, he's being—well, *trying really, really* hard to be!—'whimsical' and 'playful' here.

Vacuous claptrap. Give it up, Bob.

★

Mentioning "Mr Tambourine Man" has a nice melody gets to the heart of one of Bob's actual strengths, however. Using the basic arsenal of those 40 or so chords to which most of us in rock, folk, and country are effectively limited due to a lack of musical education, he gets some good range and variation in his tunes. He's not a great musician, and he's certainly not an adroit instrumentalist, so there's a ceiling to what he can accomplish. But within those confines he sometimes does a creditable job of legitimate melody making. One wonders what he might accomplish were he a trained musician, because there's some capability—some talent—evinced in that side of his songs. Compare his tunes to those of another songwriter who's been similarly popularly admired primarily for his lyrics, Leonard Cohen, and Dylan's songs are much the superior melodic accomplishment—even if we exclude all the many, many melodies he's outright stolen. Let's not overstate Bob's tunesmithing abilities—he ain't no Burt Bacharach—but we shall give credit where it's due.

And one advantage afforded Dylan's recordings is that he can get the eager participation of just about any instrumentalists he desires. Some absolutely first-rate players are heard throughout his recorded and live concert presentations. (In Chapter Fifty-Four, we'll look at the role of instrumental virtuosity as a contributing factor in presenting a song.)

As noted at the beginning of this chapter, Dylan has also had a major, positive influence on one especially notable aspect of songwriting. Because of his celebrity early-on, his songwriting efforts that extended well beyond radio-friendly 'three-minute songs' *got* airplay—and encouraged similar efforts. The structures were invariably quite simple (see a further discussion of structure in Chapter Fifty-Six), but the songs could, and often did, plow inexorably onward—and they got played. Add the pervasive drug culture of the time, and his light but lengthy efforts were well-suited. (Surely other influences which equally functioned to free songwriting from time constraints were extended instrumental breaks [also a by-product of drug culture?] and a society-wide simple desire for all-around 'more' than was found in late-50s and early 60s popular music. We briefly looked at this in Chapter 17.)

I think it's also fair to agree, once one dispenses with all the utterly ignorant hero-worship, that he's occasionally come up with some pleasant, amusing divertissements. Nothing of lasting literary or musical standing, perhaps, but entertaining journeyman stuff. To my mind, for instance, "Lily, Rosemary and the Jack of Hearts", with its string of fun clichés and tropes from film and TV Westerns, is likable. It's no "El Paso", but it generally entertains. And "Tangled Up in Blue", from the same album, is a clumsy but amiable account of a picaresque romance. The earlier "Desolation Row" perhaps reminds of a lesser "Hotel California" — like that far and away much better-written song it's a generally intriguing enigmatic narrative with illusory signposts along the way.[117] You really have to be indulgent to stay with the twitching gimmickry, but if you've smoked a lot of dope it can be engaging. (But then, come on. Marijuana helps *all* Bob Dylan songs — they should perhaps make it a mandatory precondition to any close listening.)

Dylan is at his best when he doesn't try to obfuscate his natural shallowness and clear intellectual limitations by piling on the verbose vapidities and non sequitur pseudo-profundities.

But unfortunately, the majority of his stuff is of the "Quinn the Eskimo", "You Ain't Goin' Nowhere", and "Tombstone Blues" variety — undexterous confusions, sometimes hyped as light and clever to mask the actual paucity of coherence and depth. But logorrhea doesn't necessarily deliver expansion; and volubility doesn't bequeath finesse. And so in their final effect his efforts are not all that different from the most basic '50s doo-wop song or children's song, in which many of the actual sounds are just that: sounds only; non-lexical vocables; "Wham-bam-shang-a-lang", "Da doo ron ron", "Hi-ho, the derry-o!", "Polly wolly doodle all the day".

It really doesn't matter what Dylan is purportedly saying, the lack of clarity and direction is typically terminal, and so the words naturally devolve into a kinda shallow, gelatinous audial mish-mash, much like those nonsense doo-wop and nursery song lyrics. Listening can be like settling into a warm bath, or going for a distracted ride in the country—it provides a pleasant, occasionally jaunty background track. Hip Muzak. There's no ultimate material difference between song lyrics that require a full-scale disembowelment and Frankensteinian reassembly—or a kilo of good dope—to 'make sense', and those simple children's songs. In both cases, the lyrics are placeholders, really—effectively *instrumental* rather than vocal, gliding and punctuating as opposed to communicating.

In a song using actual language, however, the words *are* real, of course—they obviously have individual meaning. And in a Dylan song, each line or few lines may at least scan, as a single statement or packet. It's when taken as a whole that the unmoored confusion and the 'macro-blather' in Dylan's efforts becomes apparent. We generally do indeed go nowhere. His 'Poetic Lyrics' simply evince crippling inconsonance between the micro—the wayward phrase or odd locution that makes passable idiosyncratic sense or simply entertains due to its eccentricity—and the aggregate. Note this is *not* like what one encounters in the occasional rich blues song, packed with too many powerful but entirely disconnected ideas—because the ideas in a Dylan song are usually *insubstantial*, indicative, half-baked, and without resolution other than in the most one-dimensional and pedestrian expression. The 'thinking' is negligible.[118] Of the several of his lyrical phrases sometimes found quoted elsewhere, for instance, is there even one providing actual insight into life and the workings of the world? "You don't need a weatherman to know which way the wind blows" is perhaps his best known line, and it's really just a banality; a fair example of the overall dearth of depth.

And that overall lightness—a consistent melodic but soporific breeziness in most of Dylan's songs, whether performed by him or others—helps make them such a safe choice for folks like those in my friend's band who need a song to fill out an album or a set list. The material is pretty much all critically canonized, fortunately (well, in fact, <u>un</u>fortunately); the songwriter is a fanzine celebrity; and the stolen and original tunes are sometimes attractive—so hey, who cares if the largely nonsense lyrics tumble by inconsequentially? Folks are singing along, unthinking, so fine. These are really just puffed up pop ditties; songs not requiring (nor helped by) studious attention—nor by attempts to invest authority in performance. In fact, that's when the pronounced deficiencies in the

writing become most awkwardly prominent. There's not much more trying than watching a capable singer mentally wrestling to wedge significance and authority into a slight, muddled Dylan concoction.

★

We're going to devote the next chapter to one specific lesser-known
Dylan song, as a kinda summary exemplification of the flustered cluelessness. But first, let's end this section with a quick digression and a
laugh—waddaya say? A little from Bob's Broadway musical, *The Times
They Are A-Changin'*: (YouTube title search: <u>Craig Ferguson Dylan Musi-
cal</u>) <u>https://www.youtube.com/watch?v=4Uq6RIsB0Hs</u>.[119]

[104]<u>https://en.wikipedia.org/wiki/Edward_Bulwer-Lytton</u> (web search terms: <u>Bulwer-
Lytton Wiki</u>) And in all fairness, Bulwer-Lytton really wasn't a bad writer at all.

[105]H.W. Watrous, in *Modern French Masters*, ed. John Van Dyke (London, 1896), 93

[106]<u>http://www.nobelprize.org/mediaplayer/index.php?id=2631</u> (YouTube title search:
<u>Sara Danius – interview – Nobel Prize</u>.)

[107]Even though the incident recounted here doesn't appear in the book, I highly recommend Van Ronk's autobiography, *The Mayor of MacDougal Street*, co-written with
Elijah Wald—a well-written, light-hearted, but incisive inside look at the 1960s
Greenwich Village folk scene. And while we're mentioning co-author Wald's work, two
other welcome and well-written books by him that are similarly meritorious are *How
the Beatles Destroyed Rock and Roll* (a somewhat overly provocative title, surely, but a
thoroughly excellent and enlightening history of American popular song) and *Escaping
the Delta: Robert Johnson and the Invention of the Blues*. All intelligent, informative,
worthwhile.

[108]"Hurricane", copyright 1975 by Bob Dylan and Jacques Levy. Quoted here as permitted within the Fair Use provisions of 17 U.S.C.§107.

[109]"Masters of War", copyright 1963 by Bob Dylan. Quoted here as permitted within
the Fair Use provisions of 17 U.S.C.§107.

[110]"A Hard Rain's A-Gonna Fall", copyright 1962 by Bob Dylan. Quoted here as permitted within the Fair Use provisions of 17 U.S.C.§107.

[111]"Mr. Tambourine Man", copyright 1965 by Bob Dylan. Quoted here as permitted
within the Fair Use provisions of 17 U.S.C.§107.

[112]The actual 'Mr Tambourine Man' was a guitar player named Bruce Langhorne, a
very nice fellow who died in early 2017, and spent his last many years in a pretty
house near Venice Beach in Los Angeles. He played guitar on some of Dylan's early
albums (and albums by other Greenwich Village folkies of the time), owned a large
Turkish tambourine-like instrument, and was Bob's marijuana connection during the
recording sessions. Langhorne was a singular fellow and all, and so fine; but no one
should care about all the solipsistic 'validating' information—the *song* is of a piece,
shouldn't require an appendix, and remains trivial with or without one.

[113]"Subterranean Homesick Blues", copyright 1965 by Bob Dylan. Quoted here as
permitted within the Fair Use provisions of 17 U.S.C.§107.

[114]"Lay Lady Lay", copyright 1969 by Bob Dylan. Quoted here as permitted within the Fair Use provisions of 17 U.S.C.§107.

[115]"The Times They Are A-Changin'", copyright 1963 by Bob Dylan. Quoted here as permitted within the Fair Use provisions of 17 U.S.C.§107.

[116]"You Ain't Goin' Nowhere", copyright 1967 by Bob Dylan. Quoted here as permitted within the Fair Use provisions of 17 U.S.C.§107.

[117]I promised in an earlier chapter to later extol the virtues of a song by the Eagles, despite the fact that they're surely one of the most vacuous and smugly manufactured acts in recent decades. "Hotel California" is that song. I could live a full, happy life never again hearing this incessantly, intrusively, obnoxiously overplayed record even once. But all my general distaste for the Eagles aside, I must accept that "Hotel California", written by Don Felder, Don Henley, and Glenn Frey, is first-rate work, both musically and lyrically. (And so, once again 'no', unfortunately, to those looking for easy pigeon-hole answers; life ain't all just black and white, good and bad.)

[118]There's just not enough time here to go through more of Dylan's stumblings, but if a reader is interested in a 'homework assignment', I suggest researching the actualities that Dylan glosses over, gets ignorantly wrong, or completely outright misses in "The Lonesome Death of Hattie Carroll", a song that's often pointed to, sadly, as one of his best. A helpful correspondent (who insists, fearing she'd have to 'fight off an eruption of inflamed Dylanoids', that I keep her name anonymous) sent me a penetrating analysis of it. The essay's too long to append here, unfortunately, but check out the song and the legitimate history yourself. I expect you may come to agree it's in fact yet another depressingly missed opportunity; another of Bob's bungles. (The villain in the song was most certainly that, but the facts are much larger, richer, than Dylan's sophomoric paint-by-numbers personality clash; more provocative and culturally damning.)

Or, concerning "Hurricane", research the facts of Ruben Carter's conviction—and re-conviction—for murdering three people. Shades of O.J. Simpson, with Dylan the buffoonish, dimwit apologist. Work like his over-zealous cluelessness here does a *disservice* to the nobility of progressive aspirations for racial equity and justice.

One who might aver these songs are 'artfully fabular', or similar—necessarily simplified to gain currency—is deluding himself or herself about both the results and Dylan's constrained abilities. These are flailing pop songs, *preempting* the important—and more captivating—larger issues. Larger issues that lend themselves to *actual* poetic writing, by the way, as opposed to Dylan's pedestrian recitations.

[119]For all those innocent darlings who demand, with fiercest indignation, "How could *anyone* dare think Bob's timeless brilliance is appropriate for dumbing down into a Broadway show!", it was reportedly Dylan himself who initiated and pushed 2006's gargantuan *The Times They Are A-Changin'* Broadway musical. He chose and ardently courted director/choreographer Twyla Tharpe, signed away the 'grand rights' (the necessary dramatic performing rights), and eagerly participated in hyping the excruciating extravaganza. It was his baby. Here's the whole number that was excerpted for the clip above: https://www.youtube.com/watch?v=-93Ck62tsGQ (YouTube title search: "Bob Dylan - The Musical"—with those quotation marks.)

Chapter Forty-Four

Shallowness, Thy Name Is Bob

*Success consists of going from failure to failure without
loss of enthusiasm.* — Winston Churchill

Though the overall sound of Dylan's recordings can be a pleasant background track, as noted, I find myself just exasperated by the relentlessly half-assed thinking and second-rate lyrics. So I don't ordinarily spend much time listening to his songs or reading about him.

Yet some significant research in that neighborhood was obviously required while I prepared this manifesto. And while doing so I was introduced to a song of his with which I wasn't previously familiar, entitled "Clothes Line Saga", originally called "Answer to 'Ode'". It was written as a 'response to', an 'homage to', or a 'parody of'—take your pick at this point—Bobbie Gentry's song, "Ode to Billie Joe".

What's interesting about "Clothes Line Saga" is just how incredibly, unbelievably inferior the writing is compared to the Bobbie Gentry song it supposedly parodies—or possibly attempts to mimic, essentially in tribute. The fact that critics and Dylanoids apparently even debate whether he was parodying or paying respects to "Ode to Billie Joe" inadvertently addresses yet *another* substantiation of Bob's ineptitude: often no one can at all discern for certain if he's trying to be funny or serious—there's nothing sly going on; he's simply that inarticulate, impotent. (Yet even when it's absolutely obvious that humor *is* in fact Dylan's objective, he invariably fails—we'll briefly look at his inability to write comedy in Chapter Forty-Five.)

Though Southern Gothic is not a literary genre that appeals to me personally, Bobbie Gentry's "Ode to Billie Joe" is without any doubt a stunningly successful piece from that school of storytelling; carefully, cleverly, and evocatively constructed and written. Everything in it works near-perfectly.

Dylan's creation is hack garbage—hack garbage with a big smarmy smirk on its face. And let's be clear: this *isn't* a situation in which something is 'transcendently clever' due to it *pretending* to be hack work. No, this is the real thing. The fact shallow Bob evidently thought himself capable of lampooning "Ode to Billie Joe"—or creating work of similar ethos and commensurate quality, if one wishes to assert that was his woefully unskilled aim—but ends up falling so blatantly and completely flat on his face makes the entire fiasco ever more insufferable and revealing.

Bobbie Gentry beautifully incorporates believable quotidian mundanities throughout her song, as a literary device lightly obscuring the profound confessional that's the heart of the piece—critical, pivotal facts of which she tantalizingly and skillfully never fully reveals. And, *most* substantively, to brilliantly capture the oblivious but entirely innocent self-absorption that permeates most human preoccupation and behavior.

Bungling Bob writes *only* lumbering mundanities, unfunny and unbelievable, adds in what he vaingloriously thinks is his 'killer line' about a Vice-President, and smugly presumes himself quite the clever boy—*completely* missing the point. He literally does not get what's going on. And in the end, his song is proved to be a joke—yes, he's trying to parody. But the 'joke' here is lightweight Dylan and his hubris.

So could one parody—capably parody—"Ode to Billie Joe"? Sure. The core of the story, of the song, is the uncertain twisted tale of the singer and Billie Joe MacAllister. And so the talented parodist would surely exploit that to entertainingly absurd dimensions. It's what the song is *about*. Our canny parodist might artfully insert a trivial non sequitur here and there, just as we think we may be unraveling the ever more convoluted tale—to thwart that unraveling—before galloping off to reveal more layers to the onion, more red herrings and dead ends in the evolving and ever more unbelievable tall tale.

Dylan, however, seems to think that manufacturing *any* ostensibly 'powerful event' for the center of his strutting fabrications—his idiotic one line "the Vice President's gone mad" interjection—suffices, because he doesn't understand that the day-to-day humdrum conversations he's talentlessly trying to mock are *secondary*. Making fun of those literary peripheries misses the point entirely.

Sheer incompetence.

There's not time here for me to do a deeper side-by-side analyses of the two songs, but for anyone still unconvinced of busy Bob's utterly impoverished abilities, I urge you to compare them on your own. When the gulf between brilliance and incompetence is this cavernous, it won't take long—Dylan's work is just *that incredibly bad.*

"Ode to Billie Joe":

It was the third of June, another sleepy, dusty Delta day.
I was out choppin' cotton, and my brother was balin' hay.
And at dinner time we stopped and walked back to the house to eat;
And Mama hollered out the back door, "Y'all remember to wipe your feet."
And then she said, "I got some news this mornin' from Choctaw Ridge:
Today, Billy Joe MacAllister jumped off the Tallahatchie Bridge."

And Papa said to Mama, as he passed around the blackeyed peas,
"Well, Billy Joe never had a lick of sense; pass the biscuits, please.
There's five more acres in the lower forty I've got to plow."
And Mama said it was shame about Billy Joe, anyhow.
Seems like nothin' ever comes to no good up on Choctaw Ridge;
And now Billy Joe MacAllister's jumped off the Tallahatchie Bridge.

And Brother said he recollected when he, and Tom, and Billie Joe
Put a frog down my back at the Carroll County picture show.
And wasn't I talkin' to him after church last Sunday night?
"I'll have another piece-a apple pie. You know, it don't seem right.
I saw him at the sawmill yesterday on Choctaw Ridge;
And now ya tell me Billie Joe's jumped off the Tallahatchie Bridge."

Mama said to me, "Child, what's happened to your appetite?
I've been cookin' all morning, and you haven't touched a single bite...
That nice young preacher, Brother Taylor, dropped by today;
Said he'd be pleased to have dinner on Sunday. Oh, by the way
He said he saw a girl that looked a lot like you up on Choctaw Ridge;
And she and Billy Joe was throwing somethin' off the Tallahatchie Bridge."

A year has come and gone since we heard the news 'bout Billy Joe.
And Brother married Becky Thompson; they bought a store in Tupelo.
There was a virus going 'round; papa caught it, and he died last spring;
And now Mama doesn't seem to want to do much of anything.
And me, I spend a lot of time pickin' flowers up on Choctaw Ridge,
And drop them into the muddy water off the Tallahatchie Bridge.[120]

"Clothes Line Saga":

After a while we took in the clothes;
Nobody said very much.
Just some old wild shirts and a couple pairs of pants
Which nobody really wanted to touch.
Mama come in and picked up a book
An' Papa asked her what it was.
Someone else asked, "What do you care?"
Papa said, "Well, just because."
Then they started to take back their clothes,
Hang 'em on the line.
It was January the thirtieth
And everybody was feelin' fine.

The next day everybody got up
Seein' if the clothes were dry.

The dogs were barking, a neighbor passed.
Mama, of course, she said, "Hi!"
"Have you heard the news?" he said, with a grin.
"The Vice-President's gone mad!"
"Where?" "Downtown." "When?" "Last night."
"Hmm, say, that's too bad!"
"Well, there's nothin' we can do about it," said the neighbor.
"It's just somethin' we're gonna have to forget."
"Yes, I guess so," said Ma
Then she asked me if the clothes was still wet.

I reached up, touched my shirt,
And the neighbor said, "Are those clothes yours?"
I said, "Some of 'em, not all of 'em."
He said, "Ya always help out around here with the chores?"
I said, "Sometime, not all the time."
Then my neighbor, he blew his nose,
Just as Papa yelled outside,
"Mama wants you t' come back in the house and bring them clothes."
Well, I just do what I'm told.
So, I did it, of course.
I went back in the house and Mama met me;
And then I shut all the doors.[121]

[120]"Ode to Billie Joe", copyright 1967 by Bobbie Gentry. Quoted here as permitted within the Fair Use provisions of 17 U.S.C.§107.
[121]"Clothes Line Saga", copyright 1967 by Bob Dylan. Quoted here as permitted within the Fair Use provisions of 17 U.S.C.§107.

Chapter Forty-Five

Dying is Easy, Comedy is Hard

There's nothing more difficult to do than comedy. — Robert Evans

I fart in your general direction. — Graham Chapman

I think this chapter fits naturally after our overall look at Dylan's work, because after an introductory consideration on the global difficulty of writing comedy, we'll briefly address Bob's own record of failure in the form despite his repeated attempts. And later, we'll focus in on some aspects of writing comedic songs generally.

★

It seems that comedy is *always* disparaged as a lesser accomplishment in writing—by everyone but actual writers, that is, who *know* how hard it is to create and craft something that gets an honest laugh.[122] On the other hand, there are great writers who've never written or even attempted Comedic Word One—so not having delivered real comedy can't be a definitive criterion upon which to deny this or that writer's acumen.

Dylan *is* one who's attempted to write comedy, however, but his bids have never risen above being—at the very most—just somewhat amusing. "Talkin' John Birch Paranoid Blues" and the rest of his several talkin' blues efforts, "Leopard-Skin Pill-Box Hat", "Bob Dylan's 115th Dream", "Po' Boy"—none of them elicits more than an occasional anemic smile. And, as just noted, that he so regularly, determinedly *tries* to be funny—and falls so far short—is significant; it hammers yet another nail into the coffin of that ridiculous, cringe-inducing fanboy idiotism, "The greatest living user of the English language".

We should go on a moment here to observe further that Dylan's 'humor'—if it can even be called that—is often really of the vituperative and vindictive variety. There's a whole lot of repulsive venom mixed with a whole lot of snide misogyny throughout his œuvre.

"Idiot Wind", "Like a Rolling Stone", "Leopard-Skin Pill-Box Hat", "Positively 4th Street"—the list of songs heavy on spite, retribution, and unbridled enmity is long. This alone is also not a definitive indictment of the writing—of the *execution* of all that malevolence; we've dealt with that consistent general ineptitude in previous chapters—but certainly of intent and direction. There's nothing uplifting in his unrelenting harangues—and there's no humor with which to lighten all the bitterness and resentments, *especially* in those tirades directed toward women. (Earlier we noted that Dylan's total contempt for ethical restraint resembles Donald Trump's. Add his noxious disdain for women, and the similarities between the two grow even more unfortunate.) Sneering sarcasm? Yes. Self-deprecating or affectionate levity? No. Hundreds of songs written; but to my knowledge not one engineering a genuine, intelligent laugh—and so many simply engorged with grudges, attempted smartypants denunciations, and outright ugly malice.

But strictly on the matter of actual comedy, my heart goes out to him: he sure keeps on pounding away. Perhaps one day he'll succeed, and finally earn that elusive honest, intelligent laugh.

Hey, it could happen.

★

Music and comedy are so linked. The rhythm of comedy is connected to the rhythm of music. They're both about creating tension and knowing when to let it go. I'm always surprised when someone funny isn't musical or someone musical isn't funny. — Conan O'Brien

Writing *about* comedy—well, writing coherently and insightfully about comedy, I mean—is nearly as difficult as writing comedy itself.

From Aristotle to Sigmund Freud to Lenny Bruce, great minds have tried to figure out what the hell it is that makes someone laugh.

Nevertheless, there are some aspects of comedy songwriting we can examine here; and some examples we may take as lessons, both positive and negative.

First off, one 'general rule' in a comedy song—and I mean a song that potentially delivers actual out-loud laughs—is that perfect rhymes (and generally, perfect meter) are the goal. I myself can't think of a single truly effective—guffaw-inducing—funny song that doesn't overwhelmingly rely on perfect rhyme; and if anyone reading this can, please email with that counter-example, for my edification.[123] Not to be too facile about it, but I think it's very much part of 'hitting the laugh squarely': providing both a) a fitting but unexpected resolution to preceding information, which is obviously the objective in *any* effort at humor, and b) a strong secondary surprise, because even though listeners are expecting a rhyme, the one we give them is totally unexpected—and so together doubling the enjoyment and laughter. Since we're using perfect rhymes, there's a very limited number of words—or even fanciful 'word manufactures' if we're going the Ogden Nash route[124]—that can fit. Listeners are already attempting to figure out the puzzle before the punchline rhyme arrives—they *cannot help* but be unconsciously trying to do so. And if they haven't inferred it yet—correctly deduced it before they hear it supplied by us, the songwriters—we win, earning a bigger laugh.

Another consideration of a comedy song—and one which should be obvious, but is, surprisingly, regularly neglected—is that a real joke only comes along once. Because a chorus is heard more than once in a song, if the greatest laugh is supplied there, it will be run into the ground upon repeated hearing. But even if a laugh in the chorus isn't the biggest in the song, the chorus should generally still be massaged—evolve, diverge, in its successive iterations—so the information there doesn't grow stale.

There's also the well-known Rule of Three—essentially, stacking a composition so that the strongest point, or in this case the biggest laugh, comes last, and after the 'general frame' has been properly set up.

A brilliant example of how to deal with a comedy song on pretty much all these points is Steve Sondheim's "I Never Do Anything Twice":

When I was young and simple—
I don't recall the date—
I met a handsome captain of the guard.
He visited my chambers one evening rather late,
In tandem with a husky Saint Bernard.
At first I was astonished,
And tears came to my eyes.

But, later when I asked him to resume,
He said, to my surprise,
"My dear, it isn't wise.
Where love is concerned one must freshen the bloom."

chorus 1:

"Once, yes, once for a lark.
Twice, though, loses the spark.
One must never deny it,
But after you try it you vary the diet."
Said my handsome young guard.
"Yes, I know, but it's hard.
But no matter how nice,
I never do anything twice."
La la da da de-ah da dum….

I think about the baron
Who came at my command,
And proffered me a riding crop and chains.
The evening that we shared
Was meticulously planned;
He took the most extraordinary pains.
He trembled with excitement;
His cheeks were quite aglow;
And afterword he cried to me, "Encore!"
He pleaded with me so to have another go;
I murmured caressingly, "Whatever for?"

chorus 2:

Once, yes, once for a lark.
Twice, though, loses the spark.
Once, yes, once is delicious;
But twice would be vicious—
Or just repetitious.
Someone's bound to be scarred.
Yes, I know that it's hard.
But, no matter the price,

I never do anything twice.
La la la la la la la la la la....

And then there was the abbot
Who worshipped at my feet;
Who dressed me in a wimple and in veils.
He made a proposition which
I found rather sweet—
And handed me a hammer and some nails.
In time we lay contented,
And he began again,
By fingering the beads around our waists.
I whispered to him then,
"We'll have to say amen."
For I had developed more catholic tastes.

chorus 3:
   Once, yes, once for a lark.
   Twice, though, loses the spark.
   As I said to the abbot
   "I'll get in the habit, but not in the...habit.
   You've my highest regard,
   And I know that it's hard.
   Still, no matter the price,
   I'd never do anything twice."

chorus 4:
   Once, yes, once can be nice;
   Love requires some spice.
   If you've something in view
   Or something to do, totally new,
   I'll be there in a trice.
   But I never do anything twice.
   Except—
   No, I never do anything twice![125]

If sung by a performer who can act, the laughs here begin almost from the get-go, with the second line.[126] Each of the three verses ups the comedy. And the only repeated parts of the chorus, aside from the title line itself, are the very quick "Once, yes, once for a lark / Twice, though, loses the spark," and the "Yes, I know that it's hard" — a double-entendre that's not even pushed. Everything else in each of the four runs through that chorus is entirely new information, shepherding our interest and eliciting yet more laughs. This is dazzling songwriting.[127] (Sondheim's musical setting is a perfect complement to the splendid writing, by the way. He may not have that elusive Gift For Melody — see Chapter Forty-Eight — but he is a capable, effective composer.)

One aspect of comedy songs *so* obvious and *so* easily resolved I almost roll my eyes at the necessity of addressing it concerns titling — and mis-titling. The slight but delightful "Thank God and Greyhound" (written by Larry Kingston and Earl Nix) gave the entire joke away in the song title. "Dance: Ten; Looks: Three" (Ed Kleban and Marvin Hamlisch), from the musical *A Chorus Line,* famously thudded by with nary a chuckle during preview performances — until the creative participants realized the reason for the leaden reception was that the original title, "Tits and Ass", (the recurring jocular exclamation in the lyrics) appeared right there in the printed program's song list, giving away the entire surprise before the evening even began! A simple title change turned it from show-filler into show-stopper.

A recurrent 'killer line' will certainly *still* be the 'title' used in colloquial discussions about a comedy song — no way around that. In every case where a calculatedly obfuscating Official Title *is* used, however, it's one small step in the right direction achieved by the songwriters. Obtusely broadcasting the punchline to everyone *before the joke is even introduced*, on the other hand, kinda doesn't make a whole lot of sense.

A song like, say, the Shel Silverstein penned "A Boy Named Sue" is a somewhat different animal, insofar as the title here, while obviously the crux of the story, isn't the killer laugh line in the song, but rather the device around which to hang the singer's predicament. As much fun and as entertaining as it is, this song is really more a shaggy dog story or moral fable than an outright comedy song — as is another song that's similarly conceived: Arlo Guthrie's "Alice's Restaurant".

★

Any fool with steady hands and a working set of lungs can build up a house of cards and then blow it down—but it takes a genius to make people laugh. — Stephen King

Summary question: So does a comedy song—a song intended to elicit real laughter—require adherence to the same various directions and proscriptions derived from the lessons learned in other songs we've looked at earlier?

Absolutely. In fact, how these insights all pertain to so-called 'lighter material' is that if the intent is to provoke actual laughter, then the words and arrangement of words surely require even *greater* precision and elegance, comedy being perhaps more than any other assignment of language the most dependent upon rock-solid construction and execution for effectiveness. There's no real win in a listener afterwards commenting—half-heartedly, with a forced smile—"I get what he was trying to say, and it was kinda funny."....

[122]Similarly, in just about *every* other creative exercise—from painting to dance to composing music to simple public speaking (aka stand-up comedy)—creating a presentation that gets an honest laugh is invariably recognized by actual practitioners as an exceedingly difficult challenge, and generally as *the* most satisfying accomplishment if achieved.

[123]Michael@MichaelKoppy.com

[124]Example:"Who wants my jellyfish? / I'm not sellyfish!" Or perhaps think of lyricist Yip Harburg's great use of the technique in songs he created with composer Harold Arlen for *The Wizard of Oz*.

[125]"I Never Do Anything Twice", copyright 1976 by Stephen Sondheim. Quoted here as permitted within the Fair Use provisions of 17 U.S.C.§107.

[126]I recommend a rendition done by Lara Bruckmann: https://www.youtube.com/watch?v=4mf33Lcle1A (YouTube title search: Lara Bruckmann sings "I Never Do Anything Twice"). Too many very good singers simply aren't good actors; and a song like this, so loaded with great lines, is cheated by an inferior performance.

[127]Probably the weakest manufacture here is the "fingering the beads around our waists" phrase—while it's certainly workable, it's contrived, drawing some unwanted attention to itself in the moment. And, indeed, the songwriter's eventually obvious objective here was to somehow set up the great capping line, "For I had developed more catholic tastes", a good solid laugh. (But with all the other rhymes available I wonder if this was the best that could have been achieved. Some attractive alternatives to 'waists' include chaste [or unchaste], haste, disgraced, debased, raced, erased. Sondheim, however, is a rigid traditionalist who works only in strictly perfect rhymes, and none of these choices easily becomes a plural by adding that necessary-for-a-*perfect*-rhyme 's'. Obviating that craft reservation, however—and so working for the

rhymes just offered—might have led to the final word used as a singular: "catholic taste". While the usual formulation of the phrase 'catholic tastes' is in the plural, it's arguable whether using it in the singular here would be a noticeable divergence. Yes? No? Far too much analysis for such a minor consideration?....

Well these, ladies and gentlemen, are the kinds of questions with which a true master, as Sondheim most certainly is, regularly wrestles.)

Chapter Forty-Six

If Ya Wanna Send A Message[128]....

When you cry "Forward!" you should without fail make plain what direction to go. — Anton Chekhov

I don't want to spend a lot of time here, but a quick look into songs that attempt to be anthems—songs that aspire to be political or socio-cultural proclamations—might be worthwhile.

The insight we'll derive is that there is, occasionally, a construction—and anthems are one such—in which lack of specificity can be a defensible attribute. As with any other objective, it's the *execution* of the idea that accredits authority.

★

Woody Guthrie wrote "This Land is Your Land" in 1940 as a direct response to Irving Berlin's 1938 "God Bless America", which he thought pretentiously jingoistic—perhaps especially as performed by the song's first prominent purveyor, the often bombastic Kate Smith. Unfortunately, Guthrie's effort is much the inferior to Berlin's. And I say 'unfortunately' because Guthrie's impetus and world view are so much more informed and intelligently progressive than Berlin's guileless and—well, yes, jingo-istic—boosterism.

A song that is *meant* to be a large and general exaltation, a feat to which an 'anthem' most certainly aspires, may quickly diminish by limi-tations imposed by mention of specifics. In the Guthrie, we get, almost right off the bat, "California", "New York island", "redwood forests" (read: California once again) and "Gulfstream waters". The last is the on-ly of the four that doesn't apply solely to one very small part of the wide country Guthrie wishes to address. What, ain't nothin' going on in Mon-tana? Ohio? The Appalachians lack anything to extoll? The Great Plains?

Berlin's much more expansive, *inclusive* generalized descriptions—"the mountains", "the prairies", "the oceans"—leave hardly any region unmentioned. (Well, maybe the lowlands and swamps of my native Gulf Coast Deep South, but the fact that no other actual *specifics* are noted—California, New York, etc—would tend to mitigate such reservations, as Berlin has certainly checked off most of the countryside in his lyrics.) He's also traversed the topography in logical sequence: highlands, flatlands, seaboard edges. Guthrie hops back and forth from coast to coast—and, critically, kinda innocently ignores everything in between, what's since been often pejoratively called 'flyover country'. Berlin's effort is simply much stronger—again, more inclusive via its *lack* of specificities.

What also makes "God Bless America" work far better as an anthem, frankly, is Berlin's great, rousing melody. I mean, WOW. Can anyone *not* be moved to de facto martial conceit experiencing that tune married to those lyrics? (We'll deal with the strictly musical side of songwriting later, in Part Four.) While I'm no big fan of writing that submits to "God", the pantheistic tenor of Berlin's title line, within the context of something that is frankly equally as specious and manufactured—an implied cohesive and lock-stepped national identity—seems entirely consonant. It's a great piece of work.

★

A quick glance at a few other would-be anthems may be instructive before we move on.

"We Shall Overcome", mentioned earlier, is another anthem that traffics in large generalities—even more amorphously than does the Berlin.[129] And its continued application as a political motivating and organizing tool, world-wide, speaks volumes. The Library of Congress labels it "the most powerful song of the 20th century".[130]

Dylan's superficial and leaden "The Times They Are A-Changin'", as also noted earlier, is more a disengaged shoulder shrug than something of substance. Nothing is proposed, and nothing is asserted other than muddled complaints, all capped with a *Reader's Digest* Faux-folk triviality. An awkward and dated artifact; nothing more.

John Lennon and Yoko Ono's "Give Peace a Chance" is mostly a disposable nonsense chant rather than a considered song—except for the elegantly simple and repetitively effective chorus. There's not really much going on in the verses that's worth dissecting—and it's also a dated artifact—but there *is* obviously an emphatically clear and idealistic, albeit self-aware and assertively unsophisticated, political point of view in evidence:

We don't care what makes 'expected sense'—give peace a chance.

★

The last 'would-be anthem' we'll look at here doesn't further ratify points made above, but I feel compelled to address it because it's such an unfortunate and warped failure—derived from such an outstanding inciting conception: Mick Jagger and Keith Richard's "Salt of the Earth".

Let's drink to the hard working people.
Let's drink to the lowly of birth.
Raise your glass to the good and the evil;
Let's drink to the salt of the earth.

Say a prayer for the common foot soldier;
Spare a thought for his back breaking work.
Say a prayer for his wife and his children,
Who burn the fires and who still till the earth.

chorus:
And when I search a faceless crowd;
A swirling mass of gray and
Black and white.
They don't look real to me;
In fact, they look so strange.

Raise your glass to the hard working people,
Let's drink to the uncounted heads.
Let's think of the wavering millions
Who need leaders but get gamblers instead.

Spare a thought for the stay-at-home voter.
His empty eyes gaze at strange beauty shows,
And a parade of the gray suited grafters;
A choice of cancer or polio.

chorus repeat[131].......—

This is a song idea with genuine promise…that devolves into a big stinkeroo. What a wonderful, smart idea from which to begin, though. 'Let's stand back a moment, appreciate fully what we behold—the great struggling masses of all we brothers and sisters—and proudly toast the so often overlooked, disparaged, or outright dismissed.' Great! I love this—wish I'd thought of that inspirational opening resolution and its implicit repetitive trajectory myself. But to lessen the potential distancing, I'd suggest eliminating the definite article 'the' from the first line.

However, lyricist Jagger—who frequently lards an initial intriguing idea with tripe, not really going anywhere—nowhere evinces that tendency to greater liability than here in "Salt of the Earth". What begins as a salute to—even a sanctification of—working class scruples and endurance becomes, instead, Jagger's apparent elitist consternation that such people even inhabit His World. We end, really, with nothing less than Lordly Disdain. As early as the very line, "Let's drink to the lowly of birth", there's an implicit (if not yet explicit) patronization connoted. (You've just separated yourself from those about whom you write, Mick—from 'them'—so this can be justifiably understood to be your judgment, not something fraternally descriptive.) Okay, perhaps an arguably captious and picayune objection so early on, I'll grant; yet the unavoidably clear divorce from identification and solidarity—along with the writer's barely disguised actual disgust—grows to truly colossal dimensions as the writing extends.

Just look again at those lyrics above, and especially that chorus.

What a depressing coöptation of what could have been a grand proclamation of pride, admiration and support. There's a reason one never hears the song within a political context—it's a jumbled monstrosity, really; sneering and scornful. From such a beautiful and empowering initial idea—such an inspired introductory laudation. Had Jagger continued the simple litany of admirable working class traits and accomplishments, adding in a proud and confident chorus affirming the eventual ascendance of working people and democratic values in the history-long war against oligarchy and greed, this could have grown into a majestic acclamation. Sadly, it's a missed opportunity—and a literal mess.

[128]"If you wanna send a message, use Western Union!" is a line credited, probably apocryphally, to film producer Samuel Goldwyn. No, Sam, if you wanna send a message, just do it adroitly. To quote someone on the other end of the political spectrum from Goldwyn, with a statement complementary to mine just made, here's Mao Zedong: "Works of art which lack artistic quality have no force, however progressive they are politically."

[129]This song has such a long and disputed history that for our purposes here it may be best to simply credit the writing to the four persons named on the 1960 copyright, Zilphia Horton, Guy Carawan, Frank Hamilton, and Pete Seeger, even though they carefully credited the work as an 'arrangement' of an earlier song, the authors of which were unknown to them. In 2012, Seeger—then newly familiar with Louise Shropshire's 1942 song, "If My Jesus Wills", (copyrighted in 1954) and it's obvious closeness to "We Shall Overcome"—stated she should also be credited.

The history of "We Shall Overcome", actual and surmised, is fascinating but outside the scope of what we're engaged in here—except to note that it's another example of the *real* folk process.

[130]http://www.loc.gov/teachers/lyrical/songs/overcome.html. (web search terms: Powerful Song Library Congress)

[131]"Salt of the Earth", copyright 1968 by Mick Jagger and Keith Richards. Quoted here as permitted within the Fair Use provisions of 17 U.S.C.§107.

Chapter Forty-Seven

A Songwriting Class—Taught by Professor Frank Sinatra, Doctor Elvis Presley, and Professor Marvin Gaye, with Star Student Paul McCartney

*"It's the latest popular song," declared the
phonograph, speaking in a sulky tone of voice.
"A popular song?"
"Yes. One that the feeble-minded can remember the words of and
those ignorant of music can whistle or sing. That makes a popular
song popular, and the time is coming when it will take
the place of all other songs."* — L. Frank Baum[132]

As we prepare to conclude Part Three (Lyrics), and segue into the briefer Part Four (Music and Production), two songs by Paul McCartney come to mind that in a simple, almost textbook manner may help to summarize.

There's debate within music circles about what song is the most successful in history—'most successful' being variously defined. If simple number of performances is the standard, the consensus Number One is "Happy Birthday to You", by Patty and Mildred Hill. Other contenders for 'most successful song in history' include "White Christmas" by Irving Berlin, and either "Auld Lang Syne" by Robert Burns with a traditional melody, and "For He's a Jolly Good Fellow", authors unknown. I myself remember a long time ago reading that the most successful song, monetarily—the song that had produced the most money in royalties—was

"You Are My Sunshine" by Jimmy Davis and Charles Mitchell. So who really knows? But if limited to songs from the last half-century, the general agreement is that the most successful popular song of the period—certainly the most-covered song of the period—is "Yesterday" by Paul McCartney, with upwards of two thousand recorded versions.

McCartney reported in an interview that he had once, from simple curiosity, listened sequentially to several cover versions of "Yesterday", just to enjoy the variety of performances of the song.[133] While doing so, he was surprised to discover that in renditions by three of his personal idols, Frank Sinatra, Marvin Gaye, and Elvis Presley, all three of them had changed the lyrics in the chorus, and all in the exact same manner.

Here is that chorus, as originally written by McCartney and performed by the Beatles:

Why she had to go
I don't know, she wouldn't say.
I said something wrong;
Now I long for yesterday.[134]

And as changed by Sinatra, Gaye, and Presley, with their addition underlined:

Why she had to go
I don't know, she wouldn't say.
I must have said something wrong;
Now I long for yesterday.[134]

In the interview it seemed to amuse but elude him why all three would make the alteration.

But the fact is the chorus actually doesn't hold together as written. You don't know why she "had to go", Paul, immediately followed by the unqualified assertion that you "said something wrong"? So then, you *do* know why she had to go—why did you just say you didn't? It makes no sense. His three heroes all recognized the lyrical lapse and tried to correct for it, each arriving at the same formulation to do so: "I must have said"—as opposed to McCartney's "I said". The alteration displays an uncertainty that allows the preceding "I don't know" to play believably. You absolutely don't know, but you *guess or presume* it was specifically something you may've said—as opposed to the current you absolutely *don't* know what caused the rift, but you absolutely *do* know.

Interesting, further, is to note that Sinatra's, Gaye's, and Presley's interpolation actually burdens the melody with two additional syllables that have to be squeezed into the reading—it's not at all as elegant a fit as McCartney's original. But these three performers, consummate singers all, felt the trade-off was more than necessary for them to convey an authoritative, believable rendition of the otherwise great song. The lyrics really *had* to be pounded around a bit to make the lines sensibly cohere.

And this, folks, is about as good an illustration—as good a capsule lesson—as we may find of what makes and doesn't make great songwriting.

The now well-known story of McCartney's original 'scratch' lyrics also offers us something to briefly consider. After the tune itself came to him—reportedly while he was in bed, half-asleep, and which he sang into a tape recorder he kept on a bedside table—he used a nonsense line, "Scrambled eggs, oh my darling how I love your legs", as a place holder for a few weeks, until he could come up with something he thought worthy of the strikingly original melody.

But 'scrambled eggs' actually does work—if one's willing to settle for an execution from the School of Poetic Lyrics. Hey, why not? I'm quite serious. The words sit perfectly on the melody line, and the nonsense of "scrambled eggs" *is* followed by the clearly communicated thinking of "oh my darling how I love your legs". And so how, in fact, is that materially different from any number of idiotically clunking Dylan lines praised as 'actual poetry'? I'm sure if we sit with it for a few minutes we can even 'interpret' all kinds of deep meanings from "scrambled eggs".

But let's step away for a minute to ponder the lyrics (and title) that McCartney did come up with and kept. Here's John Lennon's thoughts:

> *The lyrics to "Yesterday" don't resolve to any real sense. They're good lines—they certainly work—but if you read the whole song, they don't say anything. You don't know what happens. She left and he wishes it were yesterday—that much you get, but it doesn't really resolve.* [135]

Allowing for professional jealousy—as noted, "Yesterday" is by far the most covered Beatles song, and it is solely by McCartney—Lennon still does make a valid point.[136] The song is at most a lament and nothing more. But I think the merit in Lennon's discountenance is far outweighed by the beauty and depth of what is simply a paean to lost love, the lost love that was here but yesterday. Just the *title*, the opening word immediately followed by that brilliant strategic pause—an implied sigh, really—says everything we need to hear to ease us into the heart of the song.

★

In Chapter Eighteen, we took apart a song by McCartney that was on a much lower level of accomplishment than "Yesterday", his "And I Love Her". The lyrics to that song are, to be blunt, just plain bad.

But two and possibly three or even four aspects of the song do elevate it, somewhat—or at least merit attention. And as we're about to move on to musical matters, this is perhaps a good place to begin addressing how melody and production can ameliorate, even obscure, mediocrity.

Lead guitarist George Harrison's elegantly uncomplicated, disciplined, and repetitive four-note riff in "And I Love Her" is one of those occasional appurtenances—supporting musical flourishes—that immediately becomes embedded in the fabric of a song, a riff as integral to it as are any of the lyrics themselves. Encountering a rendition that abandoned that riff would strike one as odd or even bereft. It doesn't make the lyrics any less dumb, but it does slightly draw our attention elsewhere, away from them.

McCartney's simple and effective melody and the chords he uses to arrange it are—as with so many McCartney compositions—quite different from the obvious and predictable. And again, lightening the load of the burdensome writing.

And the final chord in "And I Love Her" is so unexpected that it alone is a noteworthy diversion and elevation from the norm.[137] I wonder if it was McCartney or Harrison—or was it maybe producer George Martin—who came up with it. Someone else?

The key change half-way through, while not at all an unusual development, also possibly deserves mention.

This is all wonderful stuff—there's really nothing second-rate or haphazard about it. But I think few can argue that those slogging and utterly artless lyrics—which are really the pretext *for* the melody, arrangement, orchestration, and performances, no?—are simply insipid. These lyrics do not even deserve hearing—much less being carried by an appealing tune and performances.

[132]*The Patchwork Girl of Oz*, published 1913.

[133]Onstage interview and discussion with Billy Collins; Rollins College, 10/23/2014.

[134]"Yesterday", copyright 1965 by John Lennon and Paul McCartney. Quoted here as permitted within the Fair Use provisions of 17 U.S.C.§107.

[135]*Playboy*, "Playboy Interview", September, 1980.

[136]"Yesterday" was a 100% McCartney written and composed song. But it is always legally credited to "John Lennon and Paul McCartney", as it is in the above foot-note—a fact that understandably continues to somewhat irk McCartney decades on.

[137]Rather than resolve on the expected tonic chord, in this case an F, it ends on a D, which is distinctively unusual and—in this situation—emotionally uplifting. Lennon and McCartney—the latter especially—regularly ventured forth with musical ideas wholly foreign to expected popular song composition at the time.

Songwriting Kit

PART FOUR: Music & Production
— PUTTING LIPSTICK ON A PIG <u>AND</u> ON A GAZELLE —

Chapter Forty-Eight

Steve Sondheim Jealously— Desperately!—Wishes He Were Right...But He's Wrong

It would be nice to accidentally overhear someone whistle something of mine, somewhere, just once. — Leonard Bernstein[138]

Time now to talk about the role of music and melody—and we'll go to Broadway and the West End for an initial insight.

The two most successful musical theater composers of recent decades, undeniably, are Stephen Sondheim, winner of the 'critics darling' sweepstakes, and Andrew Lloyd Webber, winner of the 'money in the bank' competition.[139] It's often remarked that while Lloyd Webber would surely kill to gain favor with the intelligentsia, Sondheim would surely do the same to get just one big hit song.

But when Sondheim lectures on songwriting—something he's done often during his career—one of the points he regularly makes is that *anyone* can create a memorable melody.[140]

How? By simply repeating it often enough.

There is some obvious truth in the statement, of course. Play something often enough, and people will certainly be more likely to remember it. (And as Lloyd Webber's scores do return to and reprise his themes with regularity, Sondheim's pronouncement is also, of course, a sly dig at those who, like Lloyd Webber, have achieved much wider commercial success.[141] The implication, apparently, is that if Sondheim himself were inclined to similarly reprise his themes with more regularity and prominence, he'd also have oodles of pop hits.)

But surprisingly, given his acute authority on songwriting, he ignores even mentioning (in his talks that I've heard, anyway) the actual mysterious power that a great melody has and delivers to a finished song.

Just because a musical passage is reprised, it does not at all follow that the melody must therefore innately be of lesser impact or beauty. After all, I note that while I've surely heard Sondheim's biggest 'hit', "Send in the Clowns", hundreds and *hundreds* of times over the years—which means that melody is pretty danged familiar(!)—on any given day I'm still *far* more likely to inadvertently have any of more than a dozen Lloyd Webber tunes sneak unconsciously onto my mental play list. "Don't Cry for Me Argentina", "Love Changes Everything", "I Don't Know How to Love Him", "Memory", "Another Suitcase in Another Hall", "Music of the Night", "Tell Me on a Sunday", the list goes on—and this despite the fact that lyrically, most (but definitely not all) are beneath the level of accomplishment evinced in Sondheim's better efforts.

Andrew Lloyd Webber—like lucky others in a very diverse universe, including, to greater or lesser acumen, Benny Andersson & Björn Ulvæus, David Bowie, Paul McCartney, Willie Nelson, Barry Manilow, Ric Ocasek, Brian Wilson, Jim Steinman, whoever were/are the primary composers in the Sex Pistols (presumably Glen Matlock?), and Green Day (Billie Joe Armstrong?)—was endowed with a Gift For Melody; and I put the term in majuscule advisedly. Stephen Sondheim has composed some unquestionably excellent music, and he's a peerless lyricist, but to his everlasting disappointment he wasn't awarded that Gift For Melody.

Yes, it's as simple—and as mysterious—as that. It can be a test having to acknowledge great melodies that have come from creators—acts and composers—we may personally find unbearable on most other fronts, but the gift is awarded indiscriminately.

★

One might infer the above is an argument for the primacy of melody in songwriting, but that's incorrect, and it misses the point entirely. Without melody—without the wings provided by music—lyrics can quickly lose much of their presumed superficial seductive authority.

But as we'll see in following chapters, when weighed by an intelligent audience, music is, in fact, properly subordinate.

★

Melody is god's voice. It's clothed by lyrics but melody is god's voice.
— Quincy Jones[142]

The above assertion from Mr Jones is obviously an unequivocal argument that music most certainly *is* primary. But, to reiterate the point just made, I believe he confuses what's the most *important* part of a great song with what is the most *powerful* part of a great song. And they are not the same thing.

[138] I don't think Lenny got out enough. I find many of his tunes—from *West Side Story* and *Candide* especially—delightfully memorable.

[139] Stephen Sondheim: *A Funny Thing Happened on the Way to the Forum, Into the Woods, Sweeney Todd, Company, Sunday in the Park With George, Merrily We Roll Along, Passion, A Little Night Music.* Andrew Lloyd Webber: *Jesus Christ Superstar, Evita, Cats, Starlight Express, Phantom of the Opera, Aspects of Love, Sunset Boulevard, The Woman in White.*

[140] Sondheim has also written two outstanding books that brilliantly dissect and analyze his own work and work by other lyricists: *Look, I Made a Hat: Collected Lyrics (1981–2011) with Attendant Comments, Amplifications, Dogmas, Harangues, Digressions, Anecdotes and Miscellany* and *Finishing the Hat: Collected Lyrics (1954–1981) with Attendant Comments, Principles, Heresies, Grudges, Whines and Anecdotes.* Both are highly recommended.

[141] Lloyd Webber's 'borrowings' from works by other composers notwithstanding, the melodic gift evinced in his entirely original compositions should be beyond dispute.

[142] *The National,* CBC News, 9/17/2018, interviewed by Ian Hanomansing.

Chapter Forty-Nine

Didn't I Just Hear That Song in a Commercial for Paper Towels? Life Insurance? Chewing Gum?

The song is ended, but the melody lingers on. — Irving Berlin

L et me ask the question from the other side. If music—especially melody—is the most important component in a song, with lyrics being secondary, why then aren't we all merrily strolling down the street belting out advertising jingles?

Once again, decouple yourself from extraneous considerations. Because—like it or not; and all effort to maintain 'cool' put aside—there's no doubt that inventive and affecting tunes *are* regularly composed for radio and TV commercials.

So what then, if anything, is ultimately the difference between a catchy commercial and a catchy but vacuous pop song? It's certainly nothing to do with the music.

I think one can register a definitive answer, however.

What stands in highest relief in a commercial jingle is the name of the company or product being pushed—that's obviously The Whole Idea. But few people would wish to be overheard singing the praises of Burger King, Chevy Trucks, or State Farm Insurance, whether doing so consciously or unconsciously. It'd be just a tad too boorish for even the crassest vulgarian.

It's this ultimate 'line in the sand' which well-illustrates that even the most appealing melody won't relegate what's being sung to irrelevance. There *is* a bottom line—a base level of fatuousness, of cynicism in what's being delivered in language—that we just won't allow ourselves to cross.

Good for that, I guess.

Yet, sadly, the mass of us has been conditioned to parrot, applaud—BUY—just about *any* nonsense above that line, no matter how embarrassingly incompetent, inarticulate, morally corrupt, or just plain stupid.

★

Selling out is usually more a matter of buying in. — Bill Watterson

If we go a step further, to separate out ad jingles with lyrics that mention the product being hawked—so leaving just jingles with vapid lyrics written to paint a bland serviceable background for promoting the product *without* blasting it—the difference between that latter kind of commercial jingle and run-of-the-mill pop song vacuities that folks might be heard singing or whistling on the street becomes more ambiguous.

Indeed, there's at least one ad jingle that 'crossed over' to become a major commercial hit pop song, many years back.

That was the song fragment created in 1970 solely to glorify a now-defunct California bank in a saccharine TV ad campaign. (It was subsequently rented out to other banks across the country for copy-cat regional campaigns, and used again as a commercial theme as recently as 2016, for Lowe's Building Supplies.)

The idea was that young marrieds beginning life together needed this whimsically warm and just plain wonderful bank to guide them and help them along. (Yeah, right.) On contract from the ad agency, songwriters Roger Nichols and Paul Williams composed a tune and wrote a couple of mushy verses to be heard behind various clips of a dreamy, soft-focus couple on their wedding day. And that was presumed to be the end of it.

But later, expanded, and recorded by The Carpenters (and so promoted commensurate with that act's then major weight in the music industry)—abetted as well, certainly, by the ubiquitous television commercials—the now full-fledged song became a hit. Titled "We've Only Just Begun", it did at least contain a recognizably resonant theme, albeit one streaked with pie-eyed superficiality. The song was number one on the *Billboard* charts for six weeks, Grammy-nominated for song of the year, put on *Rolling Stone's* "500 All-Time Greatest Songs" list, and etcetera.

Repeating: it was a TV commercial, folks. The line between hack sales-craft and hack songwriting isn't all that distinct after all.

★

You do a commercial, you're off the artistic roll call forever.
End of story—you're just another corporate fuckin' shill;
another whore at the capitalist gangbang. — Bill Hicks

Aside: Discussions of commercial jingles—and of popular songs used 'as is' in commercials—are generally focused on whether the songwriters and the act have Sold Out, lost whatever presumed authenticity (read 'anti-establishment cred') they may have carefully nurtured. There's a lot of money to be had, after all, if one wishes to finally cash in a purported reputation for independence acquired during an industrially successful career—be that reputation actual or (as in the great majority of cases) just hype. "We've established what you are, now we're just haggling over price", goes the old punch line. So it's certainly affirming to see Adele, the late Tom Petty, Neil Young, and a few others build so-far impenetrable walls between their songs and the always ready onslaught of lucrative commercial financial offers awaiting should they waiver. (Of course one need keep in mind that established stars are, naturally, invariably quite well-off. Still, there should be no debate that self-respect is too easily jettisoned within the maelstrom of capitalist enticement—if it was ever really there to begin with—and so hats off to those who set boundaries they actually won't cross.)

On the other hand, and as we witness every day, there are the acts crassly calculating from the actual get-go, cynically drooling over the possibility of 'branding' and selling their reputations, name, work—hell, mothers, if they can get a price—in any way, to any taker, for any purpose, anywhere.

★

But the above ponderings wander away from what we're focused on here: the strictly melodic side of songs heard in a commercial context.

And so to repeat—like it or not—some of the most memorable melodies of recent decades were created for TV and radio commercials. And while a big reason for that memorability is simple repetitive overexposure within massively expensive advertising campaigns, that's not the whole story. A good melody is a good melody—no matter whence it derives nor how it's deployed.

To dismiss or disparage a tune because it was created specifically to serve a commercial purpose is assertive foolishness—as is subordinating appreciation for a melody to one's like or dislike of the act or songwrit-er(s) who composed it and/or performed it.

Yet, yes, we do need to draw that line in the sand. The regular failure to do so is yet another unfortunate effect of post-modernist dissolution, annoyingly disguised as 'open-mindedness', or 'hip irony'.

It's neither.

And that line in the sand itself? It needs to be drawn more promi-nently, as well as higher up on the side of the dune.

Chapter Fifty

Should We Use a Number 37-A? Or a Number 37-B?

There are so many different kinds of stupidity, but cleverness is one of the worst. — Thomas Mann

A couple of personal real world instructional experiences come to mind as we move on:

I recall many years ago, working as a stagehand on a big Broadway-bound show—a show that was a mess, really; just an ego trip for the star and pretty forgettable. The specific incident that comes to mind was listening to the director, choreographer, lighting designer, and star go on for too long, debating the color of just one of the hundreds of lights in the production. "Should we use a 37-A pink gel or a 37-B pink gel?" The actual numbers of the color gels (tinted plastic sheets inserted in a holder attached to front of the lights themselves) are lost in memory, naturally, and the difference between the two colors was effectively imperceptible. But the seriousness of their debate remains. Don't misunderstand, there was no animosity or 'power-jockeying' in evidence; each professional was in good spirits and simply trying to contribute his and her best. And a great finished artistic creation most certainly *does* require attention to the smallest details.

But given the dreary show itself, and the massive amount of money already invested in it, I was tempted to stroll over, lightly tap one of 'em on the shoulder, and patiently explain—patiently but *firmly* explain: "HOLD ON. THAT'S <u>NOT</u> A PROBLEM. BUT IF YOU REALLY WANNA <u>SAVE</u> THIS CRIPPLED TURKEY, CLOSE IT DOWN AND REWRITE THE DUMB SCRIPT!"

And as you might expect, the show eventually did die on the road, long before ever seeing New York City in a far off wintery distance.

I occasionally think back to that 'life lesson' when pondering a particularly barren, but very professionally produced, popular song.

★

A complementary message comes from time doing blue-collar work in the in Hollywood studios. While, again, it's important to do professional quality work, a bottom-line resolution sometimes shared among co-workers goes basically like this: "Look, we'll do the best we can with what we have to work with. But in the end, if *anyone* notices that wall over there is tilted an eighth of an inch—or the color of the dress the actor is wearing now varies slightly from the one worn two scenes ago…there are BIG script problems with this show—and actors who can't ACT!"

In contemporary entertainment, the effort put into 'polishing the turd', 're-arranging deck chairs on the *Titanic*', 'putting lipstick on a pig'—pick your cliché—is regularly *far* out of proportion to the quality of what's being actually delivered to the audience.

★

All the musical and technical expertise and experience in the world *isn't* going to make a poorly written song any less stupid. But, no question, it *will* make a stupid song sound professional.

So hold on, what do *you* think? Should we use the 37-A pink gel, or the 37-B? Take all the time you need. It's so gosh-darn important.

Chapter Fifty-One

On Brightly Wrapped Packages

It is a tale told by an idiot, full of sound and fury, signifying nothing.
— William Shakespeare

There's a story, perhaps apocryphal, concerning the song "Moon River", by Henry Mancini and Johnny Mercer, to lead us into this section.

The wives of both men were reportedly seated together at a party one time, when another guest, upon being introduced to them, instantly and visibly brightened. To Mancini's wife, the guest raved, "Oh, your husband wrote 'Moon River'!" But before Ms Mancini could reply, Mercer's wife swiftly interjected, "No, no, no. Henry Mancini wrote, 'daaa, da, daa, da, da, da, da, daaa...' MY husband, Johnny Mercer, wrote 'Moon River'!"

There's a whole lot of important perspective wrapped up in that anecdote.

Even if a melody comes first and even if it's a truly glorious composition, once intelligible words are added they automatically become the primary partner in the combination, in the song.

The task of melody, of music, in a song with words is to support and enhance the lyrics—that is, again, especially *if the lyrics pretend to be of any actual significance.* If not—if the lyrics are just goofiness, or 'another layer of sound'—then, as we've noted earlier, the offhand argument might be made that music is actually more important. And it may also be advanced concerning agreeable trifles like, say, "Blue Suede Shoes" or "Here Comes the Sun".

But in fact even *that* argument falls flat on its face in the real world. Were it the case, vocalists wouldn't play the predominant role they do, 'fronting' just about every popular music act that has a singer—even when the lyrics are the most inane drivel or downright gibberish. The lead vocalist's *actual* forte may be as an instrumentalist—or he or she may be the weakest player in the ensemble—but if that person is also tasked with presenting the lyrics; he or she is, ipso facto, 'first among equals' to the audience. And, of course, this is because we human beings seek the direct communication that language provides. We may intuit our way through the peripherals—the music, lights, the act's mannerisms and affectations—and may find a plausible (read: personal) meaningful message therein, but we seek *confirmation* of that intuition through language, in the lyrics.

As put quite simply by storied lyricist Yip Harburg, "Music makes you feel. Words make you think. A song makes you feel a thought." But a casual inversion of that dictum—so "A song makes you think a feeling"—doesn't quite correspond.

It is a suggested motivating idea—as generally straight up indicated by the title, and then authenticated and amplified in the lyrics—that is served by the musical composition and production. Not the reverse.

Music allows lyrics to breathe; it can ingratiate them, and it may drive them as far as they can go dramatically. Music serves the lyrics—and it can do them a wonderful, powerful service, no doubt.

As we've established, however, without a capably expounded idea behind it the song is at best only a twisted folie à deux between songwriter and audience. That sometimes a great melody is saddled with lyrics that are outright abominable or downright incompetent is a particularly unfortunate fact of recent and contemporary popular song—it's the legacy bestowed by the sanctification of Poetic Lyrics and its allied affliction, the School of Not Giving A Damn. Just about *any* individual assertion of what's being delivered for our consideration, if not entirely (or even remotely) defensible, is granted public concession. Why? "Because, hell, it's got a really nice tune and we'd like to *enjoy* the danged thing without looking like complete idiots! Hey, work with us here! So let's agree that if even if this song really doesn't make any sense, that it's got—uh, er, um…a 'feeling'? Okay? Come on! Please?"

No, let's not agree to that. Because *that* is what makes us look like complete, gullible idiots.

In the contemporary culture, for a serious song to 'succeed' when the lyrics are plain stupid, the music (and after the music, the vocal and instrumental performances, and/or technical effects—and/or yes, by cascading defaults eventually devolving to just the posturing, hype, and marketing) *must* step forward to assume center stage in selling the whole package. As with "And I Love Her" or any number of similar other supposedly 'great songs', a handful of which have been looked at here, if we're going to enjoy the finished creation, we're effectively directed to *ignore* the primary raison d'être of the whole enterprise—what the song actually says—to concentrate on supporting aspects and elements.

And the number one major supporting element, obviously, is melody—the music (including arrangement, orchestration, and production).

Chapter Fifty-Two

A Blindingly Beautiful Gilded Frame Ain't No Masterpiece Painting

It's just loops, beats, rhymes and hooks...There ain't no fucking song!
The song is the power; the singer is the messenger. But the greatest sing-
er in the world cannot save a bad song. I learned that 50 years ago, and
it's the single greatest lesson I ever learned as a producer. If you don't
have a great song, it doesn't matter what else you put around it.
— Quincy Jones[143]

A nd so this is the point, production in the recording studio, where manufacturing ostinati[144] and 'hooks' becomes a primary, last-ditch task—creating musical ear worms so the song, no matter how commonplace and simplistic, becomes recognized, known, and yes, commercially 'satisfying'. This even if *both* the lyrics *and* the melody are effectively foolishness. Everyone's tried to create hooks all along, but this is the last chance to put some more in.

In Chapter Nineteen, I noted the primary difference between a song and a live performance of it is that the performance allows an act to deflect attention away from lesser songwriting through a variety of diversions—but that second-rate lyrics obviously remain *in* the actual song.

Attempts to deflect attention away from deficient writing and composing can be obtained in the recording studio as well, of course—often using many of the same diversions and evasions, along with additional avenues built into the recording process. The recording studio also allows the inclusion of whatever further musical or technical ideas can be conjured to create hooks—those catchy little audio identifiers that embed themselves in the listener's hearing and make the recording of the song 'catchy'—as noted, additional to what may've been already designed and obtained in the songwriting itself.

It's very much akin to building a memorable, occasionally even stunningly gorgeous, frame—to go around a garage-sale, paint-by-numbers 'artwork'. Current adepts—the Max Martins, Dr Lukes, et al—have this down to predictable boring rote, and it's why so many current popular songs actually *do* all sound sonically and structurally similar, be they pop, rock, country, or hip-hop. The same hack devices—for example, the so-called 'millennial whoop'[145], an insufferably bombastic over-the-top chorus, or a short rap (or 'rap-ish') section shoe-horned into a rock, pop, or even a country song—appear over and over. And over.

★

There are, of course, inherent tendencies to repetition in music itself. Our poetry, our ballads, our songs are full of repetition; nursery rhymes and the little chants and songs we use to teach young children have choruses and refrains.
We are attracted to repetition, even as adults; we want the stimulus and the reward again and again, and in music we get it. Perhaps, therefore, we should not be surprised, should not complain, if the balance sometimes shifts too far and our musical sensitivity becomes a vulnerability. — Oliver Sacks

Of course hard rock songs have long heavily relied on endlessly repeated 'signature riffs', usually though not necessarily played by electric guitar. Many (most?) hard rock songs actually *begin* gestation with a riff. That riff—and possibly the recurrently sung title line of the song—then goes on to be banged and bleated out at drunken fraternity parties and Guitar Center showrooms forever after.[146]

All too often abetting the degradation of the definition of the word 'song' (and a primary reason it really *is* just a riff and a title line—again, this especially in hard rock efforts) are *utterly* unintelligible lyrics. It's simply hard to sing or evaluate words that one just can *not*, after any number of studious listens, comprehend. ALL we're 'given' is a brick wall of incomprehensible uproar. Catchy cacophony. Amusing noise—

with what the songwriters (and the marketers) pray to God we think might be a coherent thought inside. And as noted earlier, if we don't really care what the song is about or what actual words are being sung—but are easily swept up in the manufactured excitement and innocently trust the lyrics actually do say something—we are *exactly* the audience for which the music industry (and its wannabe adherents in indie-land) zealously lusts.

So okay, now a test. We've heard it a million times, so we know all the words by heart, right? READY? Everyone sing together! "SMELLS LIKE TEEN SPIRIT"! ONE, TWO, THREE, FOUR!—

Cut to befuddled silence....

[143]Vulture.com, 2/7/2018, "In Conversation: Quincy Jones", interviewed by David Marchese: http://www.vulture.com/2018/02/quincy-jones-in-conversation.html (web search terms: Conversation Quincy Jones)

[144]Repetitive musical phrases; guitar riffs obviously being one of the most common.

[145]A short prominent 'warbling' between the third and fifth of a chord, in recent years found ubiquitously manifest in radio-friendly pop songs. Its best-known appearance is probably in the song "California Gurls", by Katy Perry, Lukasz Gottwald (aka Dr Luke), Max Martin, Bonnie McKee, and Calvin Broadus (aka Snoop Dogg).

[146]"Satisfaction", anyone? "Seven Nation Army"? "Smoke on the Water"?

Chapter Fifty-Three

Making Sausages

The tune had been haunting London for weeks past. It was one of countless similar songs published for the benefit of the proles by a subsection of the Music Department. The words of these songs were composed without any human intervention whatsoever on an instrument known as a Versificator. But the woman sang so tunefully as to turn the dreadful rubbish into an almost pleasant sound.
— George Orwell[147]

But just as with all other peripheral trappings, the production of a recording has *nothing*, obviously, to do with the actual accomplishments or deficiencies in the writing. Music and production are there to serve the idea of the song—an idea we hope has been developed into an intellectually and emotionally satisfying whole. Because the present cultural epoch exalts incoherence and encourages self-absorption, however, it's rare to find such authority in a popular song.

Successful popular songs, today, really *are* formulaic—we're back to songs like those largely hollow efforts of the 1950s. Songs utterly reliant, ultimately, on incorporating the most calculated and occasionally electronically sophisticated superficial gimmicks—in service of the most conservative hack formulae.[148] With lyrics that are getting even dumber each passing year.[149] Technically well-produced vacancies; marketed with relentless, merciless pretense.

Things which matter most must never be at the mercy of things which matter least. — Johann Wolfgang von Goethe

There's no reason to go on at more length here, but a fairly good look at much of current state-of-the-art pop music artifice and contrivance—and the desultory cynical smarminess of it all—is provided in John Seabrook's well-written but somewhat star-struck survey, *The Song Machine: Inside the Hit Factory*. While he finds it all rather mesmerizing (and, hey, in a morbid 'staring-at-a-horrible-traffic-accident' way, it kinda is), a step back allows one to jettison wide-eyed awe and see the ultimately depressing and lowest-common-denominator sweat-shop machinery for what it actually is.

Because all that stuff 'creates' is just a cheesy frame and an empty shipping crate—stamped with an ominously looming sell-by date.

[147] *Nineteen Eighty-Four*, published 1949.

[148] *Scientific Reports*, 7/26/2012, "Measuring the Evolution of Contemporary Western Popular Music" by Joan Serrà, Álvaro Corral, Marián Boguñá, Martín Haro and Josep Ll. Arcos, Spanish National Research Council. https://www.nature.com/articles/srep00521 (web search terms: Measuring Evolution Western Popular Music)

[149] "Lyric Intelligence In Popular Music: A Ten Year Analysis", 5/18/2015, by Andrew Powell-Morse. https://realestgeek.blogspot.com/2017/06/lyric-intelligence-in-popular-music-ten.html (web search terms: Lyric Intelligence Realest Geek)

Chapter Fifty-Four

Making Music

Writing music is not so much inspiration as it is hard work.
— George Gershwin

It's not really necessary that a song have a great melody for it to be significant. Though there's certainly nothing really objectionable in any of them, some (though definitely not all) of the songs forwarded in previous chapters as first-rate work might be said to be musically predictable—even musically <u>un</u>interesting, frankly.

But the addition of an affecting melody to stimulating lyrics is obviously The Gold Standard. It's why Berlin's "God Bless America" soars and why "Yesterday" captivates. A great and fitting melody adds immeasurable color and depth to quality lyrics, sweeping us along and directing our attention to the better nuances of what's being presented.

And, as we've noted earlier, a great tune *can* obviate—or better, at least mitigate—antipathy for poorly-written lyrics, just as a great performance can lift a mediocre song to temporally marginal stature. In each event, what's actually being augmented or even ennobled is the presumed intent of the song—the idea, as generally encapsulated in the title.

But it all begins with that idea, and how elegantly it has—or has not—been amplified in the lyrics.

Yes, in the end, it almost always comes down to what's being said. And when a musically engaging song is larded with bad writing, the embarrassment factor eventually enters into conscious cultural deliberations, and the song may remain in the canon being performed more commonly as primarily an instrumental (with perhaps just the chorus or the 'least objectionable verse', sung as a kinda inconsequential throw-away or introduction). This is arguably what's happened to "Alabama Jubilee", a

1915 song by George Cobb and Jack Yellen; one of the last popularly successful songs written in the black-face minstrel tradition. It's become a standard in the bluegrass music repertoire, but one rarely ever hears more than just one verse of the lyrics, because in this particular case it's now viewed as a racist relic. Yet the same holds true for lots of other older songs that don't have such obvious baggage but that are simply trite ditties—and I expect a similar fate awaits many acclaimed songs of more recent vintage, given the often particularly less than stellar writing.

★

> *To work the brain without sufficient material is like racing an engine while standing still.* — Arthur Conan Doyle

Musical erudition—a good education in the literal language and syntax of the trade—can be a great help in composing a tune, because many available options are easier to find if one knows where to look. But honestly, it's not really necessary. So many great melodies in popular song have been composed by musical illiterates. The gifted Paul McCartney— he of "Eleanor Rigby", "Yesterday", "Michelle", and "Penny Lane"—can't read or write a note. The often great Irving Berlin composed all his songs in the key of F#—*not* because he was knowledgeable enough to think F# was a particularly wonderful key, but rather because it allowed him to use mostly the easier-to-find black keys on the piano. Perhaps needless to add, he also couldn't read or write music; and so every one of his compositions was written out by an amanuensis.

And as for instrumental mastery—all too often it's not really that but rather simply remarkable manual dexterity. A guitarist may be able to play a zillion notes a minute, cleanly, clearly, all up and down the guitar neck; but without applied taste it's really not much more than noodling. And even those instrumental masters who brilliantly know both their instrument and 'when to play and when to lay back' are not necessarily going to be capable composers. Knowing an instrument has nothing to do, really, with the ability to compose an exciting or even engaging melody.

It's also something of a sad waste to use brilliant instrumental talent in service of songs that are utterly disposable—somewhat reminiscent of what you get by engaging an exceptionally talented woodworking craftsman to put together a big room full of cheap IKEA particle-board furniture. It'll all look (in our case, sound) as good as it can, yes...for cheap IKEA particle-board furniture (or our empty-headed lyrical nonsense).

I'm regularly amused when seeing or reading something about studio musicians and their often exceptional accomplishments. In the whole article or video, there may be but one sentence, spoken in passing by one of the participants, addressing the *other* side of the song, the lyrics. But then again, that's obviously not their concern—it's not why they're gathered in the recording studio. The song will be treated to the *musical* contributions of all these individual instrumental magicians, and good for that. There is almost never any corresponding study and work done by similar 'expert committee' on the lyrics, however. The writing is either a fait accompli at that point, or, if attended to on scene at all, done so by one or at most two collaborators—and on the fly, because studio time is expensive.

And, of course, the proper time to carefully, thoughtfully attend to the writing was a long time ago. Why wasn't that done?[150]

On the other end of the proficiency spectrum, the persistent popular and critical glorification of 'garage band esthetics'—lauding instrumental roughness and sloppiness that often borders on outright incompetence—is yet another illustration of the widespread posturing that infects popular music. A classic example is the citation of the Ramones as prototypically 'simple and pure' musical unsophisticates, which is actually just plain wrong. They began that way, yes, but band leader and guitarist Johnny Ramone, in particular, had a clear understanding of what the band was about, and thoughtful mastery of his instrument within the carefully delineated direction he pursued.[151] The Ramones were *not* a musically makeshift or musically undisciplined operation. But their spawn all too often are.

On balance it's good to be dismissive, or at least skeptical, of acts that essentially boast of their lack of instrumental aptitude as validation of supposed 'authenticity'.

(And, of course, this doesn't even *begin* to address pestiferous clowns like rapper, Lil Wayne, who think simply strapping on a guitar, proudly knowing *nothing* about the instrument—and obviously neither encumbered nor embarrassed by the display of complete, laughable ignorance—makes them some kinda actual Guitar God. Utter stupidity.)

★

Melody is the essence of music. — Wolfgang Amadeus Mozart

By the way, do you think it's impossible to compose a nice melody because you 'just don't have any chops'? Maybe you don't, but so what? It's not really that hard to come up with an original tune.

Before continuing, let's be quite clear I'm *not* saying it's easy to compose a Stunningly Beautiful Melody. Just—to repeat—that it's not an insurmountable challenge to create an *original* one.

How?

Begin by playing (or maybe singing) a song you know, over and over.

Then start diverting from it, going to different notes in the chords you're playing than the ones in the extant melody. Go to entirely different chords as well here and there, so *forcing* your melody into new places. Sooner or later, with enough explorations, you'll have a melody that is so different from where you started that it *is*, indeed, no longer that tune with which you began this 'journey of discovery'. Keep on modifying and molding until you're really the only one who *can* know where it all began. It can be a slow, tedious process—lots of trial and lots of error—but at the end of the slog, you'll have a new tune. Who knows how interesting it'll actually be, but it will be original—unless, that is, you've inadvertently simply stumbled onto another, different already existing song.

Back in the day, this was a practice regularly employed by Tin Pan Alley songsmiths—they'd take the chord progression of a major hit of the era and simply go to different places with it, but in this case strictly within the confines of that progression. Remember, as we noted when discussing copyright earlier, a melody can be copyrighted but a chord progression can't.

And no, there's absolutely *nothing at all* illegitimate, unethical, or even uncreative about this process, even if it is less than virginal.

An interesting variant of the old Tin Pan Alley 're-composing' technique is 'vocalese'. Most famously, surely, is a 1952 vocalese song called "Moody's Mood for Love". Its birth was a 1949 instrumental improvisation played by jazz saxophonist James Moody of the song "I'm in the Mood for Love", music by Jimmy McHugh, lyrics by Dorothy Field. Moody simply recorded his jazz take of the song, and thought that was the end of it. But singer Eddie Jefferson later wrote lyrics that strictly conformed with Moody's new off-the-cuff melody — and the resultant effort was proffered as a new song, "Moody's Mood for Love", a pop hit for a vocalist known as King Pleasure. McHugh soon after sued, and (as I understand it) due to some *lyrical* similarities — not musical ones — he and Fields won a partial judgment.

★

A correspondent proposed to me that composing a great melody and then burdening it with incoherent or plain stupid lyrics should properly be castigated as irresponsible, even reprehensible — that songwriters owe it to themselves and the world to act with inordinate care when marrying an especially pleasing melody to lyrics. That we may all sympathize with that commandment is further testament to the power of music. But unfortunately, responsibility isn't often something to expect in the desperate-to-get-rich-quick world of popular songwriting. Both critics and audiences have been conditioned to accept banalities and even incomprehensibilities, so the desire to get that powerful melody out there — with whatever passes as 'lyrics' — will likely continue to prevail.

What a song says — the inciting idea and its explication in the lyrics — is the most important component in a song.

But music is the most powerful.

[150]We'll address a large part of that question below, in Chapter Fifty-Five.

[151]Someone questioning this is directed to *Commando: The Autobiography of Johnny Ramone;* mostly an artfully compiled and edited collection of various interviews and statements Ramone (real name: John Cummings) gave during his career. In fact, however, along with the strictly personal recollections and usual lowbrow band relationship matters such a book necessarily includes, there's plenty of solid insights on performance dynamics that any act could benefit mightily from assimilating.

The Sleep of Reason Produces Monsters
Francisco Goya

Chapter Fifty-Five

Sure, 'Authenticity' is Great— But it Certainly Doesn't Guarantee Good Work

Above all, in order to be, never try to seem. — Albert Camus

Authenticity, that most prized of character traits, isn't that rare an occurrence, even in jaded 2019. It's simply the public presentation of a person as he or she truly is, and of what he or she actually, sincerely thinks. You and I know plenty of genuinely authentic people—they're the ones we tend to trust.

Yet authenticity *is* so generally rare in entertainment and the performing arts, and *especially* in popular music—and hence the value placed on finding it therein by the public so high—that an act can pretty much get away with murder so long as it retains the public perception that it's being truly, incorruptibly 'authentic'.[152] (Maybe even *literally* 'get away with murder'—cf. Jerry Lee Lewis, Snoop Dogg.)

Neil Young, his career and œuvre, come immediately to mind in this discussion, because he's managed to build an almost irreproachable public persona as one who fiercely follows his own intensely demarcated independent, uncompromising and 'fuck what's expected of me, I'll do what I want' ethos. He might understandably be cited as a textbook version of 'authentic'—or at least as close as one might encounter in popular music and songwriting.

And that's perhaps all quite laudable. To a point.

Because being authentic is really just as irrelevant to *creating significant work* as are all the apposite affectations and impostures to which it is obviously antithetical. The sad part for Young is that the effort he regularly evinced early in his career to venture outside pop song conventions, manifested in songs like "Broken Arrow", "Expecting to Fly", and "Nowadays Clancy Can't Even Sing" — efforts that were admittedly not well wrought, yet clearly ambitious and interested in *diverging* from 'standard format and themes' — has deteriorated into contentedly parading a frenetic deluge of self-indulgencies and slovenliness. The narcissistic 'authentic' Young has become the veritable King of Vanity Projects.[153]

But if even authenticity can't be counted upon to foster good work, what *is* the overarching affliction that leads to so many canonized songs of recent years, when one takes a real hard look at them, being revealed as half-baked, directionless, and even outright nonsensical? What's the fundamental imperative? Are the songwriters stupid? Lazy? Do they just not give a damn? Why are Dylan's regularly inane inflations and Bowie's mechanical gambits, songs like McCartney's "And I Love Her" and Lennon's "Come Together", clap-trap like "The Night They Drove Old Dixie Down", and so many others of similar pedigree ultimately expendable?

Yes, yes, obviously, so much of the reason for it rests with that repugnantly déclassé compact of eager lapdog fan and imperious pop idol — and all those accessory aspects of the celebrity-industrial culture at which we determinedly chipped away back in Part One.

And yes, a pretentious low-brow actualization of literary modernism and its baser trappings may also be at work here, academically and critically 'legitimizing' assertive inarticulation and sloth.

Finally, of course — and perhaps most perniciously — the cheap and cynical marketing calculations of vulgar entertainment industry marketeers deliberately, inexorably withers the entire culture.

Yet there's more to it than even all these seminal, compounding afflictions.

★

Jack Kerouac's On The Road *was supposedly written on one continuous, hundred-and-twenty-foot scroll of typing paper—a savage and unmediated burst. In 1959, Kerouac told the talk-show host Steve Allen that it took him three weeks, although this, too, was later revealed to be an ingenious bit of self-mythologizing. (It seems nothing shatters the glamour of genius more quickly than admitting that you spend*

hours every day moving commas around, or swapping out adverbs for different adverbs.) "Kerouac cultivated this myth that he was this spontaneous prose man, and that everything that he ever put down was never changed, and that's not true", the Kerouac scholar Paul Marion told NPR, in 2007. "He was really a supreme craftsman, and devoted to writing and the writing process." The book went through many drafts between 1951 and 1957, when Viking Press finally published it.
— Amanda Petrusich[154]

No matter one's opinion of Kerouac's *On the Road*, the report above gets to the heart of one of the great irritating charades of recent times, and a primary reason for the landslide of rubble that overwhelms and chokes popular songs in critical particular. Too many songwriters and fans buy into—hook, line, and 'stinker' (so to speak)—contemporary Western culture's willfully cancerous fascination with the depiction of The Tortured Artist, Bursting at the Seams with Perfectly Preformed Brilliance.

But no, Wolfgang Mozart did *not* compose his scores as if transcribing pristine results dictated to him from on high. He created working musical sketches, with trial-and-error revisions, editing them and changing them until he was satisfied with the ultimate score.[155] And yes, Kerouac's celebrated scroll manuscript for his *On the Road* in 1951 was, in fact, the stitching together of stories he'd been writing and collecting in notebooks for at least four years prior to that famous explosion of typing—and then it all went on through countless revisions before the by-then thoroughly edited book was finally published a full six years later. And concerning his technical facility which popularly actually *obscures* the quality of his writing, he was simply a first-rate, very fast, typist.

What we might call 'spontaneous faultless creation' is, at its most excusable, just a cynically fanciful bedtime tall tale for the most cluelessly, ignorantly credulous of fans. It *rarely ever occurs* in real life.

Even without the physical proofs of various creative explorations, rough outlines, notes, discarded preliminary efforts, intermediate drafts, false starts, dead ends, notes in margins, latter emendations, and last minute excisions and/or additions, what isn't documented—what *can't* be documented—are the hours, days, weeks, and months of simple, dedicated internal debate and consideration that constitute the *heart* of a masterly creative effort: the sudden notions that arrive while cooking, in conversation, walking to the store, or preparing to sleep; the ideas both fruitful and fruitless that trickle in from the most unlikely, the most unexpected, of founts; the serendipitous solutions to problems that suddenly arrive, unexpectedly, after long periods of perplexity. And then there's all the time required after, to adjust, to polish, and to Get It Right.

Inspiration—great inspiration—is as we noted earlier, truly and almost always, ninety-nine percent perspiration.

And yet, alas, even a great torrent of perspiration assures nothing.

But it is, invariably, necessary on a journey aspiring to significance.

★

*Whoever marries the spirit of this age will find himself
a widower in the next.* — William Ralph Inge

Finding a fitting Poster Boy or Poster Girl to personify what ails recent and contemporary songwriting requires looking at statements made about the creative process itself, particularly from those practitioners most prominently churning out consistently second-rate work to general critical endorsement and public regard. And while Dylan would seem to be an obvious candidate here, his comments—at least those that I've seen—on his own songs and songwriting regularly border on the downright imbecilic (or to fawning minions, perhaps they're 'delightfully Delphic'?). There's little but calculation and deflection—entirely understandable given the irritating lack of significance and coherence in the work itself, but useless to intelligent analyses of how it gets to paper.

Neil Young, on the other hand—he of famously 'keeping it real'—offers countless candid pronouncements that help illuminate the general prevailing attitude toward the creative process in contemporary songwriting. I don't think it's necessary to examine specific songs here—too many of Young's are of the 'self-help therapy / busy-work' variety, yet more proofs that sincerity is not depth, nor even necessarily interesting.[156] The failures are of the same general ilk as in so many of the efforts by others that we've already examined.

But his statements on his working methods are both directly revealing and widely emblematic.

Let's start with this one:

If I can do it [songwriting] without thinking about it, I'm doing great...I'm waiting to see what I'm gonna do next! That should give you an idea of how much planning goes into it...It doesn't have to make sense. That's not a requirement [to me]...You can follow a thought all the way through if you happen to have one. Or if you don't, you realize it doesn't matter.[157]

The notion of the 'artist' (and I'm afraid we'll here have to use that loaded term) receiving his or her individual Creative Inspiration through some sort of extra-sensory or even divine impulse perhaps achieved full efflorescence during the Romantic epoch, but it has never subsided since—probably in large part as it's such a powerfully tempting self-benediction for the self-absorbed and self-entitled. After all, if I'm simply a 'vessel'—that Extremely Rare Gifted Vessel—through which Unique and Magnificent Creative Inspiration Flows, who the fuck are you or any-one else to criticize the obviously, *necessarily* Transcendent Ideas and Works that have been transmitted through me in those Explosive Deific Revelations?!? You are mandated to obligingly Trust In My Genius. (As noted earlier, it would be folly to deny that once in a very, very great while, simple inspiration *can* carry the day and bring forth a basically fully-formed piece of work that might be considered admirable. But it's so exceedingly rare an occurrence as to be effectively irrelevant to the discussion at hand. More on this in Chapter Fifty-Eight.)

Continuing with Mr Young:

I really hate things that people work on. There's nothing about music that should be 'worked on'.[158]

And:

Editing is no good. If you're really writing, you just write— write it down and let it come out...I don't ever go back and try to change the words to a song.[159]

This is obviously much more than complacency; it's an arrogant justi-fication for egotism—and plain old indolence—masquerading as 'keeping it real'. In Young's specific case, given the generally shambolic writing in his songs, one tends to accept his assertions on his songwriting methods as candid and sincere—charitably accept them, because one certainly hopes he's capable of better work were he to actually apply himself. He's not wholly untalented.

> *If you write a song, and you don't record it right away, then you've got to carry it around with you. Who wants to carry it around? You've got to get it out and get it down while it's fresh and brand new. So that's what I try to do...That's why as soon as I write a song I've got to record it.*[160]

So, write it down as it comes; record it (i.e., preserve it forever) immediately; then squeeze out and lay down the next steaming deposit when peristalsis again compels. Never look back. It's a procedure that obviously precludes even the *idea* of rewriting, rethinking, reflection. For a man who actually *brags* that he doesn't read[161]—i.e., is proudly, entirely closed to individual or collected thinking beyond his immediate horizons—the following quote may be a crowning indictment.

> *I just keep writing. When you start thinking...you start to go down the editing path, which I don't like.*[162]

Yes, yes, Neil, asking you for actual *thinking*—and actual *work*—would be appalling insults to your genius, wouldn't they?

While Young is refreshingly, helpfully forthcoming in his self-damning admissions—and perhaps extreme in his devotion to dereliction—his general contempt for language and application (for that's what it is) falls squarely in the mainstream. He's not alone.

Here's veteran producer Todd Rundgren on still another way we get so much piss-poor writing:

> *Too often, the band comes in and they have a song—well they've got all these great chords—and no lyrics! Somebody's gotta write some lyrics—EVENTUALLY, RIGHT?!? If no one comes up with something, they're not gonna get this record done!*[163]

As implied above, at the other end of the contemporary spectrum from Young's 'writing process', and predictably yielding similarly empty results, is plastering on any words at all—quite literally *any words at all*—as deadlines threaten, just to finish the project, to complete the 'song'.

And so, something does get written, finally—with all the attention and care one expects from work done in a panic, almost grudgingly, as a menial chore and afterthought. And, for better or worse, the *quality* of the work here ends up essentially indistinguishable from Young's efforts that he so adamantly refuses to edit and hone; in this case as there's simply no *time* to edit and hone.[164]

We've been presented time and again with stories about songs the lyrics for which were written in the recording studio at the last minute; ones that were jotted down on napkins and immediately committed, unchanged, to disc; or (occasionally) whole albums, with lyrics written in motel rooms in the days immediately prior to recording.[165] Sometimes, the product is an *intentional* (or at best negligent) display of scorn for art and craft—and as with John Lennon on his "Come Together", "I Am the Walrus", and "Hey Bulldog", the farce may even be indifferently admitted.[166] Lyrics—the communication of ideas and emotions that is the ostensible purpose for the songs constituting the whole endeavor—are effectively seen as secondary, insignificant. And so they understandably and necessarily *are* secondary, insignificant.[167]

Bob Dylan reportedly simply saves things he finds in writings by others, on slips of paper, kept in a box—to be poured out onto a table later and pasted into whatever songs he's pounding together.[168] And— surprise—there's nothing wrong with using such an approach, as a subordinate adjunct that is, if the intent is to incorporate a clearly original rewrite of an occasional passing pithy locution, or to find alternative relevant framings for an idea as a guide. (Well—as we forcefully noted earlier—as long as it's not just blanket plagiarism, and so any extended or excessive 'quotations' are properly licensed and attributed.) The Achilles' heel in this approach for Dylan, however—on the strictly creative front— is that he doesn't often evince the engineering ability, the simple 'puzzle mastery', required to capably cobble together a convincingly cohesive, intelligent whole from the disparate original and 'borrowed' locutions, descriptions, lines, and vignettes. If the listener finds something he or she thinks resonates *in the conglomeration*, it's typically imputed—Dylan's basically just throwing successive random handfuls of ever more pasta (and so much of it cooked by others) against a wall and calculating that some will stick, in lieu of systematically illuminating original thinking.

David Bowie, undoubtedly an innately intelligent fellow, unfortunately regularly followed another, similarly supercilious, misguided approach to songwriting—apparently (as readily demonstrated in the songs themselves) over-relying on the results of a random gibberish-sentence generating computer program he and a friend developed to induce or expand upon his lyric-writing whims.[169] He also routinely made use of Brian Eno and Peter Schmidt's celebrated Oblique Strategies cards.[170] A third practice he favored was Tristan Tzara's (and later William Burroughs') 'cut-ups' process.[171] The critical deficiency in *any* of these measures is that while such Dada-esque applications can be temporarily stimulating, they all-too-often lead to lyrically fatal investments in the at-best obtuseness / at-worst drivel that's sometimes quickly prompted— and Bowie's efforts regularly evinced that in spades. (Another abuser was Kurt Cobain: "My lyrics are total cut-ups. I take lines from different poems that I've written... sometimes even I can't [ultimately] come up with an idea of what the song is about."[172]) The techniques—more properly, occasionally potentially helpful exercises—can indeed serve to 'shake up' the creative mind, teasing superficial explorations that ideally whet or abet the user's intent or even directed caprice; and (one hopes) initiate or nurture the journey to the eventual creation of an assembly of cohesive lyrics. But they are not shortcuts—they do not *deliver*, nor even truly accelerate the delivery of, intelligent or even intelligible writing. They just reorder options. Using them as Bowie customarily did can beget a disorganized piling on of non sequitur after non sequitur— somewhat resembling a car plastered with a schizophrenic collection of far too many gaudy bumper stickers, a surfeit of which are simply babble. Amusing? Sporadically. Essential? Rarely.

★

Rather than risk sounding dense, readers, colleagues, and critics who can't figure out what a writer is trying to say but think it sounds intelligent will typically resort to calling such work 'daring', 'provocative', or 'complex'. An unholy alliance is at work here. — Ralph Keyes

Ultimately, we listeners doggedly, indefatigably persist in the basic human quest for connection. We grasp at anything that even *remotely* resembles valuable information, to validate our possibly even inadvertent actual precipitating investment—which was (in the *absence* of such immediately resonant intelligence) in the melody, production, performance, costuming, choreography, previous efforts by the act, its physical attractiveness, biography or biographical posturing, clothes-horsing, fan community, marketing bombast, or even meretricious tabloid hype.

But in the end as in the beginning, what we yearn for is constitutional significance. We want to recognize, learn, grow. It's why we value authenticity, believing—hoping—that we'll be rewarded with coincident original wisdom.

And whether belched up in a fashion similar to Young's, shoveled out in a deadline frenzy like dirt over a shallow battlefield grave, or peremptorily slapped together in Zen-like games of Scrabble, what in each case is so often being cynically ballyhooed for our calculated acclamation (or at least acquiescence and commercial investment) is the most hasty and haphazard fripperies—*presented to us*, however and as we've observed, as Poetic Inspirations and Divine Intercessions.

The root problem in all these 'methods of writing' is the industrial-strength blend of incompetence and egotism that's run rampant in recent decades in popular songwriting—measured to varying degrees in the products promoted, but taken together dominating the process and demeaning both practitioners and audiences.

[152]My offhand theory as to why this is so has to do with the intense, pervasive insecurity endemic in entertainment and the performing arts, where the potential rewards are so great, the possibility of public failure so high, and the competition for the tawdriest markers of 'success' so unrelenting and extreme. Publically exposing one's *lack* of knowledge—or ordinary quotidian frailties—is a luxury few can afford, as it invites peer contempt and dismissal. It takes integrity to admit ignorance and uncertainties in this most competitive of industries—to be, in other words, authentic.

[153]Someone objecting to the characterizations here is advised to slog through Young's tedious autobiography, *Waging Heavy Peace: A Hippie Dream*, or, almost as tedious, *Shakey: Neil Young's Biography*, by Jimmy McDonough, as I had to do to prepare this chapter. Or hell, more directly, go back and randomly check out stuff on the mediocre-beyond-belief majority of Young's 50+ albums.

[154]*The New Yorker*, 3/15/2018, "A Slightly Embarrassing Love for Jack Kerouac", by Amanda Petrusich: https://www.newyorker.com/culture/culture-desk/a-slightly-embarrassing-love-for-jack-kerouac (web search terms: Slightly Embarrassing Kerouac)

[155]*Mozart: A Life* by Maynard Solomon, (New York, HarperCollins, 1995), 310

[156]Disagree? Well, okay—if you insist. Let's look at Young's interminable "T-bone"—a song sung, without variation in melody, over three chords that simply repeat, repeat, repeat. But, of course, that isn't an Insurmountable Deficiency—*if* the lyrics are

worthwhile, or possibly, if breathtaking instrumental mastery is displayed. Unfortunately, on both counts, we're talking about Neil Young here. Yet he apparently feels this song needs to be 9:10 long, and that we should indulge him.

I tell ya what. Here's all ten verses; you decide:

1. **Got mashed potatoes! / Got mashed potatoes! / Got mashed potatoes! / Ain't got no T-bone! / Ain't got no T-bone!**
2. **Got mashed potatoes! / Got mashed potatoes! / Got mashed potatoes! / Got mashed potatoes! / Ain't got no T-bone!**
3. **Got mashed potatoes! / Got mashed potatoes! / Got mashed potatoes! / Ain't got no T-bone! / Ain't got no T-bone!**
4. **Got mashed potatoes! / Got mashed potatoes! / Got mashed potatoes! / Ain't got no T-bone! / Ain't got no T-bone! / T-bone.**
5. **Got mashed potatoes! / Got mashed potatoes! / Got mashed potatoes! / Ain't got no T-bone! / Ain't got no T-bone! / Ain't got no T-bone! / Ain't got no T-bone! / No T-bone!**
6. **Got mashed potatoes! / Got mashed potatoes! / Got mashed potatoes! / Ain't got no T-bone! / Ain't got no T-bone!**
7. **Ain't got no T-bone! / Ain't got no T-bone! / Ain't got no T-bone! / Ain't got no T-bone!**
8. **Ain't got no T-bone!**
9. **Got mashed potatoes! / Got mashed potatoes! / Got mashed potatoes! / Ain't got no T-bone!**
10. **Got mashed potatoes! / Got mashed potatoes! / Got mashed potatoes! / Ain't got no T-bone! / Ain't got no T-bone! / Ain't got no T-bone! / Ain't got no T-bone! / Ain't got no T-bone!**

(Gee, feelin' a lotta pressure—hope I correctly transcribed these exquisite lyrics.)

If the song was worth recording—again, those three endlessly repeating chords, the occasional guitar noodlings, those 'masterful' lyrics—and requires being over nine minutes long, proudly having his name on it, and selling it to the public, it must surely be a Significant Piece of Work.

Yes? No?

To one who might contend this is just a light-hearted 'fun song', as one of my correspondents suggested, I remind that *few* of us feel the need—or imperiously decide our audiences *want*—to hear every dimwit notion that enters our heads. (As for it being intentionally out-and-out 'funny'—another reaction I've encountered—does it take nine-plus minutes to 'get' this 'joke'? Or, alternatively, is *that* the 'humor'—that it goes on for so long? To answer both questions: no. No one really wants something the caliber of a weak knock-knock joke stretched out for more than, say, oh, 10 seconds or so—eh?)

Still not convinced of Young's bankruptcy? Then maybe take a peak at his utterly insufferable 27-½ minute long "Driftin' Back"—or the equally-disqualifying and protracted "Ramada Inn". Both watery nothings—and both also pounded away ad fuckin' nauseam. Life's too short to accommodate pointless nonsense; and Young's œuvre overflows with these onanistic exhibitions. And as an instrumentalist, he simply doesn't have the chops for long exertions—that being probably another product of his unwillingness to work and learn; or, in worst case, maybe simple innate lack of ability. Who knows?

Compare "T-bone" to another song that's also repetitious and pretty much devoid of importance—"Don't You Get It" by Mark Knopfler—and the difference in what can be accomplished *musically* with a simple song notion becomes even starker. Knopfler is a first-class player and an excellent musician, eschewing the kind of swaggering posturing that Young apparently feels is a good cover—or justification?—for his own ineptitude.

One reason the blues is a form so loved by great instrumentalists is because the blues generally allows tremendous invention and variation within a strictly confined structure. A simple song notion like Young's or Knopfler's here *can* similarly serve as a basis for engaging extended instrumental exploration—but a player without musicianship or technique is quickly exposed as ineffective, incapable of rising to the occasion. In that case what we're left with is merely droning self-indulgence, presumptuous egoism—we're left with Neil Young.

"T-bone", copyright 1981 by Neil Young. Quoted here as permitted within the Fair Use provisions of 17 U.S.C.§107.

[157] *Shakey: Neil Young's Biography* by Jimmy McDonough, (New York, Random House, 2002), 127

[158] On-stage interview and discussion with Patti Smith; Book Expo America Convention, New York City, 6/11/2011.

[159] *Performing Songwriter,* 11/12/2016, "Happy Birthday, Neil Young!", interview by Lydia Hutchinson.

[160] Ibid.

[161] *The New Yorker,* 10/16/2012, "The Vexing Simplicity of Neil Young", by Alec Wilkinson.

[162] *Performing Songwriter;* Hutchinson; "Happy Birthday, Neil Young!".

[163] *WTF with Marc Maron,* 3/21/2016, interviewed by Marc Maron.

[164] A die-hard Neil Young fan may perhaps aver Young is simply *better* at the, um, 'technique', but I think the implicit underlying argument there—that unedited, 'spontaneous faultless creation' can *and does* regularly birth brilliant songwriting by this or that Great Artist, with Young's stumbling efforts forwarded as awkward 'proof' for that thesis—is foppish nineteenth century Romanticism writ XXXL, and patently spurious. To that fan I counsel reconsulting the many forewarnings back in Part One, joining us here in the twenty-first century, and indeed, 'getting real'.

[165] Such tales are currently so serviceable to claims of Creative Brilliance in the songwriter(s), that they may sometimes be manufactured for work that actually *was* carefully, deliberately written and composed; serving the dual role of both substantiation for that professed gift and de facto apologia for whatever shortcomings may be critiqued.

[166] We addressed "Come Together" and noted Lennon's comments on it in Chapter Three. Concerning "I Am the Walrus", Lennon's childhood friend, Pete Shott, recalls in *John Lennon in My Life,* (co-written with Nicholas Shaffner; London: Stein and Day, 1983) 217-218: **Though John was pleased and flattered to have his work taken seriously...it particularly irked him to have his songs subjected to the same sort of heavy-handed analysis with which our schoolmasters had**

ruined his own appreciation of [literature]. One day while dipping into his sack of fan mail...we chanced upon a letter from a student at his own old primary school, Quarry Bank. The lad revealed that his teacher was playing Beatles songs in class, and after the boys took turns analyzing the lyrics, the teacher would weigh in with his own interpretation of what the Beatles were *really* saying. John and I howled with laughter over the absurdity of it all...He found a pen and began scribbling. Inspired by the mental picture of that Quarry Bank literature teacher pontificating about all the supposed symbolism in Lennon-McCartney songs, John started [writing "I Am The Walrus"], throwing in the most ludicrous images [and the most meaningless nonsense] his imagination could conjure. "Yellow matter custard, dripping from a dead dog's eye", he began. He thought of 'semolina' (an insipid pudding we'd been forced to eat as kids) and 'pilchard' (a sardine we often fed our cats). "Semolina pilchard, climbing up the Eiffel Tower...", John intoned, writing it all down with considerable relish. He turned to me, smiling. "Let the fuckers work *that* one out!"

As concerns "Hey Bulldog" (done for the *Yellow Submarine* film), Lennon had this to say: "They wanted another song, so I just knocked off 'Hey Bulldog'...It's a good-sounding record that means nothing." *All We Are Saying: The Last Major Interview with John Lennon and Yoko Ono* by David Sheff. (New York: St Martin's Press, 2000), 204

[167]There are simply too many notices of this kind of arrogant incompetence to provide anything even approaching an all-inclusive list, but here's just one more, under the headline "Beck Admits Lyrics From Classic Songs Were Nonsense": http://www.nme.com/news/music/beck-21-1330403 (web search terms: Beck admits lyrics nonsense)

[168]*Words+Music*, NPR Radio, 10/18/1996, Joni Mitchell in conversation with Steven Morrissey: "I know Dylan said to me at one point that he, you know, he couldn't write anymore, and I said, 'Oh, what about this [song] and what about that [song]?' And he said, 'Oh, the box wrote [those].' I said, 'What do you mean 'the box'?' He said, 'I write down things from movies and things I've heard people say and I throw them into a box.'"

[169]https://motherboard.vice.com/en_us/article/xygxpn/the-verbasizer-was-david-bowies-1995-lyric-writing-mac-app (web search terms: Verbasizer David Bowie 1995)

[170]*The Guardian*, 9/7/2009, "Hey, What's That Sound: Oblique Strategies", by David McNamee: https://www.theguardian.com/music/2009/sep/07/oblique-strategies (web search terms: sound Oblique Strategies)

[171]https://en.wikipedia.org/wiki/Cut-up_technique (web search terms: cut-up Wiki)

[172]*Chicago Sun-Times*, 8/29/1993, "Smells Like A Nirvana Article", by Jim DeRogatis.

PART FIVE: Structure
— W Y S I W Y G ? —

Chapter Fifty-Six

Form Follows Function

There's a formula for success in entertainment: if it's succeeded before, beat it to death again and again. — Ernie Kovacs

What say we start this off with an easy, obvious declaration—in All Caps:

THERE WILL <u>ALWAYS</u> BE A PLACE FOR THE 'THREE-MINUTE SONG'.

And, similarly:

THERE WILL <u>ALWAYS</u> BE SONG IDEAS THAT ARE BEST CONVEYED USING 'STANDARD SONG STRUCTURES'.

When we're talking about 'song structures' or 'song constructions' here, we're concerned with how the major building blocks of a song—verses, chorus, bridge, pre-chorus, intro (or old fashioned 'introductory verse'), and so on—are scheduled, how they are sequenced, in a song.

This chapter could have properly appeared in either Part Three (on lyrics) or Part Four (on music) because it pertains to both aspects of songwriting. But I think it's also distinct from both: an independent, generally under-appreciated—under-recognized—part of songwriting. It's how the basic large building blocks of a song are arranged together, and—albeit to lesser extent—how the lyrical lines and musical attributes *within* those blocks are scheduled and work together. The actual, literal writing in those lines is another matter, of course—and we've been addressing that all along. Here we're looking at how the executed lines and the contained blocks pile up together.

We're also interested here in the marriage of music and lyrics—mostly meaning whether the music successfully supports the precipitating idea impelling the song.

So we're in the world of what might be called 'song architecture', and 'song engineering'.

Architect Louis Sullivan's famous dictum, "Form ever follows function", seems to be losing currency in that discipline, perhaps due to the flamboyance privileged by computer-aided design. In the world of songwriting, in contradistinction, it's never really had much relevance beyond the most basic. Once the 'building block structure' of a song has been established, normally the only diversions from that are either minor (for instance, perhaps an extra bar or two of music as a turn-around, or a line in the lyrics—most often at the end—repeated for emphasis) or the incorporation of another full structural building block type (such as a bridge or a pre-chorus). This *no matter what* the subject of the song and the lyrics explicating it might seem to warrant.

As for length, even with the loosening of limitations over the past few decades, the usually adhered-to model remains the 'three-minute song', with one, two or generally at-most three musical-lyrical blocks presented (those being, in descending order of application, in the verses, in the chorus, and in the bridge). It's conventional, expected—and safe.

Predictability in structure can provide a firm foundation—a kinda dependable intellectual certitude, as is found in traditional blues songs, for instance—from which successive declarations can be fired off like consecutive programmed salvos. This reliability is obviously an easy conceit within which to place any number of repetitive ideas or pronouncements—it actually reinforces the strength of each and all because they are proffered, ipso facto, as intuitively concordant, implicitly commensurate in strength. After all, each new proclamation rests on the very same bed of melody, length, rhyme scheme, and meter as the previously presented (and presumably accepted) proclamation.

The vast majority of songs created in recent decades use a structure of verse (A), chorus (B) and bridge (C) in a variation of an A-B-A-B-C-A-B construction. Understand, sometimes there'll be no C section, or there'll be two A sections before the first B—but the variety of constructs is generally rather limited, and one doesn't often find it necessary to go further into the alphabet to label a section. A, B, and C usually suffice. If a song begins with the chorus, proper scheduling (at least as I do it) would be B-A-B-A-etc, so 'B' means chorus, whether it's first in the rendition or comes in later. Traditional songs—songs which originated before the industrial revolution, or those modeled similarly—most often use a continuity of A sections, with possibly a single line repeated at the end of each; so no real chorus in the song at all, but with what's properly called a 'refrain line' providing persistence. Such a song, for instance, would be scheduled as A-A-A-A-A—and onward, to include however many verses are in the entirety.

Some of the songs we've examined earlier might be scheduled thusly:

"The Night They Drove Old Dixie Down": A-B-C-A-B-C-A-B-C-B-C

"Come Together": A-A-B-A-B-(A)-A-B-(A) (It's my practice to put instrumental passes in parentheses.)

"And I Love Her": A-A-B-A-(A)-A

"Me and Bobby McGee": A-B-A-B-(A), with that last parenthetical A here being the verse of non-lexical vocables.

"Above and Beyond" (original song): B-A-B-(B)-A-B (My revision: A-B-A-B-A-(A)-B)

"The Times They Are A-Changin'": A-A-A-A-A

"I Never Do Anything Twice": $A-B^1-A-B^2-A-B^3-B^4$, the B sections here superscripted because, unlike most chorus sections the <u>internal</u> realizations in this song differ so greatly from one chorus to the next. The ideas in verses (generally A sections) are expected to change from one to the other—the lyrics are expected to be different. But choruses (again, generally B sections) are expected to be exactly, or near-exactly, the same throughout—when they aren't, that difference should be clearly indicated in the schedule.

We could get deeper into this, of course. For instance, when an A section, a verse, *is* repeated, exactly—most often at the end of a song to bookend it—it might behoove us to specifically note that in the schedule as well. But deconstructing song structures at length is a bit outside the purview of this investigation. One quick overview of it all—of the many one could click to—is noted in footnote 173 below. It's pretty easily assimilated stuff.[173]

While a quick glance at the above schedules might lead one to presume they are each quite different from the other, the important fact is that the number of actual *available building blocks used* is quite limited. Again, none of the songs needs more than A, B, and C to name them—though the last song does note the lyrical dissimilarities in the choruses.

Even though we may have already delved into this more than necessary, I do think it germane to direct attention to some compositions by the late Roy Orbison as perfect exemplars of what *can* be accomplished when the usual, expected structures are nowhere to be found. Again, keep in mind that most songs follow one of perhaps four or five standard constructions, basics of which have been noted above. But his song, "Running Scared", for instance, is A-A-A-A-B—with the title line repeated, unusually but not uniquely, at the beginning of each A section—and a B section that is completely different, musically and lyrically, coming from out of nowhere to cap it all off and wrap it all up. I've never been all that enamored of Orbison's actual writing—the songs are *much* too cloying and maudlin for my taste—but they are, importantly, of a piece. So yes, the take on life in his songs may be mawkish, but within that syrupy world view they do regularly work. And there should be no argument that his *marriage* of music, structure, and lyrics is frequently just striking.

Other Orbison songs that defy conventional structure include "In Dreams", built in an A-B-C-D-E-F sequence—six distinctly independent musical/lyrical blocks, "Crying", which might most adequately be scheduled, believe it or not, as A-B-C-D-E-F-A-B'-C'-D'-E'-F', and "It's Over", (co-written with long-time collaborator Bill Dees), structured A-B-C-B-D. His best-known effort "Oh, Pretty Woman" is structured A-A-B-C-A-D. (By the way, this last song has always struck me as a kinda repellently gung-ho advocacy—justification?—for plain old sexual harassment. You? Think about it. The guy intrudes on, imposes himself upon, some complete stranger out on the street—and she's swept off her feet. Of course she is. Thanks for the, uh, 'dating advice', Roy.) The structures in all these songs was created to *support* his lyrics and the song's foundational precept—which is what the structure in a song should do. I think were he to have written and composed any of the aforementioned songs in a 'standard schedule' that they would have been lesser efforts.

Brian Wilson's compositions, on rare occasions at least, also present a wonderfully inventive structure—even scheduling "Surf's Up" for clear understanding of what the hell's going on can be a bit of a challenge. But, as with just so much in popular song, what's sadly—necessarily?—overlooked in most critical appreciations of his work are lyrics which are often thuddingly vapid; rhymes and statements coming at us with the shaded nuance of hand grenades, and far too often, inciting ideas themselves that are misguided or just downright inane. (No, *not* at all invariably; but yes, with eye-rolling frequency. Aside from the sporadic effort— usually, though not always, in a song that's something light—I don't feel Wilson's ever been availed of a lyricist who evinces a breadth of talent commensurate with his own generally outstanding musical abilities.)

To sum up what we've gained here, another popular hit song from a while ago comes to mind—well, because I just endured the fucking thing blasting out at me down at the 7–Eleven. It also diverges significantly from usual structural expectations—but *much* less cohesively than the Orbison songs above, or so many of Brian Wilson's. "Come On Eileen", (written and composed by Kevin Rowland, Jim Patterson, and Billy Adams, aka Dexys Midnight Runners, 1982) is a schizophrenic mess. But as with the earlier cited "Bohemian Rhapsody" and "Stairway to Heaven", the structure does not, like in the overwhelming majority of popular songs, follow an easily anticipated standard progression of successive, repeated building blocks with little subsequent variation. And it plays havoc with tempos. But also like those two songs, there's just not much truly meriting attention. Yes, it may entice us to follow along once—to see if there *might* be something worthwhile goin' on in the wreckage— but it proves to be, basically, a kinda innocuous 'carpe diem song'…with lotsa weird cancerous pustules attached.

We might properly note before closing out this section that the current acclaim for rapper Kendrick Lamar's work may be also significantly attributable to its frequent divorce from conventional structures, which thus presents overall efforts that are similarly unpredictable, as they're exposed, in real time. While this is noteworthy, again, the actual *content* within those structures—the use of language and the depth of what's conveyed—is quite over-rated.

So no, structural divergence—aimless 'eccentricity', in so many cases?—does not by itself provide a ticket to an interesting song. Yet, like melody—and as shown in the Orbison constructions above—it can go a long way to furthering a song idea that *has been* cohesively presented in the lyrics.

★

Another matter of immense importance is that a properly serious song should be a *complete* piece, not a fragment or a largely unelaborated notion—no matter how long it takes to provide that. It's a three-act play, not a two-act play, an inchoate scene, or a tautology.

I make this comparison to playwriting advisedly, because so many songs are constructed of basically just a couple of verses and a chorus—or the overall lyrical (informational) equivalent. As fundamental information tends to be provided in the verses—as opposed to the chorus, because that generally delivers a repeated summary declaration—we're often deprived of a large part of what should be the heart of the enterprise, the part that satisfies our wish for investment in A Complete Experience. To return to playwriting (or screenwriting) as a paradigm, the song may be missing the set-up (Act 1), the development and complications (Act 2), or the resolution (Act 3). It's hard to get all that into one or two verses, and why, for instance "Me and Bobby McGee" (two verses) feels somewhat incomplete despite its undeniable merits. It seems to be missing a second act. "The Gambler", on the other hand, tells a complete story; it's a fully integrated experience.

It is *far* too overly reductive to prescribe something as pat, as crudely mechanical, as 'three verses equals three acts'—for instance, "The Gambler" has five verses. So let's not marry to that *at all*. A longer verse—and/or a verse with longer individual lines—can obviously deliver more information. Yet, as a rule of thumb, it may be helpful—and much more so if we allow that 'Act 2 information', especially, may be ultimately dispensed using *several* verses.

If we get the information of Acts 1, 2, and 3 all in one or two verses, well fine—though in this hypothetical formulation my intuition would be that a) this story may not really be a whole story after all; or b) even if it is, it would benefit from elaboration and extrapolation; or c) even if it is, that it would be better presented cut into more segments—verses—so we have the time to take it all in. If it takes seven verses—most of them probably dedicated to 'Act 2 information'—then it takes seven verses. What we want is a complete experience. And the material may be so rich that one of the 'acts' may allow—or mandate—stretching over several verses, delivering a final effort of something like the 12 verses contained in "El Paso".

Thinking of the chorus as fulfilling the function of one of the acts— most often in this scenario the chorus would be presumed to effectively be an Act 3—kinda drives a square peg into a round hole. A chorus rarely provides enough basic information to replace an actual verse that wouldn't just be redundant via repetition, *and* provides the proper necessary summary overview. A chorus is generally—not always, no, but generally—a different vehicle, serving a larger, overarching objective.

The preceding paragraphs are obviously open to criticism for being *much* too programmatic and absolute, with admittedly *far* too many proven successful exceptions. That's understood, and it's offered simply as an embarkation for thought. Yet the initial statement endures, prevailing: a well-written song is a complete piece with beginning, middle, and end; a fragment generally *isn't* a complete and satisfying serious song.

★

Let's look at two songs in particular regard to the focus of this chapter, "Fairytale of New York" by Jem Finer and Shane MacGowan (1987) and "California Cotton Fields" by Dallas Frazier and Earl Montgomery (1969)— once again, older songs with which I hope most readers are familiar.

First up, "California Cotton Fields":

My driftin' memory goes back to the spring of '43,
When I was just a child in Mama's arms.
My daddy plowed the ground and prayed that someday we would leave
This run-down, mortgaged Oklahoma farm.
Then one night I heard my daddy sayin' to my momma
That he finally saved enough for us to go.
California was his dream, a paradise, for he had seen
Pictures in magazines that told him so.

chorus:
California cotton fields:
Where labor camps were full of weary men with broken dreams.
California cotton fields:
As close to wealth as Daddy ever came.

Almost everything we had was sold or left behind,
From Daddy's plow to the fruit that Mama canned.
Some folks came to say farewell or see what all we had to sell;
Some just came to shake my daddy's hand.
The Model A was loaded down and California bound;
A change of luck was just four days away!
But the only change that I remember seeing for my daddy
Was when his dark hair turned to silver grey.

chorus repeat[174]

Before we get into this, let's examine the structural schedule. It's either A-B-A-B, or—if we decide the fifth line in each verse actually begins a separate, individual section (as a pre-chorus, perhaps)—A-B-C-A-B-C.

Talking once with Dallas Frazier, who was the primary songwriter, I asked if he'd written more than the two verses appearing in the finished song, or had ever considered doing so, since the vein of historical material was so extensive. After what seemed to be a self-reflective pause, he quietly responded that the notion had never occurred to him, nor to Earl Montgomery, who latterly helped complete it. The song generally plays between just 2:15–2:45 minutes, depending on the tempo chosen—so easily within 'standard expectations'—and they were professional songwriters, providing material solidly within those conventional demands of the industry and concomitant expectations of the public at the time.

(By the way, offhand comparison might be made of this song to Woody Guthrie's "Tom Joad" (1940) and, to a lesser extent, to Bruce Springsteen's "The Ghost of Tom Joad" (1995), but keep in mind the former is a pretty faithful recapitulation of Nunnally Johnson's film script adaptation of John Steinbeck's *The Grapes of Wrath*; and the latter song is a further extension on that work—so both, as well as Johnson's 1940 screenplay, are successive inventions emerging from Steinbeck's 1939 novel, and so independent of facts recounted in "California Cotton

Fields". In other words, that whole line of descent, beginning with Steinbeck's original narrative—as solid as each successive effort has been—remains fictional and illustrative, as opposed to documentary, extending outward and onward from the dramatic parameters originally set by Steinbeck. Frazier wrote "California Cotton Fields" about *his own* actual life experiences—born in 1939, when he was a child his family really did migrate from Oklahoma to California in a Model A Ford [with a mattress tied to the top, according to Frazier]. The song is probably best known in the rendition by Merle Haggard—his family incidentally *also* having been Dust Bowl refugees, so again there's that complementary depth. This does add a layer of underlying 'legitimacy' to "California Cotton Fields", in its association both with Frazier and with Haggard. But once again, as concerns all such peripheral matters—and that's strictly what this background information remains—it should still be placed at arm's length when discussing the song itself.)

There's two points I think pertinent for consideration here about this marvelous piece of lyric writing. We'll get to the second in the following chapter, but the first, as implied by my question to Frazier—as well as by similar comments earlier about "Me and Bobby McGee", in particular—is that this song could, surely, have been longer. Though the chorus tells us the denouement of events, both at the half-way point and repeated again at the end, I feel we're deprived of a missing 'act'—in this case, actually, one or several intermediary 'second acts'—that might provide a fuller experience than the excellent exposition there now.[175] It would have lost nothing in punch and could have gained much in scope in a longer execution. I'm interested in what happened to the mother, the trip to California itself, the later moments of key realization and disappointment, old neighbors perhaps subsequently encountered again—even where now sits that presumably rusted Model A Ford. Agree? There's a wealth of material from which to add color, and to draw wisdom.

★

And now, "Fairytale of New York":

It was Christmas Eve, babe,
In the drunk tank.
An old man said to me, "Won't see another one."
And then he sang a song:

"The Rare Old Mountain Dew".
I turned my face away
And dreamed about you.

Got on a lucky one;
Came in eighteen to one.
I've got a feeling
This year's for me and you.
So happy Christmas.
I love you baby.
I can see a better time
When all our dreams come true.

They've got cars big as bars;
They've got rivers of gold;
But the wind goes right through you;
It's no place for the old.
When you first took my hand
On a cold Christmas Eve,
You promised me
Broadway was waiting for me.

—You were handsome.
—You were pretty,
Queen of New York City.
When the band finished playing
They howled out for more.
Sinatra was swinging,
All the drunks they were singing.
We kissed on a corner
Then danced through the night.

chorus:
    The boys of the NYPD choir
    Were singing "Galway Bay";
    And the bells were ringing out
    For Christmas Day.
    —You're a bum!

—You're a punk!
—You're an old slut on junk,
Lying there almost dead on a drip in that bed.
—You scumbag, you maggot,
You cheap lousy faggot!
Happy Christmas your arse—
I pray God it's our last.

<u>chorus repeat</u>

—I could have been someone.
—Well so could anyone!
You took my dreams from me
When I first found you.
—I kept them with me, babe;
I put them with my own.
Can't make it all alone;
I've built my dreams around you.

<u>chorus repeat</u>[176]

(Before we get into the song, am I the only one who thinks setting up the female character [and her alone, by the way] as a junkie—"You're an old slut on junk / Lying there almost dead on a drip in that bed."—is an unfortunate writing choice? Even though I'm a kinda 'straight arrow' throw-back to an earlier sensibility in many ways, I still certainly did more than my share of drugs—primarily psychedelics—back when. So I'm not making a pejorative judgment on the characters' activities. There's simply something incomplete, I think, in outlining characters on the margins of prevailing culture without incorporating an awareness in the writer's oversight—and/or a self-awareness in the characters themselves—that the context and events are atypical, vagarious. Maybe I'm wrong, but I offer the consideration. And in any event, the songwriting remains admirable.)

In "Fairytale of New York" I don't think we find musical ambiguity; the score works to excellent effect throughout. The three quite distinct musical parts perfectly underscore and tie together the disparate aspects of the story. (And, by the way, what a strong title for a song— presumably taken from J.P. Donleavy's unrelated novel, *A Fairy Tale of*

New York, no? Not sure how I feel about that—since the song certainly doesn't adapt the book, and so would seem to intrude on a potential such effort. But ya can't copyright a title, and it's a great one—so there you go.)

It's a synergetic marriage of lyrics and music; however, the story itself feels truncated. Unlike "California Cotton Fields"—which delivers an excellent Act 1 and a solid Act 3 (though in the chorus)—"Fairytale of New York" seems arbitrarily lopped off. We get an Act 1, and all or an abbreviated part of an Act 2—without an Act 3. What happened to these folks? Where are they going; what *are* their options? We're introduced to them; we witness a dramatic, vitriolic argument; we learn of their respective self-reflections and aspirations—and then…pfft. What we get is quite good, yes—but ultimately, once again, it's somewhat short-changed.

It may be argued, as it was in a letter to me, that what's been presented is enough—that there's nothing at all missing by leaving off where it does. The listener has enough information, and his or her own projections and reflections—the listener's active involvement—are better elicited by ending the presentation at this point. While the strength of what is there *is* complete—as far as it goes—my suspicion remains that this song would both easily allow and forcefully benefit from further exploration, and not preclude our extended active emotional and intellectual investment. What happened next?[177]

★

I think it's critically important to fully divorce from the choking mandates of the 'three-minute song', no matter how ingrained general expectations have become. But it's an admittedly difficult thing to scrap. A song of my own called "Nineteen Years Old", in a simple A-A-A-(A)-A schedule, plays nearly six and a half minutes long, and I've occasionally offered that I wish to hell it were shorter—evidence of my *own* inculcated partiality to the 'three-minute song'. But I always add that there's really not a single line I think unnecessary and would therefore be willing to cut. Excising anything in "Nineteen Years Old", I believe, would be a diminution. Even the instrumental pass (about 20% of the overall length) is integral as it properly, necessarily, postpones the payoff of the story, a story in which one presumes—hopes—listeners have by then become involved.

Might be I'm just too close to it? Okay, possibly. Hell—*you* tell me what to cut:

When she was just nineteen years old and I was twenty-three,
It seemed the right place and time for us to part company.
No arguments, no big regrets, perhaps we'd meet again.
And small town life was closin' in, a world without enough oxygen.
While a voice kept whisperin' to me, "Go find your great grand destiny".
An' what with all the other fish out in the sea,
She bein' just nineteen years old; me just twenty-three.

"Join the Navy, See the World!": turned out just Vietnam.
Came back worked factories, fields, and farms, across this great wide land.
A man believes what he wants to believe, but he becomes what he does.
After too many battles, so many scars, his reasons devolve into "just because".
But in my mind from time to time, she'd still appear to me,
Smilin' back there in my memory,
When she was just nineteen years old, and I was twenty-three.

I heard she'd married, raised two sons; now full-grown, on their own.
Divorced and teachin' school these years; comfortable, alone.
Me I'd gone from gal to gal, with impatience I couldn't shake.
I don't really know what I was lookin' for, were the decades—just a mistake?
If we'd stayed on those years ago, how different might things be?
Oh, the effect she'd had on me,
When she was just nineteen years old, and I was twenty-three.

instrumental verse

Now I'm back here in this place I thought I'd never see again.
Buildings and streets all put in since I left way back then.
My ragged shoes retrace the stones that lead to her front door.
I guess what I left so long ago was what I ran off lookin' for.
Once fancy-free, now refugee; then a kind woman opens the door to me.
And behind all the lines in her smile I see,
She's still just nineteen years old...
And to her, I'm twenty-three.

Maybe you found some dross—some 'filler'. If so, you can lemme know. But as far as I can determine, this song—this complete story—needs to be that six and a half minutes long. Q.E.D.[178]

I've also written and recorded a song called "All in the Timing: A Hollywood Romance in Seven Chapters", that is 27–½ minutes long—with over 500 lines of non-repeating lyrics.[179] And on my next album is a song called "Prison Break", that lasts less than a minute, with but one line of lyrics. I believe that in *both* cases the songs are the proper length for the information delivered and the emotions imparted. Yet someone exposed to them might quickly cite lines in the longer song—hell, whole gigantic passels of lines I'm sure—that he or she thought superfluous (or even just poorly written) and that could (should!) be cut; and confidently suggest any number of lines and ideas that could be profitably added to the shorter song. I accept both possibilities, naturally. But in each case, worrying about simple length when working on them was an immaterial consideration.

★

In summary, the proper length of a song is rightfully, overwhelmingly dependent on the intrinsic communicative requirements of the lyrics, with allowance for instrumental passes and flourishes if warranted. Repetition simply to lengthen without new information is usually evidence of an impoverished inciting idea.[180] The same holds, generally at least, and as noted earlier, for a song padded out—degraded into sing-along—with non-lexical vocables.

Form follows function.

[173]http://www.songwriting.net/blog/bid/207339/Songwriting-Tip-Understanding-the-Most-Common-Song-Structures (web search terms: Understanding Common Song Structures)

[174]"California Cotton Fields", copyright 1969 by Dallas Frazier and Earl Montgomery. Quoted here as permitted within the Fair Use provisions of 17 U.S.C.§107.

[175]As the chorus in this song *does* provide an integral part of the story—the 'Act 3 summation', revealing that Daddy never found the Arcadian life he believed California promised—if we kept the A-B-A-B scheduling, that in itself would militate against there being additional verses. The resolution in the chorus would be unnecessary, redundant, if brought to us even more than the two appearances there now. So rather than continuing the present A-B-A-B construction, an expanded song would surely work best in a final schedule of something like, say, A-A-B-A-A-A-B, or similar, with perhaps a bridge and/or an instrumental pass added in as well. As noted earlier, a

chorus generally serves a different end than verses. (And if we split the current song into <u>three</u> sections, as we noted was possible—so presently scheduled A-B-C-A-B-C—our hypothetical expanded song would perhaps end up scheduled something like A-B-A-B-C-A-B-A-B-A-B-C, with maybe an added bridge section. In any event, the same primary objective obviously remains: to place the song's 'title line section'—its chorus—sparingly, effectively. Too much analysis and conjecture here? No. This is what 'in the trenches' song criticism is about. Yet *none* of this should be inferred to be hardline criticism of the great song that exists as is.)

[176]"Fairytale of New York", copyright 1985 by Jem Finer and Shane MacGowan. Quoted here as permitted within the Fair Use provisions of 17 U.S.C.§107.

[177]I've myself several times created an additional verse for this or that well-known song that I perform. There's obviously no payment for it, nor any share in writing credits (see Chapter Forty-Two), but what's gained is the satisfaction that the extant song—which I obviously like or wouldn't have even given a second look—has been given a sense of fullness or completion that was previously lacking.

[178]"Nineteen Years Old" can be heard here: http://www.michaelkoppy.com/. (web search terms: Michael Koppy)

[179]I just recall that in footnote 156, Neil Young's "Driftin' Back" (27:36 long) was mentioned. Given that the length of the two songs is almost exactly the same, a side-by-side 'quality comparison' might be made between "Driftin' Back" and "All in the Timing: A Hollywood Romance in Seven Chapters (27:26 long). Believe me, length is the *only* thing they have in common.

[180]My own 'go-to nominee' for Most Irritating Pop Song in this category (and you most surely have your own; lemme know and we'll compare) is probably "Old Time Rock and Roll", written and composed by George Jackson and Thomas E. Jones III—particularly as performed by Bob Seger, whose recording of it is scheduled A-B-A-B-B-B-B-(B). That utterly insipid, truly idiotic goddamn fuckin' chorus Just Will Not Stop. Where's my gun?

Chapter Fifty-Seven

Music Seeks Words.
Object: Matrimony.

A means can be justified only by its end.
But the end in its turn needs to be justified. — Leon Trotsky

The second point concerning "California Cotton Fields"—and this is very much a question, really—has to do with the tune behind the lyrics. The song is usually played up-tempo—Haggard's rendition is the slowest I've encountered (at a still fairly brisk 93 beats per minute)—which seems to my ears to be counterproductive, given the measure of events detailed in the lyrics. The song has even become a staple for blue-grass bands, usually quite unfortunately. There's a strong tendency in poorly played bluegrass to scrap all other considerations in the mad quest for blind speed—reminiscent of the similarly corrosive breakneck electric guitar showboating rampant in poorly played hard rock.

But my question concerns the tune itself—and I repeat that it's just inquiry. I wonder if an entirely different musical setting might have provided better agency for the great story, as there is a gut intuition here that while slowing something down is easily done, that this tune 'wants' to be played at a clip that's too vigorous. And when presented at the tempo at which the tune and chords behind it seem to be most comfortably performed, the story becomes somewhat flattened, tossed off.

As "California Cotton Fields" is primarily known via recording by Merle Haggard, I'm reminded of another song—one written and composed by Haggard himself—which may warrant likewise consideration. His well-known "Mama Tried", also a great piece of writing, strikes me as similarly uncertain musically, coincidentally due to the very same concern. It's also a song regularly murdered by bluegrass ensembles, by the way; but they're not the only culprits—just about every live performance strikes as hurried, and leads one to submit these lyrics might *also* be better served in a modified or even entirely different musical setting. Again, sure, it's possible to Slow Things Down—obviously—but am I the only one to whom the musical side of things in these two great songs does seem to curve the intention of the lyrics?

Music is *secondary* in a serious song, yes, but it's absolutely, critically important. Yet it's the mysterious, magical nature of music that makes suggestions of alternative musical ideas and settings so debatable; and ultimately even futile.

Would "California Cotton Fields" (or "Mama Tried") work better by marrying them to a melody in a minor key? The serious reflection in both might dispose one to consider that option, yes, though there's zillions of examples in which deep sentiment is carried by a tune in a major key. So that's just one option, and hard to discern with certainty—a priori, simply because it's so profoundly difficult to forget what's already there! But it must remain a question. No answer can be definitively lodged, I admit—because we're once again staring into the Mystery of Music. It's always easier to intuit—to believe—that maybe something doesn't work as well as it could musically than to know how to improve it.

None of my many correspondents was able to help take this topic any further than we've done here. But a song we looked at earlier that may provide some insight on the matter is "The House of the Rising Sun". As noted, it was traditionally performed using three chords—until Dave Van Ronk completely rearranged the song, sharpening the melody and available harmonies by spreading it over five chords. His effort has pretty much completely transformed that song, so much so that it effectively no longer exists in its former guise, even being performed by hardcore traditionalists in that 'new and improved arrangement'. (We might also point out that it was Bob Dylan who first introduced Van Ronk's effort to a wider audience, by including it on his first album—unbeknownst to Van Ronk, who wasn't happy about the de facto piracy, since he was himself preparing to record the revised song as a centerpiece on his *own* first album. I think Dylan turned in a better actual performance of it than Van Ronk recorded several weeks later, but that's ultimately secondary, and the duplicity is lamentable.)[181]

I've done something similar to what Van Ronk did to "The House of the Rising Sun" with my work on "You Are My Sunshine". In both cases, the melody remains but the chords upon which it lies are changed. There is *nothing at all unusual* about such work—it's done all the time in jazz, obviously, and with much greater musical sophistication. (Sometimes that applied layer of 'jazz sophistication' can be ultimately counterproductive, however, taking the heart from a song and turning it into lounge lizard mush.) What *is* important is how effective the new arrangement works with the lyrics—the lyrics that are the argument for the song in the first place. Paul McCartney—he who can't read music—gives an excellent lesson on this discussing his "Yesterday" and how it *might* have been set to music.[182] It's a song—like most others—that could be played using just three or four chords. It'd be boring as all hell—laughably so, given what we know and are accustomed to—but it could be done.

The melody of Steve Sondheim's "I Never Do Anything Twice", examined earlier, is neither sweeping nor grand. Frankly, on its own it's pretty forgettable. But it's an *ideal* bed upon which to spread the story that's told. The music serves the entirety perfectly. (I think my own melody employed in the aforementioned "Nineteen Years Old" is also forgettable—quite ordinary. Yet I believe the point of the song—and the lyrics conveying that point—are well-served by it being so, well, 'nondescript'.)

The proper question, always, is Does the musical composition work with the lyrics? Does it *help*?

Melody and harmony are the setting for what's being sung; they should easily fit—contribute to—the emotional and literal direction of the idea of the song, and the development of that idea in the lyrics. If the music 'fights' the lyrics—absent the occasional exception of a carefully reasoned rationale for such a discordance or misalignment (as perhaps in a comedy song)—the entire effort is diminished.

★

Yes, as was noted earlier, music is the most powerful element in a song. But music alone is wide open to subjectivity—so lacking in literal intelligence while potentially so extravagantly rich in emotional carriage—that it is more a sea voyage left to the whims of a capricious wind than an elegantly charted passage. Words—again, even just a title— provide us with actual direction. We see that in what's called classical 'program music'—where just a title for the composition intends to direct our focus during the flood of music washing by. Think of *The Moldau* by Bedřich Smetana, in which the title—the name of the longest river in the Czech Republic—directs us to imagine the rains and rivulets that come together, gather other tributaries, and evolve into a latterly mighty river. Great music—and great framing, via the fitting, evocative title.

So many great classical compositions aim at similar effect—a title, not required in classical music but certainly not unwelcomed—is intended to guide us. The difference between this and so many popular songs is that in program music and similar, there is generally *no* other language involved other than that pointedly, often elegantly suggestive title. In the popular song, on the other hand, after even an undeniably felicitous title we're all too regularly *then* hammered with ancillary blather which actually *detracts* from—confuses—whatever substantive content was promised. Think of "Time to Say Goodbye", addressed in Chapter Twenty-Four. (As for instrumental songs, so obviously without lyrics, they're often titled to careless or off-hand effect. This can be a missed opportunity, I think—perhaps even a de facto admission that the music isn't really that coherent or intrinsically interesting after all. It need not last beyond a couple of minutes or so—and, because instrumentals are also invariably created with conventional structures and within standard time constraints, it rarely does. It's a trifle, a throw-away; even if an amusing or diverting one.)

As Susan Sontag astutely points out in her outstanding *On Photography*, while a picture may be worth a thousand words, it is the caption—some very few *actual* words—that define, even confine, that picture.[183] They inform and firmly instruct our emotional-intellectual cooperation.

A title serves analogous purpose for a musical composition. Words—a song title—direct our imagination and perception. So when a title is followed by a set of lyrics, it's important that the lyrics expand upon the inciting direction proclaimed by that title; not just fill space. And, reciprocally, that the music *serves* that directed expansion; doesn't contest it.

---

[181] On the other hand, *most* renditions of Van Ronk's arrangement sound better, to my ears, than his own effort.

[182] McCartney briefly—very briefly—addresses this in Part 2 of *The Rhythm of Life*, a 1997 BBC documentary hosted by George Martin. (YouTube title search: <u>Rhythm of Life - Part 2 of 3</u>)

[183] *On Photography* by Susan Sontag. (New York: Farrar, Strauss and Giroux, 1973), 108

PART SIX: Toward A New Songwriting

— AND A WAY FORWARD —

Chapter Fifty-Eight

Rules Were Made to Be Broken. However...

One moment of incompetence can be fatal. — Frank Herbert

A reader who hasn't just jumped straight to this chapter—to see what all the fuss was about, perhaps, and save time—may peremptorily decide the various prescriptions and songwriting guidelines here following are obvious; or, conversely, lacking foundation.

I have conflicting thoughts on how this concluding material should be presented.

Folks, *surely* the basic thrust of what's been advocated all through this monograph—citing examples of key deficiencies found throughout contemporary and recent popular songwriting (and 'songwriting culture') and ways to mitigate, even rectify, those pernicious tendencies— has been pretty plainly addressed. Occasional positive examples have also been presented, and their stellar attributes commended. To justify the following summary findings and directives one by one again would be redundant. The cases have been made. (So if this is your first stop, you will be better served by returning to the beginning and reading your way back here.)

On another aspect, there really are *no* pat remedies to the predicament in which we currently find ourselves in regards to the low quality of writing in popular songs. There'll be exceptions to any—*and every*— 'rule' advanced, and brilliant works that incorporate one or more of every one of those vexing 'exceptions'. This fact should not be discounted.

But as we're attempting to provide *general* directions here, for song writers, critics, and fans—well, *thinking* songwriters, critics, and fans, that is—one hopes with that goal firmly in mind it's possible to proceed free of charges of doctrinaire pedantry. And if below I've neglected repeating a prescription that's been touched upon earlier, so be it—again, surely the positions have been fairly explained or implied.

Finally—as noted, and certainly adding to any sense of anticlimax—is the point that almost everything here can be fairly characterized as obvious. That *doesn't* mean, however, any and all of it doesn't goddam merit pounding home. Just look and listen to all the crap dumped on the public day in and day out for confirmation of what we're up against.

★

The only thing that counts are ideas. And behind ideas are moral principles. Either one is serious or one is not. — Susan Sontag

The first 'requirement' we'll make about the qualities of a worthwhile song is that it should have a clear and encompassing objective, a productive point of view, a defined direction. What's the <u>reason</u> for it? What is the actual message that it's delivering? Colorful observations, without those observations contributing to a culminating 'call to action' or summary insight derived from them, is usually mush. Simply retreading boilerplate platitudes, without original enhancing intelligence, is an admission of vacancy and a waste of everyone's time. It's also possibly a sad misuse of what might be a great melody.

(Yes, some—no, *most*—of the prescriptions in this chapter will indeed be as simple as the above. Please continue….)

★

A song deserving our attention delivers <u>new</u> information—a new insight or a locution with a twist that causes the listener to appreciate the objective or proposal of the song in a new or different way. It provides a distinctively fresh appraisal of the (perhaps prosaic) subject of the song. To cite a song that's an example of exactly the opposite, and so a dead end, see "Forever Young", examined earlier.

A medium requires a message—or it's no longer actually mediating anything. In popular song, the medium has, pace McLuhan, become the message—which in our case means the message has become peripheral, irrelevant. It's no longer serious communication; just clamor and trivia.

★

Every word has an individual and distinct definitions, connotations, and nuances. Imprecise use of language is not poetic. It is the exact *opposite* of poetic.

Words *do* have meaning, sentences *do* provide consistent direction, and a serious song *does* have a substantive purpose.

Similarly, Faux-folk affectations generally detract from whatever elegance and eloquence a song may contain. Use advisedly.

★

If all a song delivers in originality, or focuses attention on, is one clever turn of phrase or assertive declaration, with the rest pretty much forgettable padding, we're possibly being taken *for* lightweights *by* lightweights. While not definitive of depth, if the strongest line *isn't* the recurrent title passage—or if there are several independently strong lines found throughout—it can be a helpful indication that the whole is probably greater than the sum of its parts, and merits our attention.

★

There is nothing worse than a sharp image of a fuzzy concept.
— Ansel Adams

On the other hand, a song arraying several independently strong ideas—well-expressed pieces of information—that are non sequitur is like a collection of unfocused punchlines. Little is gained beyond momentary amusement. If the verbal collage isn't tied together into a resonant larger whole—given a *reason* to exist in conglomeration—the work is more accurately just a pasted-together dodge; not an essential song. Music and melody and performance and production can each and all mitigate such poverty, but they can't eliminate it.

★

Even if a listener is ignorant of an allusion or reference in a song, that allusion or reference should be to universally available knowledge, ideally even readily discernible within the context of surrounding information. If a reference is to something *so* solipsistic that we need to be told what the hell it's talking about, the lyrics are obviously not truly communicating. A song requiring knowledge of the songwriter's intimate personal life—or requiring unhinged 'wishful thinking' interpretations—is not an example of good songwriting.

★

If something is well written, I always find it too short. — Jane Austen

1. A complete song can last *exactly* three minutes.

2. A cohesively complete song can go on and On and ON—if continually delivering new, substantive information and insights.

3. A song can be short and still be complete.

What we want is an *integrated* presentation, engaging our intelligence, teasing our emotions. The time it takes to bring us that is a secondary, unnecessary—even counterproductive—consideration.

★

Reveal some of yourself in each of your songs. — Jack Clement

While sincerity is not depth—no need to rail further on that, eh?—it is personal experience that guides most writing, even in situations in which the writer has no background, and characters with whom the writer has no communion. Maybe "California Cotton Fields" gains ulterior currency because it illuminates the songwriter's direct experience, but my expectation is that it was the songwriter's direct experience—his personal investment—that simply *propelled his diligence,* his dedication to achieving his goal, his sense of 'mission' with the song. Descriptions in that song are certainly not privileged, specialized knowledge, limited to those having lived them. But personal investment *can* beget superior application.

So, to add a corollary—and more valuably pertinent—directive to the epigraph above, "*Invest yourself fully* into each of your songs".

★

Appearance blinds, whereas words reveal. — Oscar Wilde

As concerns public presentation, while there's nothing actually wrong with silly affectations and performance theatrics, a serious song should be able to stand—and *should* stand—on its own, understood and delivering essential illumination, free from performance circusry.

The utterly empty—culturally, intellectually impoverished—parading of self-indulgent costuming and attendant performance preening generally indicates a *lack* of substance, an *absence* of insight in the material itself, meriting little other than passing eye-rolling indulgence. As a general rule, drag, and its vocal equivalents, are for the superficial and the supercilious.

★

The difference between the right word and the almost right word is really a large matter—it's the difference between lightning and the lightning bug. — Mark Twain

Every single word in a song lyric requires attention. Even the simplest matter—like just going from one line to the next—demands considered scrutiny, as there are so many different ways to conjoin and elide one thought into another. There should be conscientious, deliberate weighing of which is best: 'and', 'but', 'or', 'nor', 'yet', 'although', 'though', and so on. They are not all the same, interchangeable. Each is unique.

Does the first *thought* end precisely coincident with the end of the *line*, or would it benefit by enjambing into the following line without weakening the following thought? Maybe the juncture between the two pronouncements should be the equivalent of a dash, or maybe a full stop, or perhaps a measured pause. Each option presents slightly different—possibly *profoundly* nuanced—meanings to what sits on either side.

If great care is taken on such ostensibly minor matters, one may presume the pivotal ideas and statements will be even more carefully curated—as they most certainly should be. If that's the case and they are, good.

★

Most writers...prefer having it believed that they compose by a species of fine frenzy—an ecstatic intuition—and would positively shudder at letting the public take a peek behind the scenes at the elaborate and vacillating crudities of thought—at the true purposes seized only at the last moment—at the innumerable glimpses of ideas arrived at not at the maturity of full view—at the fully matured fancies discarded in despair as unmanageable—at the cautious selections and rejections—at the painful erasures and interpolations—in a word, at the wheels and pinions—the tackle for scene-shifting—the step-ladders and demon-traps—the cock's feathers, the red paint and the black patches, which, in ninety-nine cases out of a hundred, constitute the properties of the literary histrio. — Edgar Allen Poe[184]

Good writing is achieved through hard work. So let's relegate the obtuse delusional reveries of romantic consumerism to the obstinate twentieth century. Good work almost always takes time and application. Yes, it is possible to occasionally—once in a great, great while—come up with something truly meritorious, even inspired, kinda 'on the fly'.[185]

But I'm reminded, similarly, of an old show biz adage concerning spontaneous, purportedly 'unscripted' remarks. The rare offhand comment *can* sometimes entertain; but "The best ad-libs are well-rehearsed".

And as a rule, the best songs are carefully, deliberately created.

★

> *First drafts are for learning what your story is about.*
> — Bernard Malamud

The insertion of punctuation—as has been done on the songs quoted in this treatise and manifesto—can be a helpful tool in determining a song's coherence and arc. A song lyric is closer to poetry in construction than it is to prose, yes, but treating it as prose can be enlightening—both for songwriter, and eventually, for audience.

★

> *What I write is smarter than I am—because I rewrite it.*
> — Susan Sontag

An instructive anecdote: A friend, preparing some songs for his next album, asked me to look them over and offer suggestions. Along with all the other comments, positive and negative, I noted my objection to one line that I thought was particularly weak in one of his songs. It was just a passing line, sure, but I felt it was a big step down from its surroundings.

When the album came out months later, he and I spoke about it and I then noted a specific line in one of the songs on the album that I thought was especially good—even brilliant.

It turned out (and of course, I didn't remember all the specifics of our conversation months earlier) that this great line of lyrics was actually the *replacement* for that very same weak line I'd noted back then! Because it had been identified, and he'd accepted it was deficient, he'd not only eliminated a weak place in the song, he had turned *that exact place* into a notable strength. This is what it's all about.

And it's a textbook illustration of what intelligent application can deliver. There's only so much room in any song lyric. Nothing in a song should be haphazard; nothing left unexamined.

★

Opportunity is missed by most people because it is dressed in overalls and looks like work — Thomas Edison

Vermeer is not known to have painted more than 34 paintings. Salinger wrote just one published novel, and Chaplin created just one memorable character.

Johannes Vermeer clearly took immense pains to achieve his masterful paintings, which of course means it would have been impossible to simply churn them out. His work will likely be held in awe for centuries.

People continue to purchase over a million copies of J.D. Salinger's *The Catcher in the Rye* every year, three generations after it first appeared, and it's been translated into over 30 languages, from Mandarin to Farsi.[186]

The often-inventive comedian Jackie Gleason once disparaged Charles Chaplin's work, observing that Chaplin had really only created one notable comedic character while Gleason had created several. But it seems Chaplin's Little Tramp will live in human imagination forever.[187]

In any creative effort, quantity and quality should almost always be considered mutually exclusive.

And in songwriting it's better to have created One Truly Great Song than to have pumped out album after album of mediocrities.

[184]This is excerpted from Poe's fascinating "The Philosophy of Composition", a piece of literary self-analysis and self-reflection so revealing—and so programmatic—that

there's significant debate as to whether he was being candid or possibly even sarcastic in his recounting of the planning for and writing of his well-known poem, "The Raven". My expectation is that the stunningly detailed calculations explained in "The Philosophy of Composition" on how "The Raven" was conceived and executed were thoughts that arrived *throughout* his creative enterprise with the poem: some general and specific aims clear in advance, many derived in partial retrospect in the midst of writing the poem, and some after the fact when looking over the work at his desk. So not quite as carefully deduced as he himself may have honestly thought, in retrospect, when writing "Composition". A capable creative writer tends to initiate an architectural idea independent of engineering considerations, but that capable writer almost *immediately* turns attention to such matters, attempting to solve them and/or reconcile the ambition with those actualities and limitations. It's a parallel, on-going process, as integral to the entirety as keeping the ultimate objective itself constantly in view.

[185]I hesitate to suddenly cite an example of something unique and lasting that *was*— apparently, anyway, albeit not entirely—sorta 'created on the fly', as doing so here might tend to undercut the absolute fact that such occurrences are profoundly rare. But sure, it *can* happen. When it does, however, an honest, self-aware practitioner is as properly surprised by the good fortune as anyone else who somewhere, unexpectedly, stumbles upon serendipity. Tammy Wynette's and Billy Sherrill's writing and composition of "Stand By Your Man" really was, by every account, crafted together in "a half hour" (or "15 minutes", or "20 minutes", or "in less than an hour", reports do vary), at the end of a recording session, when all parties realized they needed one more song to fill out the album, the rest of which they'd just finished recording. Note, however— and something that's invariably neglected when the story is recounted—that Sherrill *did already have* many or most of the lyrics worked out. No, it wasn't a finished song, but he *was* well on his way to that point. (How far along the supporting music, the melody, was in gestation is unknown to me.) But the professionals involved here were not Great Beatified Receptacles Simply Transmitting God's Divine Message. They were experienced, working practitioners, with command of the tools—in this case primarily musical knowledge, and secondarily, instrumental mastery—who applied themselves toward an already-evolving song idea and its consistent lyrical exposition, that fortuitously meshed with Wynette's extraordinarily powerful vocal, to end up with a song that seems to be standing the test of time (even despite its retrograde gender implications). The band's strong lead into the chorus each time through, and producer Sherrill's attention to dynamics certainly helped. It's a great all-around package that hit the right note at the right time for the right people, and continues to resonate today.

One would be remiss to under-state that timing, and the original market positioning of the song. Like, perhaps, the play *Angels in America* some years later (and I don't think the comparison too tenuous, as we're addressing large generalities here, and even though the two works clearly address rather antithetical political world views) the song came along at a befitting historical moment, with enough message for a broad and very ready societal reception, to become a powerful cultural touchstone.

[186]The closest Salinger came to publishing another complete novel was *Franny and Zooey* or *Raise High the Roof Beam, Carpenters and Seymour: An Introduction*, but each are in fact comprised of two individual and independent novellas. He also published a few collections of short stories.

[187]One might reasonably argue that Chaplin's title portrayal in *The Great Dictator* was a second memorable character.

Chapter Fifty-Nine

Swan Song

*Where people unanimously maintain a conspiracy of silence, one word
of truth sounds like a pistol shot.* — Czeslaw Milosz

Songs can be better—much better. And we deserve much better.
The First Step to that end is to put to death the automatic consecration of the usually tawdry, swaggering drivel the celebrity-industrial complex ferociously inflicts on the general culture. (And enough with all the performer pomposities, and all the fan idolatries. Jeesh.)

The second is recognizing that a serious song is more—should be more—than whatever stray words come to mind, left unattended, layered on top of whatever chords quickly burble into semi-consciousness, and an unrelenting riff.

We live in an era of exponentially expanding options; and it's time for songwriting to rise to the implicit challenges, to grasp the wider opportunities, and to regularly achieve true legitimacy as, yes, an art. There will no doubt always be fleeting, humdrum commerce, and there will always be parading idiocy; but it is a larger share of intelligence and actual poetry, amidst all the inconsequence and posturing, that is in order.

★

What began as an essay—thoughts I simply wanted to get off my chest—gained so much encouragement as it was exposed, debated, and evolved on my web site that it progressively grew into this book. It could be said I've actually been preparing it, writing it, since I was that perplexed teenager recalled in Chapter Four.

I hope it may provoke other worthy inquiries and examinations—and if it does, then good.

If it helps to actually bring forth better songwriting and better song criticism, then great.

A revolution begins with a spark.

As for me, it's time to get back to my own work. And so I'll leave you with this exquisite caution from Nikos Kazantzakis:

Beauty is merciless. You do not look at it; it looks at you.
And it does not forgive.

Melencolia I
Albrecht Dürer

Appendix I: Recordings of Songs Quoted

Song	Performed by	Initial Release Album	Recording Company (USA)
"American Pie"	Don McLean	*American Pie*	United Artists
"The Night They Drove Old Dixie Down"	The Band	*The Band*	Capitol
"Come Together"	The Beatles	*Abbey Road*	Apple
"Small Town"	John Mellencamp	*Scarecrow*	Mercury
"Forever Young"	Bob Dylan	*Planet Waves*	Asylum
"Where Does the Good Times Go?"	Buck Owens and The Buckaroos	*It Takes People Like You*	Capitol
"And I Love Her"	The Beatles	*A Hard Day's Night*	Parlaphone
"Time To Say Goodbye"	Sarah Brightman**	*Timeless*	East West
"Lula Walls"	The Carter Family	*The Original and Great Carter Family**	RCA Victor
"The Cuckoo"	Clarence Ashley	*Old Time Music at Clarence Ashley's**	Folkways
"Brown Eyed Girl"	Van Morrison	*Blowin' Your Mind!*	Bang
"I Will Turn Your Money Green"	Furry Lewis	*Furry Lewis**	Folkways
"These Days"	Jackson Browne	*For Everyman*	Asylum
"Me and Bobby McGee"	Kris Kristofferson	*Kristofferson*	Monument
"El Paso"	Marty Robbins	*Gunfighter Ballads and Trail Songs*	Columbia
"Down the Old Road to Home"	Jimmie Rodgers	*Train Whistle Blues**	RCA Victor
"The Gambler"	Kenny Rogers**	*The Gambler*	United Artists
"Above and Beyond"	Buck Owens and The Buckaroos**	*Buck Owens*	Capitol
"Hurricane"	Bob Dylan	*Desire*	Columbia

Song	Performed by	Initial Release Album	Recording Company (USA)
"Masters of War"	Bob Dylan	*The Freewheelin' Bob Dylan*	Columbia
"A Hard Rain's A-Gonna Fall"	Bob Dylan	*The Freewheelin' Bob Dylan*	Columbia
"Mr Tambourine Man"	Bob Dylan	*Bringing it All Back Home*	Columbia
"Subterranean Homesick Blues"	Bob Dylan	*Bringing it All Back Home*	Columbia
"Lay Lady Lay"	Bob Dylan	*Nashville Skyline*	Columbia
"The Times They Are A-Changin'"	Bob Dylan	*The Times They Are A-Changin'*	Columbia
"You Ain't Goin' Nowhere"	Bob Dylan	*Bob Dylan's Greatest Hits Vol. II*	Columbia
"Ode to Billie Joe"	Bobbie Gentry	*Ode to Billie Joe*	Capitol
"Clothes Line Saga"	Bob Dylan	*The Basement Tapes*	Columbia
"I Never Do Anything Twice"	Millicent Martin**	*Side by Side by Sondheim*	RCA Red Seal
"Salt of the Earth"	The Rolling Stones	*Beggars Banquet*	London
"Yesterday"	The Beatles	*Help!*	Capitol
"T-bone"	Neil Young	*Re-ac-tor*	Reprise
"California Cotton Fields"	Merle Haggard and The Strangers**	*Someday We'll Look Back*	Capitol
"Nineteen Years Old"	Michael Koppy	*Ashmore's Store*	Good Track
"Fairytale of New York"	The Pogues	*If I Should Fall from Grace with God*	Island

*With these songs it would be misleading to cite the 'initial release album', as they were often first available solely as 78 rpm single records, and have appeared on multiple albums—those generally all being collections, such as these—in later years.

**With these songs I've deliberately chosen renditions that are 'best known' and not by the original writer(s) and composer(s). Versions by the creators may be found, but in all likelihood they would be collector's items rather than commonly available.

Appendix II: Songs Cited But Not Quoted

Song	Recommended Rendition	Writer(s) and Composer(s)	Year Created / Rendition Released
"Lucy In the Sky With Diamonds"	The Beatles	John Lennon	1967
"Turn Around"	Harry Belafonte	Malvina Reynolds, Alan Greene	1959
"Hurt"	Johnny Cash	Trent Reznor	1994 / 2003
"Don't Fence Me In"	Roy Rogers	Cole Porter, Robert Fletcher	1934 / 1944
"The House of the Rising Sun"	The Animals	traditional	1964
	Dave Van Ronk		1962
	Bob Dylan		1962
	Dolly Parton		1980
"I Will Always Love You"	Dolly Parton	Dolly Parton	1973
	Whitney Houston		1992
"Proud Mary"	Creedence Clearwater Revival	John Fogerty	1969
"Nessun Dorma"	Luciano Pavarotti	Giacomo Puccini, Giuseppi Adami, Renato Simoni	1926 / 1975
"Time To Say Goodbye"	Sarah Brightman, Andrea Bocelli	Francesco Sartori, Lucio Quarantotto	1995 / 1996
"Nine Below Zero"	Sonny Boy Williamson	Sonny Boy Williamson	1963
"Wildwood Flower"	The Carter Family	A.P. Carter	1928
"I'll Twine Mid the Ringlets"		Joseph Webster, Maud Irving	1860
Hamilton	Broadway Cast	Lin-Manuel Miranda	2015 / 2016
In The Heights	Broadway Cast	Lin-Manuel Miranda	2005 / 2008
"Talking Blues"	Christopher Bouchillon	Christopher Bouchillon	1926

Song	Recommended Rendition	Writer(s) and Composer(s)	Year Created	Rendition Released
"Don't Cry for Me, Argentina"	Julie Covington	Andrew Lloyd Webber, Tim Rice	1976	
"One Night in Bangkok"	Murray Head	Tim Rice, Björn Ulvaeus Benny Andersson	1984	
"Homeward Bound"	Simon & Garfunkel	Paul Simon	1964	1966
"Crocodile Rock"	Elton John	Elton John, Bernie Taupin	1972	
"Happiness is a Warm Gun"	The Beatles	John Lennon	1968	
"Stand By Me"	Ben E. King	Ben E. King, Jerry Lieber, Mike Stoller	1960	
"Bench Scene"	*Carousel* Broadway Cast	Richard Rodgers, Oscar Hammerstein II	1945	
"Color and Light"	*Sunday in the Park With George* Broadway Cast	Stephen Sondheim, James Lapine	1984	
"Prologue"	*Into the Woods* Broadway Cast	Stephen Sondheim, James Lapine	1986	1987
"All-American Prophet"	*The Book of Mormon* Broadway Cast	Trey Parker, Matt Stone, Robert Lopez	2011	
"Bohemian Rhapsody"	Queen	Freddie Mercury	1975	
"Stairway to Heaven"	Led Zeppelin	Jimmy Page, Robert Plant	1971	
"Don't Look Back in Anger"	Oasis	Noel Gallagher	1995	
"I Can See For Miles"	The Who	Pete Townsend	1967	
"Masters of War"	Bob Dylan	Bob Dylan	1963	
"Nottamun Town"		traditional		
"Blowin' in the Wind"	Bob Dylan	Bob Dylan	1962	1963
"No More Auction Block"		traditional		
"With God On Our Side"	Bob Dylan	Bob Dylan	1963	1964
"The Patriot Game"		traditional, Dominic Behan		
"Restless Farewell"	Bob Dylan	Bob Dylan	1963	1964

Song	Recommended Rendition	Writer(s) and Composer(s)	Year Created	Rendition Released
"The Parting Glass"		traditional		
"Bob Dylan's Dream"	Bob Dylan	Bob Dylan	1963	
"Lord Franklin's Lament"		traditional		
"Farewell, Angelina"	Joan Baez	Bob Dylan	1965	
"Farewell to Tarwathie"		traditional		
"This Land is Your Land"	Woody Guthrie	Woody Guthrie	1940	
"When the World's On Fire"	The Carter Family	traditional	1929	
"Little Darlin' Pal of Mine"	The Carter Family	A.P. Carter	1929	
"A Few Words in Defense of Our Country"	Randy Newman	Randy Newman	2008	
"MacArthur Park"	Richard Harris	Jimmy Webb	1967	1968
"Memory"	Elaine Page	Andrew Lloyd Webber, Trevor Nunn	1981	
"Moonlight in Vermont"	Margaret Whiting	John Blackburn, Karl Suessdorf	1944	
"Fields of Gold"	Sting	Sting	1992	1993
"America"	Simon & Garfunkel	Paul Simon	1968	
"Across the Universe"	The Beatles	John Lennon	1968	1969
"Lady"	Kenny Rogers	Lionel Richie	1980	
"Frank Mills"	Shelley Plimpton	James Rado, Gerome Ragni, Galt MacDermot	1967	1968
"The Cloths of Heaven"	Michael Koppy	William Yeats, Michael Koppy	1899	2012
"Hey Jude"	The Beatles	Paul McCartney	1968	
"The Boxer"	Simon & Garfunkel	Paul Simon	1968	1968

Song	Recommended Rendition	Writer(s) and Composer(s)	Year Created	/	Rendition Released
"Bad Romance"	Lady Gaga	Stefani Germanotta, Nadir Khayat	2009		
"Zip-a-Dee-Doo-Dah"	James Baskett	Allie Wrubel, Ray Gilbert	1946		
"Chim-Chim-Cher-ee"	Dick Van Dyke, Julie Andrews	Robert Sherman, Richard Sherman	1964		
"I Walk the Line"	Johnny Cash	Johnny Cash	1956		
"The Dance"	Garth Brooks	Tony Arata	1988	/	1990
"I Can't Make You Love Me"	Bonnie Raitt	Mike Reid, Allen Shamblin	1990	/	1991
"Travelin' Soldier"	The Dixie Chicks	Bruce Robison	1996	/	2002
"Green, Green Grass Of Home"	Tom Jones	Claude Putman	1964	/	1966
"Blurred Lines"	Robin Thicke	Pharrell Williams, Robin Thicke, Clifford Harris Jr	2012	/	2013
"Got To Give It Up"	Marvin Gaye	Marvin Gaye	1976	/	1977
"The Twelve Days Of Christmas"	traditional				
"Lily, Rosemary and the Jack of Hearts"	Bob Dylan	Bob Dylan	1974	/	1975
"Tangled Up in Blue"	Bob Dylan	Bob Dylan	1974	/	1975
"Desolation Row"	Bob Dylan	Bob Dylan	1965		
"Hotel California"	The Eagles	Don Felder, Glenn Frey, Don Henley	1977		
"Quinn the Eskimo"	Manfred Mann	Bob Dylan	1967	/	1968
"Tombstone Blues"	Bob Dylan	Bob Dylan	1965		
"Talkin' John Birch Paranoid Blues"	Bob Dylan	Bob Dylan	1962		
"Leopard-Skin Pill-Box Hat"	Bob Dylan	Bob Dylan	1966	/	1967

Song	Recommended Rendition	Writer(s) and Composer(s)	Year Created / Released	Rendition
"Bob Dylan's 115th Dream"	Bob Dylan	Bob Dylan	1965	
"Po' Boy"	Bob Dylan	Bob Dylan	2001	
"Idiot Wind"	Bob Dylan	Bob Dylan	1974 / 1975	
"Like a Rolling Stone"	Bob Dylan	Bob Dylan	1965	
"Positively 4th Street"	Bob Dylan	Bob Dylan	1965	
"Thank God and Greyhound"	Roy Clark	Larry Kingston, Earl Nix	1969	
"Dance: Ten; Looks: Three"	Audrey Landers	Marvin Hamlisch, Edward Kleban	1975 / 1985	
"A Boy Named Sue"	Johnny Cash	Shel Silverstein	1969	
"Alice's Restaurant Massacree"	Arlo Guthrie	Arlo Guthrie	1967	
"God Bless America"	Kate Smith	Irving Berlin	1928 / 1938	
"We Shall Overcome"		traditional		
"Give Peace a Chance"	Plastic Ono Band	John Lennon	1969	
"Salt of the Earth"	The Rolling Stones	Mick Jagger, Keith Richards	1968	
"Happy Birthday to You"		Patty Hill, Mildred Hill	1893	
"White Christmas"	Bing Crosby	Irving Berlin	1942	
"Auld Lang Syne"		traditional, Robert Burns		
"For He's a Jolly Good Fellow"		traditional		
"You Are My Sunshine"	Gene Autry	Jimmy Davis, Charles Mitchell	1939 / 1941	
	Michael Koppy		2006	
"Send in the Clowns"	Glynis Johns	Stephen Sondheim	1973	
"Love Changes Everything"	Michael Ball	Andrew Lloyd Webber, Charles Hart, Don Black	1989	
"I Don't Know How to Love Him"	Yvonne Elliman	Andrew Lloyd Webber, Tim Rice	1970	

Song	Recommended Rendition	Writer(s) and Composer(s)	Year Created /	Rendition Released
"Another Suitcase in Another Hall"	Barbara Dickson	Andrew Lloyd Webber, Tim Rice	1976	
"Music of the Night"	Michael Crawford	Andrew Lloyd Webber, Charles Hart	1986	
"Tell Me on a Sunday"	Marti Webb	Andrew Lloyd Webber, Don Black	1979	
"We've Only Just Begun"	The Carpenters	Roger Nichols, Paul Williams	1970	
"Moon River"	Audrey Hepburn	Henry Mancini, Johnny Mercer	1960 / 1961	
"Blue Suede Shoes"	Carl Perkins	Carl Perkins	1955 / 1956	
"Here Comes the Sun"	The Beatles	George Harrison	1969	
"Smells Like Teen Spirit"	Nirvana	Kurt Cobain, Dave Grohl, Krist Novoselic	1991	
"Satisfaction"	The Rolling Stones	Mick Jagger, Keith Richards	1965	
"Seven Nation Army"	The White Stripes	Jack White	2002 / 2003	
"Smoke on the Water"	Deep Purple	Ritchie Blackmore, Ian Gillan, Roger Glover, Ian Paice	1971 / 1972	
"Alabama Jubilee"	Red Foley	George L. Cobb, Jack Yellen	1915 / 1951	
"Eleanor Rigby"	The Beatles	Paul McCartney, John Lennon	1966	
"Michelle"	The Beatles	Paul McCartney, John Lennon	1965	
"Penny Lane"	The Beatles	Paul McCartney, John Lennon	1967	
"Moody's Mood for Love"	King Pleasure	Eddie Jefferson, James Moody	1952 / 1954	
"I'm in the Mood for Love"	Louis Armstrong	Jimmy McHugh, Dorothy Field	1935	

Song	Recommended Rendition	Writer(s) and Composer(s)	Year Created / Released
"Broken Arrow"	Buffalo Springfield	Neil Young	1967
"Expecting to Fly"	Buffalo Springfield	Neil Young	1967
"Nowadays Clancy Can't Even Sing"	Buffalo Springfield	Neil Young	1966
"I Am the Walrus"	The Beatles	John Lennon	1967
"Driftin' Back"	Neil Young and Crazy Horse	Neil Young	2012
"Ramada Inn"	Neil Young and Crazy Horse	Neil Young	2012
"Don't You Get It"	Mark Knopfler	Mark Knopfler	1996
"Running Scared"	Roy Orbison	Roy Orbison, Joe Melson	1961
"In Dreams"	Roy Orbison	Roy Orbison	1963
"Crying"	Roy Orbison	Roy Orbison, Joe Melson	1961
"It's Over"	Roy Orbison	Roy Orbison, Bill Dees	1964
"Oh, Pretty Woman"	Roy Orbison	Roy Orbison, Bill Dees	1964
"Come On Eileen"	Dexys Midnight Runners	Kevin Rowland, Jim Paterson, Billy Adams	1982
"All in the Timing: A Hollywood Romance in Seven Chapters"	Michael Koppy	Michael Koppy	2012
"Prison Break"	Michael Koppy	Michael Koppy	2019
"Mama Tried"	Merle Haggard and The Strangers	Merle Haggard	1968
"Stand By Your Man"	Tammy Wynette	Billy Sherrill, Tammy Wynette	1968

Appendix III: Notes on the Epigraph Authors

Just for fun....

I've used a boatload of authoritative quotations throughout this effort, primarily as epigraphs—in an attempt to quickly set the stage for material immediately following. Though most sources are well-known, some aren't—and it seems some biographical information about each might be of interest; even appropriately appreciative in a small way. So here's a little—very little, admittedly and unfortunately, but with some attempt to not simply provide conventional boilerplate—about those whose words have been quoted.

Ansel Adams (1902–1984; p. 301) American photographer, born and died in California, noted for his photographs of American landscapes, especially Yosemite Valley. His first camera was a Kodak Number 1 Brownie, a mass-market camera made of cardboard.

François-Marie Arouet (1694–1778; p. 41) took the name Voltaire at age 26, while imprisoned in the Bastille, and along with voluminous published writings, wrote over 20,000 letters—a life devoted to the pen so deeply that he spent as much as 18 hours a day at the task.

Jane Austen (1775–1817; p. 302) is one of the most popular western writers in present day China, with her *Pride and Prejudice* having been translated into Chinese over 50 times and *Sense and Sensibility* translated at least 10 times.

Lester Bangs (1948–1982; p. 85) pop music critic and writer. He was fired from *Rolling Stone* by editor Jann Wenner for 'disrespecting musicians'.

L. Frank Baum (1856–1919; p. 235) author of *The Wizard of Oz*, which he then followed with 13 other books set in the Land of Oz. But before Oz, he collaborated on his first book, an adaptation of Mother Goose stories, with a then also unknown, illustrator Maxfield Parrish.

Irving Berlin (1888–1989; p. 92, 245) lived to 101, and was, according to George Gershwin, "The greatest songwriter who ever lived".

Leonard Bernstein (1918–1990; p. 241) died just five days after officially retiring; perhaps as good an anecdotal argument against ever 'retiring' as may be found.

Napoleon Bonaparte (1769–1821; p. 57) is remembered in mathematics for the Napoleon Theorem; and in urban design for the now near-universal address numbering system of even house numbers on one side of the street, odd on the other.

Michelangelo Buonarroti (1475–1564; p. 169) considered himself a sculptor first, a painter second. And he really wasn't all that enthused about painting the ceiling of the Sistine Chapel—in fact he just didn't want the job at all.

Marlon Brando (1924–2004; p. 81) held four patents for devices he invented to tune conga drums. But musical instrument companies considered them too expensive to manufacture, so he was never able to license them.

Bertolt Brecht (1898–1956; p. 30) usurped—stole—much of his credited work from female collaborators, including from Ruth Berlau, Margarete Steffin, and Elisabeth Hauptmann, among others. One has to wonder if he could get away with that in today's world.

David Byrne (b. 1952; p. 89) founding member of The Talking Heads in 1975, along with Tina Weymouth, Chris Franz, and Jerry Harrison. Like me, he prefers riding a bicycle for daily transportation over driving a damn car.

Albert Camus (1913–1960; p. 267) was ethnically French-Algerian, but Algerian at his core—and after only Saint Augustine of Hippo probably the most famed writer in history from that part of the world.

George Carlin (1937–2008; p. 28, 49) wrote all his own stand-up material, resulting in six books, 14 hour-long television specials, and 20 full-length audio albums. He considered himself a writer foremost; a performer secondarily.

Lewis Carroll (1832–1898; p. 117) made his primary continuing income not as a writer but as Professor of Mathematics at Oxford University. Along with his 12 books of fiction, he authored 11 books on mathematics.

Graham Chapman (1941–1989; p. 221) one of the six members of Monty Python, played the title role in *Monty Python's Life of Brian* and the lead in *Monty Python and the Holy Grail*.

Anton Chekhov (1860–1904; p. 229) was a physician, but as he made a lucrative income from his writing, he regularly treated patients without charge. "Medicine is my lawful wife, and literature is my mistress."

Winston Churchill (1874–1965; p. 215) was the chief proponent of England's Gallipoli military campaign of World War I, which was a spectacular defeat, a disaster claiming nearly half a million casualties on both sides including the slaughter of over 50,000 Allied soldiers.

Eric Clapton (b. 1945; p. 103) was neither lead vocalist or nor main songwriter in Cream (both those tasks being essayed by bassist Jack Bruce) which very much perturbed his record company, banking on Clapton to be the 'star'.

Jack Clement (1931–2013; p. 302) was a long-time highly successful producer and songwriter in Nashville. He got his start when Sam Phillips hired him to be an engineer at Sun Records in Memphis.

George M. Cohan (1878–1942; p. 115) songwriter ("Give My Regards to Broadway", "Over There", "You're A Grand Old Flag", more), actor, playwright, dancer, singer, producer. His statue stands in New York City near Times Square.

Christopher Columbus (1451–1506; p. 101) was a lousy (or at best wildly mistaken) geographer—and a worse governor of New World lands he was charged with administering, infamous for his cruelty.

Arthur Conan Doyle (1859–1930; p. 262) made a fortune from his Sherlock Holmes creation, writing 56 stories and four novels, though he grew to utterly detest the demands for ever more work on it.

Alexandre Dumas (1802–1870; p. 26) wrote over 200 books, more than 20 plays, and operated a veritable, very profitable 'writing factory', employing a large staff to write stories for newspaper serializations. He himself was talented, but if he had no creative ability, in today's world he'd surely be running a movie studio.

Thomas Edison (1847–1931; p. 305) famously spent over a year, every single day, testing over 6,000 different materials before finding the one, carbonized bamboo, that proved long-lasting enough (burning for over 1,200 hours) to be efficient in his invention of the practical electric light bulb.

Robert Evans (b. 1930; p. 221), producer, farsightedly told director Francis Coppola that the first edit of *The Godfather* made it too short, and ordered him to add almost an hour's material back into the film that was then finally released.

Anatole France (1844–1924; p. 45), son of a bookseller, spent his own entire life devoted to literature; professionally as a journalist and librarian, and as author of poetry, plays, fiction, biography, and criticism.

Benjamin Franklin (1706–1790; p. 161) invented a completely re-thought and radically-improved glass harmonica, a musical instrument for which pieces were subsequently composed by Mozart and Beethoven, among others.

Jonathan Franzen (b. 1959; p. 155) is a famously avid birder, having sighted at least 2,600 different species (as of 2014, anyway) on his 'birding life list'.

George Gershwin (1898–1937; p. 261) was rejected for tutoring by French composer Nadia Boulanger, as she feared classical study would deleteriously affect his jazz orientation, which she admired.

Johann Wolfgang von Goethe (1749–1832; p. 260) wrote his best-known work, *The Sorrows of Young Werther,* at age 24, which caused an outsized sensation, to the point of young men across Europe dressing as the title character, and (reputedly) even to a few 'copy-cat suicides' inspired by the title character's demise in the novel.

Ben Greenman (b. 1969; p. 149) co-writes a lot of pop celebrity autobiographies, including ones with Gene Simmons, Mariel Hemmingway, and Simon Cowell.

Walter Gropius (1883–1969; p. 40) founded the Bauhaus in 1919, after serving in the German Army during the first World War, where his experiences, like those of so many others confronted with the mechanized horrors of 'The Great War', gave a messianic urgency to his immediate post-war work.

Merle Haggard (1937–2016; p. 97) grew up in a house that was converted from a railroad box car. The first time he saw Johnny Cash was when Cash played a show at San Quentin Prison, where Haggard was an inmate serving time—for a previous attempted jailbreak while incarcerated for burglary.

Frank Herbert (1920–1986; p. 299) was best known for his six *Dune* science fiction novels, for which he was first inspired while reporting on shifting sand dunes on the Oregon coast. The first book in the series was published by Chilton Books, which had previously only published automobile repair manuals.

Bill Hicks (1961–1994; p. 247) was banned from David Letterman's talk show, after 11 previous appearances, for doing comedy takedowns of religion and the anti-abortion movement that the gutless producers feared were too hard-hitting.

Christopher Hitchens (1949–2011; p. 139) wrote *God is Not Great: How Religion Poisons Everything*, among other brilliant and iconoclastic non-fiction books.

Harlan Howard (1927–2002; p. 177) once had 15 songs that he wrote and composed on the country music Top 40 simultaneously. He was arguably the most successful songwriter in the history of country music.

William Ralph Inge (1860–1954; p. 270) was nicknamed "The Gloomy Dean" because of his pessimistic view of humankind. "We have enslaved the rest of the creation, and have treated animals so badly that if they were able to formulate a religion, they would depict the Devil in human form."

Quincy Jones (b. 1933; p. 243, 255) apparently didn't really like Michael Jackson all that much personally, if between-the-lines readings of his various comments on the pop star since Jackson's death are correct.

Nikos Kazantzakis (1883–1957; p. 308) was born and is buried in Heraklion, Crete, Greece. His self-penned epitaph reads, "I hope for nothing / I fear nothing / I am free".

Ralph Keyes (b. 1945; p. 274) wrote, among many other books, *Is There Life After High School?*, in which he emphasizes that *every* student thinks he or she isn't 'cool' or in the 'right crowd'.

Stephen King (b. 1947; p. 227) absolutely hated Stanley Kubrick's film version of *The Shining*, particularly criticizing how Kubrick directed the character played by Shelley Duvall. "She's basically just there to scream and be stupid, and that's not the woman that I wrote about."

Rudyard Kipling (1865–1936; p. 111) was perhaps history's greatest propagandist for European and American colonial imperialism; and author of the poem "The White Man's Burden".

Ernie Kovacs (1919–1962; p. 279) was one of the first great comedic talents in television. His brilliantly underplayed "Nairobi Trio" skit should live forever.

Jon Landau (b. 1947; p. 64) manages or has managed Shania Twain, Bruce Springsteen, and other major acts; and heads the Rock and Roll Hall of Fame Nominating Committee. He's perhaps as fair an embodiment of The Establishment as can be found in current popular music.

John Lennon (1940–1980; p. 60) wanted Jesus Christ and Adolph Hitler to be in the collage of personalities pictured on the Beatles' *Sgt Pepper's Lonely Hearts Club Band* album cover, but was out-voted.

Abraham Lincoln (1809–1865; p. 75) never said the quote attributed to him here, though he's almost always cited as its author. It was actually first attributed to him 20 years after his death by Prohibition Party speakers wishing to graft greater moral suasion to their cause.

John Lomax (1867–1948; p. 103) always insisted that Lead Belly perform in a prison uniform costume, to 'fit the image' of a romanticized dangerous desperado. He was generally more interested in popularizing traditional songs than in simply preserving them.

Marika Lundeberg (b. 1995; p. 71) is my niece, and a recent graduate of St Olaf College in Northfield, Minnesota. And I love her very much.

John Lydon (b. 1956; p. 51) (aka Johnny Rotten) was cast to play King Herod in a 2014 North American touring production of the Tim Rice-Andrew Lloyd Webber musical, *Jesus Christ Superstar*, but the show was scuttled before opening.

Bernard Malamud (1914–1986; p. 303) was born and died in New York City. But when he saw the film adaptation of his book, *The Natural*, he said to his daughter, "At last, I'm an American writer".

Thomas Mann (1875–1955; p. 249) was a German political conservative during World War I, but his views evolved into liberal and finally strong leftist convictions as the century continued. He was anti-communist due to its failure to arrest authoritarianism, but thought Nazism much worse.

Marshall McLuhan (1911–1980; p. 135) kept his television in the basement, didn't drive a car, and—quite to the contrary of his image as a cutting edge technological guru—generally altogether avoided engagement with technology.

H.L. Mencken (1880–1956; p. 63) is sometimes credited (castigated) by religious fundamentalists as the journalist whose reports swung the nation against Biblical literalism and to the side of teacher John Scopes in the famous 1925 "Scopes Monkey Trial".

Czeslaw Milosz (1911–2004; p. 307) lived the first half of his life under Russian Czarist feudalism, in Poland through the NAZI German invasion and brutality, and finally Stalinist oppression—before defecting to the West.

Joan Miró (1893–1983; p. 7) painted *The Farm*, today considered to be his masterpiece, which depicted his family farm in Spain, in 1926. It was first bought by Ernest Hemingway, for 5,000 francs, as a birthday present for his wife.

Steven Moore (b.1951; p. 39) wrote two landmark studies, *The Novel: An Alternative History: Beginnings to 1600*, and the following *1600–1800*, which total over 1,800 pages. He won't write a third. (presumably *1800–Present*?), because "I finally had to admit that I'd bitten off more than I could chew".

Wolfgang Amadeus Mozart (1756–1791; p. 264) started playing piano at age three, composed his first minuets at age five, his first complete mass *and* his first three symphonies at age 12, and his first opera at age 14.

Martin Mull (b. 1943; p. 59) likes to price his paintings like commercial commodities—so, for instance, having a picture listed at a price of $499.95 instead of $500.00.

Robin Nagle (b. 1961; p. 50) is an *actual* garbologist; the New York City De-- partment of Sanitation's official, salaried, Anthropologist-in-Residence.

Edwin Newman (1919–2010; p. 198) had a sign posted in his office, reflecting his disdain for misused words, that read "Abandon 'Hopefully' All Ye Who Enter Here".

Conan O'Brien (b. 1963; p. 222) began his television hosting on a literal week-to-week contract, while NBC sought to find a suitable permanent host.

George Orwell (1903–1950; p. 31, 260) came home one day in 1944 to find his home destroyed by a German V-1 rocket, and he only found his then still unpublished manuscript for *Animal Farm* after hours of searching the rubble.

Thomas Paine (1737–1809; p. 3) is probably the best candidate for the title The Father of the American Revolution; yet only six people attended his funeral, three of whom were former slaves.

Paul of Tarsus (c. 4 BCE–c. 67; p. 23) basically pretty much made Christianity viable, through his tireless evangelizing, traveling, and correspondences. He's credited with 14 of the 27 books in the *Bible New Testament*.

Amanda Petrusich (b. 1980; p. 268-269) is a staff writer for *The New Yorker*, editor at *The Oxford American*, and contributor to *Pitchfork*.

Plato (428–348 BCE; p. 77) began writing only after the death of his teacher, Socrates, during 12 years in which he left Athens to travel around the Mediterranean world. So his works are all recollections, reconstructions—or, in some cases, possibly fabrications.

Edgar Allen Poe (1809–1849; p. 49, 303) was found wandering the streets of Baltimore in a delirium, and died four days later, at the age of 40, penniless and alone. The cause of his death has never been ascertained.

Pythagoras of Samos (c. 570–495 BCE; p. 33) is credited with the philosophical notion called "The Harmony (or Music) of the Spheres", in which the planets and stars all move in quantifiable mathematical relationships to each other, corresponding to relationships between musical notes.

Oliver Sacks (1933–2013; p. 256) authored 12 books, including *The Mind's Eye*, *Musicophilia*, *Awakenings*, and *The Man Who Mistook His Wife For A Hat*, all dealing in the field of what has become known as 'neurological anthropology'.

Carl Sagan (1934–1996; p. 25, 193) was not a fan of *Star Trek*, thinking the cast entirely unrepresentative of humanity because it was almost entirely Caucasian and Anglo-American. "And only two of 12 or 14 interstellar vessels are given non-English names, *Kongo* and *Potemkin*," he wrote.

Antoine de Saint-Exupéry (1900–1944; p. 165) wrote and illustrated his most lasting work, *The Little Prince*, while in the United States in 1942, and it wasn't published in his native France until after his death in the crash of a plane he was piloting. It is now the world's most translated book.

George Bernard Shaw (1856–1950; p. 61) wrote 62 plays, two novels, and countless book and music reviews. He never stopped working—and died from a fall off a ladder, at age 94.

Percy Bysshe Shelley (1792–1822; p. 47) and his wife, author Mary Shelley, were committed animal rights advocates and vegetarians throughout their adult lives, and he was also an early champion of non-violent political resistance.

William Shakespeare (1564–1616; p. 251) famously left his 'second best bed' to his wife of 34 years. It's thought customs of time mandated the 'best bed' be an heirloom, so presumably assigned to his eldest progeny. So the 'second best bed' was, in fact, the one Bill and wife Anne used.

Johnny Shines (1915–1992; p. 123) was a blues musician, and for three years the traveling companion of the legendary Robert Johnson, performing with him as far away as Windsor, Ontario, where they appeared together on radio.

Edith Sitwell (1887–1944; p. 15) was a writer known for her commanding rejection of misogynist prohibitions. "There was no one to point the way. I had to learn everything—learn, amongst other things, not to be timid."

Stephen Sondheim (b. 1930; p. 143) is a famously avid puzzle enthusiast, even having created 42 crossword puzzles for *New York Magazine* in the 1960s. "The nice thing about doing a crossword puzzle is that you know there is a solution."

Susan Sontag (1933–2004; p. 300, 304) wrote at least 17,198 emails in the 1990s and early 2000s, which are now held by the UCLA Library Special Collections. Her computer's small digital music library was dominated by works by Édith Piaf and Jacques Brel.

Hunter S. Thompson (1937–2005; p. 55) liked to re-type out, word for word, novels that he particularly liked, including fiction by Faulkner, Hemingway, Mailer, and Fitzgerald, simply to vicariously enjoy great writing and to learn what it may have felt like to create a masterpiece.

Leon Trotsky (1879–1940; p. 295) was, as is well known, assassinated by Stalin's agents following several failed attempts, but he actually lived a whole day after being slammed in the head with an ice axe by the assassin.

Mark Twain (1835–1910; p. 303) based the character of Huckleberry Finn on a childhood friend named Tom Blankenship. "He was ignorant, unwashed; but he had as good a heart as ever any boy had. He was the only really independent person, boy or man, in the community and by consequence, he was tranquilly and continuously happy and envied by the rest of us."

Paul Valéry (1871–1945; p. 86) arose every morning for 51 years to spend two hours in solitary monkish contemplation before beginning his day. At 21, on October 4, 1892, during a heavy storm in Genoa, he experienced a deep existential crisis that made him stop writing poetry ever again.

Gore Vidal (1925–2012; p. 157) probably would have lost the fist fight William F. Buckley threatened him with during the 1968 Democratic Party Convention, but he clearly bested the right-wing darling in their intellectual confrontation.

Leonardo da Vinci (1452–1519; p. 187) was asked to draw an angel by his teacher, Andrea del Verrocchio, and the result was so good del Verocchio decided to never paint again. (This according to Giorgio Vasari in his *Lives of the Most Excellent Painters*, first published in 1550.)

Andy Warhol (1928–1987; p. 67) was a lapsed Roman Catholic, and interestingly perhaps, the majority of those who worked in his 'factory' were reportedly also lapsed Catholics.

Bill Watterson (b. 1958; p. 246) created the daily comic strip *Calvin and Hobbes*, which he stopped after almost exactly 10 years. "By the end of it, I'd said pretty much everything I had come there to say. It's always better to leave the party a little early."

Daniel Webster (1782–1852; p. 91), known as The Great Orator, died in 1852, but was so influential in US history that he has appeared on a total of seven different US postage stamps, issued from 1870 to1969.

Oscar Wilde (1854–1900; p. 302) was (in the judgment of admiring critic Harold Bloom) "most at home as a celebrity, a precursor to Truman Capote, Andy Warhol, and a host of other aesthetic superstars...his genius was larger than his chosen role could accommodate".

Your Mother (presumably living a full and happy life this very minute; p. 27) turns out to be The Greatest Mother Ever, although there was certainly never a doubt. She loves you very much, and expects you to return home this Christmas. Don't disappoint her.

Appendix IV: Ancillary Acknowledgements

Much effort was made to properly cite sources in this book. A reader discerning, or even suspecting, that a properly due citation may be missing, or that a citation that appears may be incorrectly attributed, is asked to contact the author, so that corrections may be made in a subsequent printing.

As concerns artwork used, the majority of illustrations used were stumbled upon via the internet, and confounded all efforts to track down origin and creator(s), presumably because they've been appropriated so many times since creation that they've been effectively stripped of information on provenance. If a copyrighted image was used, it was done from ignorance and the simple inability to locate proper authority. In any case in which a reader may know the creator and/or rights holder for an image appearing herein, the reader is again asked to contact the author, so that it can be properly addressed.

There are almost always going to be the odd misspellings or grammatical errors in just about any manuscript, no matter how carefully edited. Readers spotting them in this book are humbly asked to please inform the author, and are sincerely thanked in advance for that kind assistance.

Illustrations:
"Protest Guitars" (front cover) illustration (©2018) by Edel Rodriguez (b.1971), originally for *The Los Angeles Times*. Used with permission.
"Not Bad, Fellas" (page 2) cartoon (©1998) by Tom Cheney (b.1954), originally for *The New Yorker*. Used with permission.
"Fall of Richmond" (page 9) Currier & Ives lithograph, 1865.
William Wordsworth (page 27) painting (1798) by William Shuter (1771–1798), hangs in the National Portrait Gallery, London.
Francois Truffaut (page 28) photographer unknown, c.1963.
Saltines and milk (page 37) photograph by the author.
Wildebeests (page 45) photographer unknown.
Peed pants (page 47) photographer unknown.
Awards (page 51) illustrator unknown.
"The Parable of the Blind Leading the Blind" (page 65) painting (1568) by Peter Breughel the Elder (c.1525–1569), hangs in the National Museum of Capodimonte, Naples.
Ostrich (page 69) photographer unknown.
Dance steps (page 89) illustrator unknown.
Charleston dancers (page 90) photographer unknown, c.1926.
Fortune cookies (page 98) photographer unknown.
Pablum (page 120) photographer unknown.
"Mona Lisa Paint-by-Numbers" (page 127) illustrator unknown.
"Mona Lisa" (page 128) painting (1503–1519) by Leonardo da Vinci (1452–1519), hangs in the Louvre, Paris.

Empty box (page 142) photographer unknown.

Greeting cards (page 156) photographer unknown.

Fuel gauge (page 209) photographer unknown.

Dumpster fire (page 216) photographer unknown.

Alphabet soup (page 233) photographer unknown.

"Songwriting Kit" (page 240) photographer unknown; title added by the author.

Direction signs (page 250) illustrator unknown.

Roulette wheel (page 257) photographer unknown.

Framed dollar sign (page 260) illustrator unknown.

"The Sleep of Reason Produces Monsters" (page 266) etching (1799) by Francisco Goya (1746–1828), prints of which are in the Museo del Prado, Madrid; the Metropolitan Museum of Art, New York City; the National Gallery of Canada, Ottawa; and elsewhere.

Charles Chaplin (page 305) still from *A Dog's Life* (1918) by cinematographer Roland Totheroh (1890–1967).

"Melencolia I", (page 308) engraving (1514) by Albrecht Dürer (1471–1578), prints of which are in the Metropolitan Museum of Art, New York City; the Museum of New Zealand, Wellington; the Scottish National Gallery, Edinburgh; and elsewhere.

"Tonto National Forest, Arizona" (page 327) photograph (©2018) by Ganapathy Kumar (b.1978). Used with permission.

Typeset in Palatino, Garamond, Gill Sans, and Times Roman.

Finally, there were so many people who emailed in with comments as this was being written and posted on my web site—causing no end to positive changes in the text—that to try to list them all would be a fruitless endeavor, and perhaps even an invasion of privacy in some cases. Those who can be acknowledged and can not be left unnamed, however, include Nancy Logan, Tim Jahns, Gregory Van Zuyen, Kim Fay, Pete Petroski, Michael Stearns, John Bertucci, Charles Gary, Michael Goldman, Jerry Hastings, DJ Baffy, Twyla Griffin, Kisha Mmari, Eshe Alter, Joe Offer (of the often helpful Mudcat.org web site), Linda Harkey, Tommy Warren, Kathy Villacorta, Don Swenholt, Michael Tola, David Channel, Jerome Szymczak, Art Kempf, Mike Rudicell, Eric Marin, Cliff Carothers, Howard Petrik, Mary Etta Moose, John Vestman, Tonda Marton, John Carlson, Patrick Riley, Jon Devirian, Joan Matey, Howard Vertner, Martha Weeks, Dominique Benichetti, Mireschen Troskie, Steve Winchester, Dominique Courtois, Tony Porter, and Wayne Sietle.

To they and the many others without whom this danged thing would never have been completed, much less inclusive of so many intelligent contributions, I can offer is my sincerest appreciation, and the promise that when we meet in person, down the road…I'll buy the first round.*

Michael Koppy, West Hollywood, 2019

---

*Draft beer, domestic brand, eight-ounce glass, happy hour—you leave the tip….

Index

Biographical information
can be found on my web site:

www.MichaelKoppy.com